RAYNES MINNS was born in 1946 and grew up in Hampstead, the eldest of a family of three children. Educated at various convents, she studied art at Hornsey College of Art and theatre design at the Central School of Art and Design in London. She has worked as a theatre designer for television, the Young Vic, the Northern Dance Theatre, Inter-Action and the Theatre for the Deaf. In the late sixties she lived for a time in Paris, buying and designing theatricalities for the Prop Shop and Thea Porter.

Bombers and Mash, her first book, is the result of a fascination over many years with wartime cookery books. An excellent and imaginative cook herself, Raynes Minns became intrigued by these recipes for a fuelless, meatless and sugarless world, and began to investigate the Domestic Front further. Using a vast number of sources and talking to women all over the country, she gradually built up a picture of the deprivations and dramas of the women's war. She now lives in London with her husband and two sons, and spends her spare time painting and illustrating.

For my Mother, Patrick, Ned and Inigo

Bombers and Mash

The Domestic Front 1939–45

Raynes Minns

Virago

Published by VIRAGO PRESS Limited 1980
41 William IV Street, London WC2N 4DB
Reprinted 1981, 1985
Copyright © Raynes Minns 1980

All *Food Facts* reproduced are Crown Copyright.

British Library Cataloguing in Publication Data
Minns, Raynes
  Bombers and mash.
    1. World War, 1939–45 – Women
    2. Women – Great Britain – Social conditions
    3. World War, 1939–45 – Great Britain
    4. Cookery, British
    I. Title
  941.084   D810.W7
  ISBN 0-86068-041-X

Typesetting by Jubal Multiwrite Limited,
printed and bound by Whitstable Litho Limited.
Additional camera work by The Graphic Unit

Contents

Abbreviations and Cookery Measurements
A Woman's Chronology of the War
Acknowledgements

Preface   1

Introduction   3

1. Give them a chance of safety and health   17
   Evacuation and the war nurseries

2. Women of Britain – Go to it!   31
   Into the factories

3. This is the Army, Mrs Jones   43
   The Women's Auxiliary Forces

4. Your gas mask will take care of you   53
   Women in Civil Defence

5. Over to you!   65
   Behind the scenes: the voluntary groups

6. Lend a hand on the land   75
   The Women's Land Army

7. Food is a munition of war   85
   Food and rationing

8. Sow, grow and add Oxo   95
   The Dig for Victory campaign

9. Women, save your bacon!   103
   Cooking in wartime

10. Start a rag bag   143
    The Salvage drives

11. Wot, no rags?   149
    'Lend don't spend': household shortages

12. The parasites are at their filthy work   159
    Under the counter: The Black Market

13. Crossing the ocean doesn't make you a hero   163
    The GIs

14. Airgraphs get priority   175
    Marriage, sex and the family

15. Living together again   187
    The psychological effects of war

    Select Bibliography   201
    Index   203

List of Abbreviations

AFS	Auxiliary Fire Service
ARP	Air Raid Precautions
ATS	Auxiliary Territorial Service
CAB	Citizen's Advice Bureau
CD	Civil Defence
ENSA	Entertainments National Service Association
GP	General Practitioner
HE	High Explosive
HG	Home Guard
ILP	Independent Labour Party
LCC	London County Council
LDV	Local Defence Volunteers
LEA	Local Education Authority
MAP	Ministry of Aircraft Production
MOF	Ministry of Food
MOI	Ministry of Information
NFS	National Fire Service
ROF	Royal Ordnance Factory
SFP	Supplementary Fire Party
TUC	Trades Union Congress
WAAF	Women's Auxiliary Air Force
WI	Women's Institute
WLA	Women's Land Army
WRNS	Women's Royal Naval Service
WVS	Women's Voluntary Service
VAD	Voluntary Aid Detachment

Comparative Cookery Terms and Measures

BRITISH MEASURES	AMERICAN MEASURES	APPROX METRIC MEASURES
1 pint	= 1¼ US pints/2½ cups	= .568 litre
1¾ pints	= 2 US pints	= 1 litre
4 fluid ounces	= 8 tablespoons	= 120 cc
1 teaspoon	= 1½ teaspoons	= 6 cc
1 tablespoon	= 1¼ tablespoon/½oz	= 17 cc
1 lb fat	= 2 cups	
1 oz fat	= 2 tablespoons	
1 lb sugar	= 2⅓ cups	
1 oz sugar	= 2 tablespoons	
1 lb sieved flour	= 4½ cups	
1 oz sieved flour	= 4 tablespoons	
1 lb grated cheese	= 4 cups	

BRITISH AND AMERICAN WEIGHTS AND THE APPROXIMATE METRIC EQUIVALENTS

1 ounce	=	30 grammes
16 ounces or 1 lb	=	480 grammes
2 lb 3 oz	=	1 kilogram

A Woman's Chronology of the War

1937
April Budget provides for a National Defence Contribution.

1938
March Car manufacturers switch to aircraft part production.

Sept. 29 Munich Agreement signed by Great Britain, France, Italy & Germany.

Nov. Sir John Anderson takes charge of Air Raid Precautions (ARP) and makes evacuation plans.

1939
1½ million men & women volunteer for Civil Defence (over a million unpaid)

March Hitler invades Czechoslovakia.

April 27 Ministry of Supply set up and compulsory conscription for men aged 20–21.

Aug. 23 Ribbentrop and Molotov sign the USSR – German non-aggression pact.

Aug. 24 Emergency Powers Defence Act passed. Military reservists called up.

Aug. 25 Treaty of Alliance between Poland & England.

Aug. 31 Only 1 person in 5 interviewed by Opinion Poll anticipates war.

Sept. Control of Employment Act.

Sept. 4 out of 6 London schools requisitioned for other purposes. (6 out of 10 in Manchester.)

Sept. 1 German troops move into Poland. Evacuation of millions of children, expectant mothers & the blind. Blackout enforced. All windows papered, painted or sealed. Estimated 140,000 hospital patients discharged (including 7–8,000 T.B. patients 'not on a peace-time standard of fitness for discharge'.) 187–195,000 new and old beds made ready for air raid casualties.

Sept. 3 War declared. Anderson shelters delivered. Cinemas, theatres, public places closed. BBC closes all channels except Home Service. Massive civilian casualties, neurosis and panic expected. Gas masks to be carried at all times.

Sept. 4 Start of phoney war. No bombardment.

Sept. 29 National Registration: identity cards issued.

Sept./Oct. War Cabinet sets up new Ministries of Food, Shipping, Economic Warfare, Information. Sir John Anderson takes over amalgamated Ministries of Home Office and Home Security. The Ministry of National Service extends call-up age from 27 to 41.

Oct. Appeals for war workers, salvage and savings groups.

Nov. National Savings Movement launched.

Nov. 23 Last date to register for ration books.

Dec. Many evacuees return for Christmas. Most places of entertainment reopen. A million people still unemployed.

1940
Jan. Two fifths of all evacuee children and nine tenths of mothers return home. 430,000 children getting no schooling, over a million very scant schooling.

Jan. 8 Food rationing begins: 4 ozs ham, 4 ozs bacon, 12 ozs sugar, 4 ozs butter per adult person per week.

March Meat rationed to 1s 10d-worth a week for adults (about 1 lb in weight): 11d-worth for young children.

April 3 Lord Woolton becomes Minister of Food.

April 9 Germany invades Denmark and Norway.

May 10 Chamberlain resigns. Germany invades Belgium, Luxemburg and Holland. Churchill forms National Government. Local Defence Volunteers (later the Home Guard) formed.

May 13 Churchill gives his 'blood, sweat and tears' speech.

May 15 Holland surrenders.

May 22 Emergency Powers Act passed.

May 28 Belgium surrenders.

May 29–June 3 Evacuation of British and Allied troops from Dunkirk.

June Lord Beaverbrook, Minister of Aircraft Production, appeals for scrap metal. Aircraft industry working 10 hours a day, 7 days a week.

June 5,306,000 women in civil employment.

June 14 Germans enter Paris.

July Tea, margarine and cooking fats rationed to 2 ozs a week. Illegal to serve protein in more than one course in restaurants. Cheese ration fluctuates between 2 ozs and 8 ozs per week. Supply of timber for furniture cut off. Internment begins in Great Britain of all German nationals.

July 23 Imposition of purchase tax.

Aug. Over 2 million still needed for Forces and Civil Defence.

Aug. 13 Battle of Britain: full scale air attack on South-east England.

Aug. 18 Enemy losses – 236 planes, British losses 95 planes and 160,000 tons of shipping.

Sept. 7 Blitz begins on London. People take to underground shelters on own initiative. Half a million fewer people leave London during the Blitz than at outbreak of war. Serious welfare problems develop.

Sept. 17 Battle of Britain won.

Sept. 23 George Cross introduced for acts of civil gallantry.

Sept.–Oct. Anti-air raid services properly co-ordinated.

Sept.–Nov. London bombed every night. Over 3 million homes damaged or destroyed. 30,000 dead from bombing.

Oct. 15 Peak bombing, 538 tons dropped. (Average 200 tons per 24 hours at this time.)

Oct. Maximum Price Orders on many foods. Rural nurseries (residential) too full to take more children.

Nov. 68% of mothers and children say they will not or cannot re-evacuate. Almost as many children returning to towns as leaving. 8% sleeping in public shelters. 4% in tubes. 1% in surface shelters. 13% sharing shelters. 27% in Anderson or domestic shelters. 6 out of 10 Londoners still sleeping in unsafe homes.

1941

Jan. 400,000 Morrison (inside) shelters on order. Air Training Corps launched for boys 16–18 (200,000 recruits in 6 months).

Feb. Plea from TUC to Ministry of Health for (Beveridge) report on inadequate Health Insurance.

March Battle of the Atlantic begins. Registration of Employment Order for women 20–21, later extended to 30 and men over 41. More appeals for 'immobile' women to volunteer for work. Preserves, margarine, treacles etc. rationed to maximum of 8 ozs a month.

March 5 Essential Work Order controls employed workers.

March 7 Budget raises income tax to 6s 6d in the pound minimum, 10s maximum. 4,000,000 new tax payers created.

April 700,000 tons of British shipping sunk. Women's Services become part of armed forces subject to military discipline, to check flow of those wishing to resign.

May Cheese ration down to 1 oz a week. Clothes prices 175% higher than pre-war. Wholesale goods about 50% higher than pre-war.

June 1 Clothes rationing introduced. Controlled distribution of eggs.

June 10 William Beveridge appointed to head enquiry into inadequate Social Insurance schemes.

June 22 Germany invades Russia.

June Board of Trade introduces Utility Scheme for retail goods.

July Bevin recalls 30,000 men to work in the coal mines.

Aug. Shortages result in black market and longer queues. (17/6d for 1 lb grapes, £2 for a melon.) Extra cheese rations for heavy workers.

Sept. As many civilians as soldiers have been killed up to this point.

Nov. Controlled distribution of milk. Cosmetics very scarce. Increase in juvenile delinquency of 33%, in petty thefts 200%, in malicious damage 70% since 1939.

Dec. VD statistics rise, 63% for women, 113% for men. 19,918 civilian deaths since 1940. Registration of girls and boys 16–18. Cheap milk and vitamins become available for children. National dried milk available. Magistrates orders for birching of boys under 14 increased 600% in 1941. Decreased thereafter.

Dec. 1 Points scheme introduced to complement rations.

Dec. 6 Japanese bomb Pearl Harbor.

Dec. 9 Conscription for single women between 20 and 30, liable for military service or other work. Call up age for men lowered to 18.

Dec. 10 Japanese bombers sink H.M.S. Prince of Wales and H.M.S. Repulse.

Dec. 11 U.S.A. declares war on Germany and Italy.

1942

Jan. Austerity starts in earnest. Thousands of GIs arrive in U.K.

Feb. Soap rationed to 3 ozs a month. Single bananas and onions used as raffle prizes. Home Guards recruited to serve at ack-ack batteries. Clothing ration reduced to 48 coupons a year.

Feb. 15 Fall of Singapore.

March Fuel rationing discussed in House of Commons: stocks very low.

April 6 No more white bread.

June Hugh Dalton's Austerity regulations ban pockets, pleats, long socks. Dried egg packets appear. Restaurants allowed to charge maximum price of 5s per meal.

July 32,000 people compulsorily directed to work since June 1941. (1 million by 1945.)

Aug. Only 22 furniture designs produced on Utility Scheme.

Sept. More soldiers than women and children killed in war at this point.

Oct.–Nov. Battle of El Alamein.

Dec. Civilian deaths since 1941: 3,236.

1943

Jan. No unemployment. 300,000 savings groups in action. Retail prices 42% higher than pre-war. Wages 35% higher than pre-war. 'Wings for Victory' weeks. Government White Paper shows that a quarter of 611,000 boys and girls under 18 already had such long hours or travel that no extra war effort is possible on their part.

March–Sept. Major offensive by RAF Bomber Command against German towns.

April 20 cigarettes cost 1s 9d. Cosmetics very scarce. Pipe cleaners in use as hairpins. 'Victory Roll' hairstyle eliminates need for pins.

June 9 out of 10 single women, 8 out of 10 married women aged 18–40, in Forces or industry: remainder caring for young or old, or billetors, doing part-time work and out-work at home.

July Petrol, fuel, blankets, beer, food very scarce.

July 10 Allies land in Sicily.

Aug. Women and men at Rolls Royce factory strike for one week for equal pay for equal work – and get it. Female suicide figures 32% lower than 1938.

Sept. Pay as You Earn (PAYE) scheme introduced for tax payers.

Sept. 7 Italy surrenders. Number of doctors in public health service has fallen by 20% since 1939.

Dec. 1,870,000 women in trade unions.

1944

"Salute the Soldier" weeks. Women teachers' claim for equal pay rejected by Churchill as "impertinence".

Jan. Average women's wage in engineering £3.10s: average men's wage in engineering £7. Only 4 cwt of coal allowed per month.

Jan. 21 Start of 'Little Blitz'.

Jan. 22 Anzio landings.

Spring 140,000 Home Guard serving on ack-ack batteries. 1,421,000 non-British troops stationed in UK, majority American GIs. Great shortage of cots, bottle teats, rubber sheets, chamber pots. Bottles only replaced when proof presented of their breakage. Cinema audiences rise to 25–30 million a week: mostly American films.

June Peak of industrial activity in all fields. Air raid siren in Paddington fails to disperse fish queue.

June 6 D-Day. Allies land in Normandy.

June 13 First flying bomb hits London. Fresh evacuation of 1½ million from city.

Aug. 25 Liberation of Paris.

Sept. 8 First V-2 rocket reaches Britain.

Sept. 17 Arnheim air-borne raid fails.

Dec. 1 oz of extra tea for 70-year-olds and older.

1945

Jan. 12 Representation of the People Bill. Whalemeat available in fish shops – shortly followed by 'snoek' or barracuda.

Feb. 4 Yalta conference, Stalin, Churchill and Roosevelt attending.

Feb. 14 Devastation of Dresden by bombing.

April 20 Russians reach Berlin.

April 30 Hitler commits suicide.

May 7 Germany surrenders.

May 8 V-E Day. Victory in Europe.

Aug. 6 USA drops atomic bomb on Hiroshima.

Aug. 9 USA drops second atomic bomb on Nagasaki.

Aug. 14 Japan surrenders.

1940–1945

Average warnings of danger: 1 every 36 hours for 5 years. Over half the mothers of 'irregularly' conceived children were thought to have husbands in the Services. 264,444 members of Armed Forces killed during war, 277,077 wounded.

1945

25,000 divorce petitions filed (10,000 in 1938), 70% on grounds of adultery: 58% filed by husbands.

1948

March 31 46,000 war pensions awarded to civilians – widows, disabled, orphans and members of Civil Defence under the Personal Injuries (civilian) scheme.

July 5 National Insurance Scheme and National Health Service come into operation.

Acknowledgements

My very grateful thanks are due to the following people for their invaluable contributions, recollections and advice: Sybil Ashdown, Catherine Athill, Ronald Ayres, Beryl Bainbridge, Simon Bargate, Nan Berger, Rose Bevan, Hilda Budd, Mary Cadogan, Frances Carpenter, Joanna Catois, Billie Chandler, Daphne Charlton, George Clout, Zaleed Cohen, Biddy Cook, John Cooper, Dame Margery Corbett Ashby, Jane Cousins, Sarah Craddock, Mr Crawford, Reginald Cuthbert, Anna Davin, Denise Dawkins, Francoise Ducrocq, Elaine Ellis, Mary Evans, Bunnie Grossman, Cecile Halle, Jane Henderson, Miss Ruth Hendrie, Barbara Henson, Andrew Hewson, Margaret Hewson, Corin Hughes-Stanton, Lady Mary John, Rebecca John, Valerie Keegan, Liz Kinnersley, Mary Knapp (my mother), Marjorie Laws, Eva Lerner, Jean Liddiard, Mr Loucas, Elsie Magarshack, Jane Mendelsohn, Bianca Minns, Margaret Minns, Harry Mister, Peace News, Phyllis Morrell, Sybil Morrison, Trevor Mostyn, Joan Munt, Osiokowski, Ursula Owen, Peace Pledge Union, 'Pickled Annie', Mary Prideaux, Madame Prunier, Mary Rich, Hon. Mrs Mary Rous, Nomi Rowe, Elizabeth Russell Taylor, David Sharp, Liz Shelburne, Susie Slack, Christine Smith, Deanna Smith, Miss Dodie Snew, Harriet Spicer, Mary Stott, Pat Thane, Anne Waugh, Bill Webb, Anne White, Anne Whitehouse, Helen Whittick, Susan Wilby, May Wilkinson, Jane Willby, and almost every woman of the war years that I have encountered in various queues over the past three years. My special thanks to all the women I spoke to at the WLA Reunion at the Albert Hall. Some others wish to remain anonymous either because of their wartime oaths of secrecy, or because they think that their feelings about the war are 'unpatriotic'. Many organisations and institutions have given me invaluable help: Advertiser's Association, Central Office of Information, Citizen's Advice Bureau, Ephemera Society, Fawcett Library, Girl Guide's Association, HMSO, Imperial War Museum, Labour History Library, Ministry of Agriculture, Fisheries and Food, Ministry of Defence, Peace News, British Red Cross Society (Truro), Syndication International, Women's Royal Voluntary Service.

I have made every effort to find the owners of copyright of all the material in this book, and apologise to any I may have missed.

For permission to reproduce the illustrations, acknowledgements are due to the following: BBC Hulton Picture Library (pp 7 top and bottom, 12, 33, 35 bottom, 38 & 39, 52, 54, 55 top and bottom, 71 top and bottom, 78 & 79, 80, 84, 92, 146 bottom, 155, 181 top and bottom, 186, 188, 198 & 199); Ephemera Society (pp 6, 28, 30, 102, 165, 185, 197); Girl Guide's Association (p 146 top); Hamlyn Books (pp 35 top, 42); *Illustrated London News* (p 195 top and bottom); Imperial War Museum (pp 76, 87, 119, 145); Mary Knapp (pp 40, 96, 161); Mrs Laws (p 176); National Museum of Labour History (p 200); *Parade* (p 45 bottom); Val Parker (p 177); Popperfoto (pp 2, 16, 41, 64, 150, 153 top, 162, 168&169); *Punch* (pp 152, 158); Salvation Army (pp 45 top, 46, 58, 67, 167 top); Sarah Schofield (p 48); Liz Shelburne (p 172); Alan Spain (pp 11, 94); Mrs Spicer (p 49); Topix (p 4); Trades Union Congress (pp 74, 109, 191 bottom); Mrs Wiremu (p 177 top).

For permission to reproduce the following recipes, grateful thanks to *Farmer's Weekly*: Fish Puffs, Salmon in Custard, Rabbit Pudding with Mushrooms, Two Dishes from One Fowl, Honey Nut Tartlets, Christmas Cake without Eggs, Health Bread, Carrot Jam, Furniture Cream, Farmhouse Herb Salve, A Good Liniment, Medicinal Jam, Parsnip Wine, Gorse Wine, Ginger Beer

For permission to reproduce advertisements, acknowledgements are due to the manufacturers of the following: Acme, Beecham's, Birds', Bourn-Vita, Celanese, Decca, Frys, Hoover, Horlicks, HP Sauce, Irium, James Cycles, Kent, Lifebuoy, LRC Products (Glymiel), Mansion House, Miner's, Mrs Peek's Puddings, Murphy Radio, Odo Ro No, OK Sauce, Ovaltine, Oxo, Phillips, Pyrex, Sanatogen, Sparva, Stork, Sunlight Soap, Tattoo, Wren's Polish, Wright's Coal Tar, Zixt

Preface

This is not a comprehensive history of women during the Second World War but an attempt to delve beneath the propaganda and statistics to discover the impact of war on ordinary women of all classes, in towns, cities and villages. For them it was not a war of pitched battles between armies but one of wrecked plumbing, substitute egg powder, frightened children and fearsome austerity measures – orchestrated by enemy bombs and British bureaucracy.

It was through my research into wartime cooking, when my own children were babies, that I discovered more of what lay behind the fuelless, meatless and sugarless recipes of the war. I began to talk to women about their wartime experiences and how they coped with shortages of every kind, with queuing and rationing, with scrimping and saving and making do. On the whole I have kept away from the official histories (though Angus Calder's *The People's War* and Norman Longmate's *How We Lived Then* have been inspirations and companions throughout), but have focused on the voices of the women themselves, their stories, their reactions, their memories, their diaries. In the government literature of the period we see what Britain expected of her women: from the women themselves we learn how they actually experienced the war.

Food was only part of the story of the Domestic Front. There was separation from families, long hours of work, loneliness, exhaustion and fear. It is difficult in writing on this subject to show the infinite variety of women's responses and experiences. For of course they varied hugely – from class to class, from area to area, from individual to individual. What seems clear is that women learnt, whether by the infusion of patriotic fervour through government propaganda or something more complex, to handle and sometimes repair the almost total breakdown of normal life. And they did it with extraordinary spirit.

But the strain was enormous and a price was paid. Some may recall those days as the best of their lives: there was comradeship, good humour, a new independence which came with new responsibilities. But for many women the breaking point was never far away. Some of the stories are all the more heroic for that. Although women often lived through each day exhausted and in terror of what the night would bring, most of them continued to respond to the pleas to 'Keep up the good fight', to 'Keep smiling', to 'Win through'.

After six years of war, many women were sickened by the devastation they had lived through, and exhausted by their efforts to keep any sort of ordinary life going. And when the war ended, there was the business of living together again, children reunited with parents, men back from the Front needing jobs and understanding, government promises of new solutions to old social problems. Living together again was by no means always simple.

The years of the war demanded from women a strength, resourcefulness and tolerance which sometimes seemed superhuman. They responded with amazing fortitude and determination, with humour and energy, with imagination and love. If I haven't always stressed the cheerful aspects it is because these are already well documented. I have tried to find out what was going on behind the stiff upper lip and the determined smile. I am deeply grateful to the women I talked to for their help and support in this, and I hope I have represented them as they would wish. Any errors or failures to do this are my own.

Raynes Minns, London 1980

This typical open trench for emergency shelter, a feature of both park and field, afforded little protection from bombs. These children of hop pickers in Kent are watching one of the numerous aerial flights overhead, a common occurrence in the South-eastern counties.

Introduction

Everything from the biggest factory to the smallest village workshop is turning out something for the war, so that Britain can supply arms for herself, for Libya, India, Russia and every front. Hundreds of thousands of women have gone to work in factories or joined the many military auxiliary forces. Old time social distinctions are being forgotten, as the sons of factory workers rise to be officers in the forces, and the daughters of noblemen get jobs in the munitions factories... The British have been bombed night after night and month after month. Thousands of them have lost their possessions, their houses, their families. Gasoline, clothes and railroad travel are hard to come by and incomes are cut by taxes, and food is more strictly rationed than anything else. One of the things the English had enough of in the past was soap. Now it is so scarce that girls working in the factories often cannot get the grease off their hands or out of their hair.

These words, from a Washington War Department leaflet issued to American GIS in early 1942, attempted to sharpen American sensibilities to the daily problems of a country at war. In the Britain that welcomed these American troops seven and a half million men were posted away, and women had been forced to make drastic adjustments to cope with the upheavals of war.

Women had not entered war altogether without protest. There were numerous pleas to stop the war by the Women's International League for Peace and Freedom, the Women's Freedom League, Pax International, the Peace Pledge Union and the National Peace Council as well as various Church groups. Some of these women wondered why a 'civilised' world could find no better way out than 'competition in reciprocal slaughter and destruction'. The League of Nations and the US government were appealed to as mediators to cease hostilities and to form a 'constructive peace'.

The feelings of many women whose relatives had been slaughtered only twenty years previously were recorded in the (unpublished) minutes of 'Women's Organisations in Wartime'. 'Women are feeling sore and bitter against they don't know whom. Those who have been living on a mere pittance since the last war and whose husbands are still disabled from it and whose sons are now being called up, take some persuading before they'll get enthusiastic this time.' They also voiced a profound mistrust of a government which had championed peace and democracy and yet failed to prevent another war.

By the winter of 1939 a meeting of women's organisations agreed that 'Universally women feel that men are responsible for the war... as every opportunity for co-operative prevention has been wasted.' The Chamberlain government had not only inflicted war on the nation 'through weakness', but had also 'mishandled women's passion to end it'.

But such protest was on the whole unpopular, and war propaganda throughout 1939 became increasingly effective – 'intellectual pollution' was how Tom Harrison (author of the candid public opinion poll, Mass Observation*) described it. Although on the day the Nobel peace prize was to have been awarded in Norway a large procession of silent women from international

* Mass Observation, a social survey organisation, was set up in 1937 by Tom Harrisson and Charles Madge as a 'reaction to the disturbed condition of Western Europe under the growing threat of fascism.' Among other things, they invited ordinary people to write accounts of their daily lives, 'recording the voice of the people'. Using full-time and voluntary observers and diarists, they collected together unique and extraordinarily candid information on everyday life and public mood before and during the war.

Queue for the cinema after they reopened. Note the gas masks in boxes.

organisations formed a protest, urgent appeals had already swept most women towards the industry of war.

The Munich crisis in September 1938 had given the British an important breathing space to roll very limited resources into action. In November, handbooks were distributed to all households listing essential war jobs – the only alternative (for men) to military conscription. By the end of 1938, 1½ million people had enrolled for Civil Defence Work. The part-time ranks of the Territorial Army and the RAF Volunteer Reserve began to swell, and over 300,000 volunteered for the Armed Forces. In April 1939 the Military Training Act conscripted men of 20 and 21 years to six months' compulsory military training. The Emergency Powers Act of August concluded the Defence Regulations that were to dominate civilian life for the next six years.

These changes were effected with a flood of forms, posters and leaflets, broadcasts about national security (ie. defence) and identity cards necessary for National Registration and consequent mobilisation into war work. With the inexorable process that eventually left them with 7½ million of their youngest and fittest men conspicuously absent, British women began to prepare for the domestic upheavals to come, adjustments that were to be their 'finest hour'. Throughout 1939, gradually increasing numbers of women responded to appeals for war work. In every field in which they could replace a man for active service they did so, joining government training schemes if necessary. Some 'joined up' for patriotic reasons, others because they needed the money urgently. Local authorities were advised by the Ministries of Information, Home Security, Food and Agriculture and the War Office on the formation of Invasion Committees to cover all parts of the country. The Home Guard, the Police, Civil Defence, the Fire, Casualty and Messenger Services as well as a Fire Guard all had to be coordinated, using women as well as men to cover every emergency from bombing to invasion.

There was much to be planned. Church bells were to be silenced except to announce the landing of the enemy. Emergency transport was to include tractors, traction engines, lorries, cars, farm carts, horses and hand carts. Lists of wells, springs, ponds and rivers were noted and guarded, if necessary, for civilian and fire service use (not forgetting sea water for pumps) should the water supply fail. For the anticipated masses of casualties, emergency cottage hospitals had to be organised, in homes if need be, with whatever vehicles could serve as ambulances. Improvised stretchers had to be made, chemist stock and invalid food listed, collapsible cardboard coffins, common burial grounds and morgues needed organisation. The Red Cross and St John's Ambulance Corps were reminded that 'immediate evacuation to outside hospitals will often be impossible', and 'in addition to provision for our own civil and military casualties, arrangements must be adequate for dealing with large numbers of enemy dead'. Hospital entrances presented stark reminders to those who had served in the First World War. New signboards directed women ambulance drivers to wards for gas casualties without wounds, casualties without gas, and to the general clearing station. Student nurses and doctors piled mountains of heavy sandbags against outer walls while patients (even those awaiting operations) were sent home to make room for war casualties, and wards on higher floors were emptied to reduce the danger from bombs or blast.

Civilians had been prepared for gas and chemical warfare since Munich, when 38 million gas masks were issued. They were told that rattles would announce the presence of dangerous gases and decontamination treatment would be made publicly available. Gas masks of the latest model were advertised by the Ministry of Defence, despite the millions issued during the Munich Crisis.

Better Safe Than Sorry –
It comes in six sizes:
New line for babies and children 2–5
with Mickey Mouse boxes;
for bedridden patients;
for walking casualties;
and for the General Public over 5 years.
15s each

Like identity papers, it was to be illegal not to carry them at all times, (although many forgot or refused after a few months of a gasless war). A mother and child on their way to the corner shop without a gas mask were told to report to the police station and had to walk 1½ miles since transport too was curtailed and petrol allowed for 'essential' travel only. 'Inessential' vehicles were immobilised and civilians learnt from yet more pamphlets how to sabotage them if the invader was around. 'To put your vehicles out of action, remove the distributor head and leads and either empty the tank or remove the carburettor'. The parts were to be hidden well away. Plans for strict food and clothing rationing were made known and all these rulings were to be subject to fines if disregarded until eventually (under Security Regulations) everything from

feeding bread to birds to chatting about a boyfriend's whereabouts became a fineable offence.

Both children and adults were to be clearly labelled in case of accident; and women were constantly reminded to make their homes available to capacity for billetors or refugees. Invasion committees 'must not rest satisfied until they have convinced every householder that it is his (sic) inescapable duty to provide food, shelter and succour for every homeless person until other arrangements can be made.' Rest centres in schools, barns and halls were the only alternatives in emergency and these were supposed to shelter the homeless for a few hours' respite with a little food if possible, but like most other social services they were quite inadequate for the homeless and were organised by women themselves as the need arose, in horrifying proportions.

Holidaymakers returning in August 1939 to share the last moments of peace with husbands, fathers, sons and brothers saw familiar parts of the country signposted

'To the trenches'; nameless signposts and stations and camouflaged landmarks Stirrup pumps and Anderson shelters (two curved walls of corrugated steel joined at the top and bolted to stout rails, to be sunk 3 feet into the ground and covered with 18 inches of earth) were being delivered. Steeples or towers that might collapse through bomb blast were dismantled, while brick street shelters (very unsafe, as it turned out) and slit trenches were constructed. Underground, some factories, offices and shops made their own air raid shelters and factory managers were told to organise their own defence systems. Furthermore, factories were later informed that only where 'existing shelters cannot be used as emergency cover should work cease when the siren sounds'. Below ground, workers practised their Air Raid Drill accordingly in the new shelters. 'In the event of an Air Raid, visitors will conform to the staff regulations for Air Raid Precautions. No one may leave this building.'

The London Underground was not intended for use, as the possibility of hysteria or even subversion through a 'deep shelter mentality' was, along with mass death, to be avoided at all costs. But thousands of people took over the Tube themselves when the Blitz actually came, angry at the lack of adequate shelter provided. According to the Stand Firm Policy of the government, a leaflet, 'Your Home as an Air Raid Shelter', suggested protection against 'stray shots and falling metal' as well as the collapse of the house. 'If you can have a trench ready in your garden or field, so much the better, especially if you live where there is danger from shell fire' – which of course affected most families in overcrowded industrial districts where gardens and fields were rare.

In villages, people clubbed together to buy their own sirens and worked out how to barricade village streets with carts, bedsteads, ancient prams – a useless tactic but officially encouraged for its contribution to morale. Pill-boxes merged with hillocks and aircraft hangars were camouflaged as grassy fields. Space was soon at a premium as private evacuees, hospitals and military depots installed themselves in safe or strategic parts of the countryside. Farmers could now get gas masks for their cart horses and a special version was designed for dogs. Some people evacuated their pets, including goldfish and canaries, and 400,000 London pets were humanely gassed by the RSPCA during the first four days of war, in a patriotic gesture to save food.

On a domestic level, women faced conflicting advice; to mobilise themselves for war work, to evacuate the children, to stay put and to 'stand firm', and, moreover, to save bread and give to National Savings. Many were still hoping that war would somehow be averted. But at the end of August 1939, Parliament was recalled, all leave cancelled, the British Fleet mobilised and teachers told to prepare for evacuation with their classes. As Hitler invaded Poland on 1 September millions of children and mothers gathered at railway stations to

Two types of shelter: a highly modernised version built by employers for 2000 factory workers (here rehearsing), and the famous Anderson shelter issued to householders, in this case Mrs Rowe and Mrs Threadwell of Islington who are measuring their height. Some made their shelters quite cosy – others preferred to shelter under the stairs.

Life was simple in the golden morning of the world. To-day, in wartime, it has become more nerve-racking than ever before. The article below tells you how an eight weeks' course of 'Sanatogen' Nerve-Tonic Food can restore your natural reserve of energy and vitality.

What doctors say
about *next Winter*

make their awful farewells, uncertain whether they would ever meet again. Wives, sisters and mothers of young men waved them off as bravely as they could with the memory of the First World War in the minds of many. Now they faced the horror of war on an even greater scale – a war that was to be fought against civilians also.

Those still at home finished sewing their blackout curtains and shared wireless sets with a foretaste of the intimacy war was to bring. On 1 September the BBC announced a single wartime channel of programmes and the television channel was closed down at 11 minutes past 11 in the morning – 'for the duration of the war'. On 3 September Chamberlain announced that war against Germany was declared. Eight minutes later, sirens sounded to bewildered and assorted reactions – of stupefaction, sang-froid, panic. Mothers donned gas masks and forced babies into their anti-gas suits and wondered whether to run to the public shelter or hide under the stairs. But the bombers did not arrive for almost a year. It was the start of 'this strangest of wars', the phoney war. (There were three minor attacks in the provinces between March and May 1940). The constant strain of waiting for bombardment was such that some women recall almost wishing something would happen. A nurse, Kate Phipps, wrote in her diary from her 'depressing sand-bagged wards' that 'This crisis business, hanging over us is very nerve-racking. I haven't slept at all these last few weeks and some people are getting a bit jittery, expecting to be annihilated at any moment'.

The Emergency Powers Act now enforced blackout regulations, to include masked torches and headlights and thick white lines on pavement kerbs. Driving accidents increased temporarily. Families could also be fined if any light glimmered from their windows as 'easy enemy targets'. Women taped glass panes so that they could not shatter and faced their gloomy interiors with ever more economical amounts of light, heat, comfort and company. Places of public entertainment, cinemas, theatres, football grounds or mass meetings were immediately closed 'until further notice', to prevent large numbers of people being killed. (They reopened in December 1939). Newspapers and trunk calls were censored and appeals made to limit telephone calls and post to a minimum. The fourth army, the Home Guard, complete with broomsticks, chairlegs and women's homemade Molotov cocktails, rolled not into action but into the nervous waiting period of the phoney war.

But these months were vital in allowing British factories to produce necessary military equipment. In spite of considerable output of aeroplanes, warships, submarines and tanks the previous year, Britain had only a tiny proportion of equipment compared to the enemy. From the first day of the war all healthy men between the ages of eighteen and forty-one were to be conscripted under the National Services (Armed Forces) Act, unless their jobs were in essential 'reserved' occupations.

Women under the age of forty were categorised into 'mobile' or 'immobile' groups – the latter constituted the 10 million women 'already doing their own form of National Service' in caring for the 9 million young (under fourteen), the 6 million old or the millions of war workers and evacuees. Women who had not already joined the Auxiliary Armed Forces answered Chamberlain's War Workers Campaign to work in Royal Ordnance Factories, the Women's Land Army, in Civil Defence, in hospitals and the ambulance corps – though it was a slow and frustrating business. Most 'immobile' women too, from young mothers to eighty-year-olds, pleaded for part-time work (almost impossible to find at first) or volunteered for work, often with the voluntary groups that almost single-handed were to provide the only social services for the population at war. The Women's Voluntary Service, the Women's Institutes, the Townswomen's Guilds, the

Salvation Army and the Red Cross had somehow to transform their peacetime activities to cope with a state of national emergency. By 13 September the *Women's Newspaper* announced that 'So great was the wish to join the WVS that a one way traffic system had to be put into operation along the headquarters' corridors at Tothill St Westminster.'

But government advice was conflicting. Two months later, after millions of women had requested war work, the Ministry of Information announced that women, unless particularly well qualified, were to stick to their jobs and their homes. 'The woman who carries on with her job and does voluntary work in her spare time is doing her full share.'

The Chairman of the Women's Liberal Federation contested the government attitude to women.

> Listening to the BBC conversation a few days ago between the Ministry of Food and two tame housewives, I got more and more angry. For twenty years since the last war, women have proved their fitness in one big job after the other and women are especially good with a clear experience of how rules and regulations affect real people in the home. But now, in this great crisis . . . the Ministry of Food has no use for women except to tell each one in her own kitchen to make the best of short rations . . . It is a deplorable wastage of brains to give us no opportunity in our own field. Unemployment among women is proportionally heavier than among men, and especially heavy among those with the *most* experience.

Nevertheless, posters clamoured for still more hands. Women (and men not conscripted into the Forces) were mobilised into one of the 'reserve' occupations like engineering, farming, medicine or civilian administration. Tanks, guns, aeroplanes, warships, bullets, bombs, uniforms, camouflage nets, parachutes, kit bags and kit, medical supplies and submarines had all to be produced with a dreadful urgency. Britain produced only 40 per cent of her foodstuffs, and farm workers were now obliged to plough by night, through air raids if neces-

sary, to reach the new food production target. Imports were too dangerous with seas guarded by the Luftwaffe and submarines. Food was expensive in seamen's lives as well as money, warned the Ministry of Food.

Women's attitudes to war work varied. For some it brought a new prosperity and independence and opened doors to many a job, hitherto strictly male. In fact greater acceptance by the general public of women working was one of the greatest changes brought about by the war. Women from the heavy industrial areas had suffered dreadful poverty in the decade before the war, and these in particular welcomed the extra income from their war work, as did widows from the First World War. Only seven years previously, in 1932, 2¾ million insured workers had suffered the ignominy of the dole queue. A third of all Welsh workers, and a quarter of all Scots had been out of work, with between 15 per cent and 25 per cent unemployment in much of the North, the Midlands and the South-West of Britain. Elsewhere, light industry had actually flourished, with the novel and prospering manufacture of cars, wireless sets, electric irons and bicycles, producing boom towns like Coventry and Luton. Wages for those employed rose, with only one person in eight out of work in the South-east. Jobs for women had already started to expand. However, among the more genteel the notion still prevailed that, firstly, it was 'not done' for a married woman to work, and, secondly, in the white collar occupations, that a married woman would be usurping the job of a male wage-earner. At a time when jobs were hard to find, it was thought unfair for a household to have two incomes. Accordingly, women teachers, nurses, civil servants and so on were obliged to resign on marriage, a course which further encouraged the concept of the 'little woman', housebound and dependent. The extent to which opposition to this concept existed among women is illustrated by Margery Corbett Ashby's records of women's reactions to the bad management of their war work, which she provided for the official wartime public opinion poll and for Mass Observation in January 1941:

> Furious that the Government has learnt so little about the value of women's work... Status is very bad and pay worse while there is a strong tendency to lower both with a flat rate of £1 18s 6d, a week, without regard to training or responsibility. This will be very dangerous socially... Women over 35 are not wanted. New ministries refuse women in responsible jobs.

During the first months of the war women had to fight hard to get work at all. They were shuffled backwards and forwards between Town Hall and Employment Exchange where little help was given by inexperienced staff grappling with the tediously impersonal and bureaucratic forms of wartime life. Some were allocated work they were quite unsuited for. Others were frustrated or daunted by the conflict between rude officialdom and their desire to fight for victory. Once 'mobilised', a woman could be directed anywhere, ie. a Cornish woman could be sent to the Midlands where the quota of local women was not yet fully employed, or had themselves been posted to the Land Army or a factory elsewhere. Sometimes the work itself had not been properly organised. On 11 November, a farmer, Miss Calmody Hamlyn resigned from the Devon Women's Land Army Committee, rather than persuade any more girls to leave their homes on promise of non-existent jobs. 'I was sent out to recruit them promising work, badges and uniforms, and now they have been trained, am I to tell them they must go to the unemployment exchange?'

The Women's Freedom League complained in December that 'The tragedy of war overshadows all our hopes and efforts for the Women's Cause. Women as responsible citizens are taking a big share in Civil Defence but it cannot be claimed that the Government is making anything like the full use of the Woman Power of the country.' Those already in factories (where at least the wages were tempting) and others

YOUR COURAGE
YOUR CHEERFULNESS
YOUR RESOLUTION
WILL BRING
US VICTORY

This poster, the first of the war, annoyed people more than any other: they felt it typified the THEM and US tactics of the government.

HOW TO CHALLENGE AN INVADER.

Hands up!	*Hande hoch!* (Henda hoch).
Hand over your weapons!	*Ubergeben sie ihre waffen!* Ubergayben zee eerer vuffen).
Surrender or I shoot!	*Ergeben sie sich, oder ich schiesse!* (Airgayben zee zich ohder ich sheesa).
Quick march!	*Vorwarts marsch!* (Forvairts marsh).
Turn round!	*Umdrehen!* (Oomdrayen).
Left turn!	*Links um!* (Links oom).
Right turn!	*Rechts um!* (Rechts oom).

Recruiting van draws women to war work.

like nurses in hospitals, found hours and conditions worsening. Day or night shifts of ten to twelve hours were now the norm. It was a period of physical adjustment to the new strain of unfamiliar work schedules. Women and men on bomber production lines were on duty from 8 am. until midnight for seven days a week and without Bank Holidays to recuperate. In June 1940 Ernest Bevin tried to introduce a 60-hour working week, since the fervour of sleepless war workers often negated itself. Nurses with empty wards (until the summer of 1940) complained of their barrack-like conditions and depressed wages in *Woman Today*, a magazine in which Edith Summerskill pointed out in December that married women and their children had hitherto been denied the medical health benefits that their insured husbands had enjoyed under the 1911 National Insurance Act. Those women in the Royal Ordnance Factories realised t' at the Personal Injuries (Emergency Provisions) Act placed a lower price on their injuries than on those of their husbands. Disablement was a very real possibility, not simply through the bombardment of factories as prime targets, but also through the dangerous nature of the work itself – handling ammunition, making bombs and working with the unfamiliar hazards of wartime working conditions. They demanded that married women had the right to earn, with equal status and equal pay for equal work in secure and healthy premises.

Many younger women were already mechanics, engineers or lorry drivers. Others manned barges on the Manchester Ship Canal. With the first air raids, those who were already coping with the strain of broken homes, evacuated children, restricted shopping, fear, lack of sleep and loneliness had to take on more unusual posts. With increasing pressure on women to relieve men for the Forces they repaired rooms, became chimney sweeps, porters at stations, repaired gas pipes and unloaded cargo at docks. With devastation around them they tried to set up emergency nurseries for unevacuated children, managed mass emergency feeding in the streets, drove 'corpse wagons' and joined the Fire Service.

By October 1941, a Ministry of Labour survey showed a deficit of two million workers for the Forces and munition production. Murmurings of conscription for women had made headlines throughout the year – disturbing news for mothers or those already working long hours. Mass Observation, however, reported that most women wondered why the move to conscript women had not been taken earlier than 1941, and that 97 per cent of all British women would be happy to take what they felt to be positive steps towards Victory over Nazism. The complete disruption of family life seemed imminent. Ernest Bevin began 'Calling all Women' from the Ministry of Labour to join the 'Bevin Beauties' (women workers) in the heroic fight. Not surprisingly,

women at the Ministry accused him of approaching women in the wrong way. In December, the Second National Service Act banished some doubts. Women would definitely not be sent to the military front to fight. Hitherto women had been 'freely directed' to civilian work of all kinds. Now the Women's Services were included, with Civil Defence and industry as the only alternatives.

Women realised that with a controlled labour force they might be sent away from whatever was left of their families to wherever they were needed. The wives of servicemen faced particular problems: it was perhaps ironic that these women, who sacrificed their husbands to possible death at any instant, were not directed to work, since it was they (the lowest paid) who most needed a share in the prosperity brought by wartime industries and distraction from their personal anxieties. In 1939, the lower ranks of the Services were only paid 2s a day, of which eventually a proportion went to the

3 women from different homes — 3 women with different problems — 3 women with different incomes

Four-figure income :
(And yet Mrs. S.-H. feels the pinch) *But expenses are heavier these days, and there's less help. So some washing must be done at home. That's where the Acme helps — gives the inexperienced woman almost professional washing, makes work lighter, easier.*

'Middling' salary :
(It's a close call for Mrs. K.) *Keeping a home going these days takes some doing — particularly when some less fortunate ones are sharing it with you. Still, one can always do even the heavy washing oneself — provided you've an Acme as an ever-present help.*

A Wage-earner :
(It's wonderful how Mrs. B. 'manages') : *Every minute of the day precious. Not an ounce of energy to waste. The home and children to be kept proudly, spotlessly clean. Washing, that everlasting call on the working woman, is made almost light work when you have an Acme to help.*

but the answer's the same for all —
an Acme !

WHEN a woman first uses an Acme, one thing astonishes her. How on earth, why on earth, did she muddle along without one ! For it only takes you one washday with an Acme to realise what a necessity it is.

One other thing may surprise you when you first see an Acme. How simple it looks ! And yet the simple-looking, effortless Acme conceals the finest engineering design known — the cantilever system. Turn that screw on top. It regulates with unerring accuracy the controlled pressure which is exerted along the whole length of Acme's two rubber rollers. That accounts for the Acme *cleansing* as well as wringing. At every point, from its pressed steel frame to its 10 year guarantee, the Acme is the finest wringer you can buy.

Why not decide at once ? Why not go straight to your hardware dealer and buy the finest wringer in the world — the Acme !

The Portable Acme illustrated below costs 47/6 for the 16-inch size : 45/6 for the 14-inch size. If you have more room, choose the Acme Folding Stand model — 80/-. All three models are fully described in booklet C.5. obtainable from your Hardware Dealer or post free from Acme Wringers, Ltd., David Street, Glasgow, S.E.

The Acme Lion gives you:
Cantilever pressure. Cushion rubber rollers. Patent reversible drain. Turning handle folds away. Unbreakable pressed steel frame. Rust-proof, chip-proof finish. Die-cast cog wheels. Rustless " oiled " bearings. Choice of 9 clamp fittings. 10 year guarantee.

An Acme will wring, mangle, cleanse, your wash all in one — quicker and better than you could ever do it.

THE ACME LION

family each week along with a government allowance of 25s for a wife with two children. (Decent wages at the time varied between £3 and £10 a week, the best-paid being men in shipyards and munition works.) Only in 1943 was the serviceman's wife given a War Service Grant of £3 a week. These 'immobile' women, left to their own resources, undertook out-work and part-time work as far as they were able. (The Ministry of Information's statistics are confusing as they count two part-time workers as one, which sheds a false light on how many women were subsidising their meagre grants.) These War Service Grants were extended to cover the dependants of Civil Defence workers and farm workers. Mass Observation reported women's attitudes:

> It was said that the women must get older women in to look after their homes. So, a childless woman whose husband is away, perhaps out East, may stay at home and do nothing, unless she volunteers, and at least *be* at home if she works, but a woman whose husband is both able to join up or is doing war work at home, must leave him to another woman and go away from home.

A retired nurse in the same survey spoke angrily on a friend's behalf: 'Her husband was injured in the last war and needs careful feeding, and she is driving a tractor on a farm, and may be forced to leave him with some strange woman to look after – and sleep with I suppose.'

From the outbreak of war, women trained themselves to cope, to work long hours doing vital war work, to try and remain calm, never to break down in an emergency and sometimes to accept the break-up of their families and separation from their children.

And, inevitably, it was women who filled the increasing gaps in the wartime industries. At first they enrolled for work through choice (whether classified as 'mobile' or 'immobile') until conscription of women aged 19 to 30 was brought into force in December 1941. After this the only choice for 'mobile' women of these ages was between essential work in industry and essential work in the Forces. Age limits for women workers were extended. By 1943, of Britain's 17 million women between the ages of fourteen and sixty-four, nine out of ten single women and eight out of ten married women with children over fourteen were working in the Forces or in 'essential work'. Three million married women and widows were working, more than double the pre-war figure. Most of the 10 million 'immobile' women were employed in outwork in their homes, in part-time work or had joined the Civil Defence or the voluntary and auxiliary nursing services, sometimes combining more than one of these occupations, for which their wages were either low or non-existent.

Although they detested a war that divided their families and often left them to suffer alone, women were to prove their capabilities in many former male strongholds. Only with the help of these millions of women was the wartime economy able to function. And in turn, women's wartime experiences had a profound and permanent effect on them.

Labelled children arriving at their billet.

1. Give them a chance of safety and health

EVACUATION AND WAR NURSERIES

During the winter of 1938–39, discreet enquiries were made in 1,760 local government areas to find out how many refugees could be received into each rural district in the event of aerial bombardment. Aided by billeting officers and the newly formed Women's Voluntary Service, county authorities made a surreptitious survey of all country households. Bicycling or walking from house to house, they were often met with incredulity and a dusty, or at any rate a hasty, answer, but it was estimated that some extra 4,800,000 people could be rehoused in the so-called surplus accommodation of the countryside.

But for unsophisticated and understaffed rural authorities the prospect of providing millions of blankets and mattresses, medical supplies, extra water and food was daunting, especially since war had not even been declared, and most people were hoping it could still be avoided.

Britain was divided into reception, evacuation and neutral areas, but much of the better accommodation was booked for military or medical purposes, for factories or institutions. Space was at a premium. Large institutions like the Bank of England, the BBC, and Billingsgate Fish Market arranged evacuation into the more secure parts of the countryside. Museum treasures were buried deep in vaults or, in the case of the National Gallery, winched on to lorries and hidden in Welsh caves. In Oxford, Nuffield College became a tank factory, Balliol College housed the Royal Institute for National Affairs and Ruskin College became a maternity home. Borstals, prisons and hospitals (including mental hospitals) made useful barracks, as their inmates were turfed out. Some 5,600 criminals were released as war

workers, while hospital patients were sent home, 'operations pending', to make room for anticipated military casualties. Women all over Britain were obliged to billet the odd assortment of war workers which included miners, mothers, professors, ex-convicts, students, salesmen and labourers who worked cheek by jowl in the name of patriotism. They were paid a 'government guinea' a week (unless it was a private arrangement) to accommodate, feed and launder for the unnerving intrusion into their already disrupted lives. In September 1939 a third of all Britons changed address and in the course of the war sixty million changes of address in a population of thirty-five million were registered. Normal life ceased as schools, homes, places of work, pubs and cinemas closed or were filled with strangers.

The three authorities involved in the evacuation of children – the Ministries of Health and Transport and the Board of Education – were almost completely unprepared for the results of their schemes. The chaos which followed the city exodus in the first few days of war was for the most part dealt with by women who chose to help voluntarily. The largest group, the Women's Voluntary Service (WVS), and its offshoots such as the Housewives' Service, had recruited almost a million helpers by 1941. Other groups included the Red Cross, Salvation Army, St John's Ambulance Brigade and the Women's Institutes. These women struggled to co-ordinate and supplement the foster homes, grants advisors and meagre welfare services which were all overwhelmed by the mass of social problems exposed by evacuation. Essential zones to be evacuated were also the poorest. Resi-

It went with the pram...

in spite of father's protests. And Mrs. Higgins was right as usual. Her Acme has been a blessing to her, down in the

country—*and* to her neighbours. It makes light of the wash of half-a-dozen crowded cottages. You see, just now, there simply aren't any Acmes to buy. But when the war is won, well, we know of at least six housewives who won't be without an Acme of their own for a minute longer than they —.or we — can help !

dential areas were less likely to be targets than those near docks, gasworks and railways, where the poorest and largest families were housed. Many women were deeply shocked at the physical condition of their charges from such areas. Malnutrition was common, some children suffered from scabies and rickets, many had lice. There were children who had never used a lavatory, squatting instead on a newspaper on the floor or bed. Though this was perhaps less surprising in such a time of stress, so many evacuees were said to be suffering from bed-wetting (something like 33 per cent), that a laundry allowance of 3s 6d a week was added to the billeting grant of 10s 6d per child (8s 6d for more than one child). There were stories of foster parents who found children peeling off the wall-paper to look for bugs as their mothers did at home, or sleeping on the floor because at home they were used to sleeping under their parents' bed. Such stories made headlines, and once again, as in 1914, when the physical condition of army recruits was found to be so poor, war forced a British government to recognise the extremes of poverty and neglect that still survived in our cities, and eventually to act by expanding the limited welfare services.

A classic account of such urban poverty is given in *Our Towns 1939–42*. It described, for example, the condition of the water supply in Shoreditch, where one house had no indoor supply; 30 per cent had to carry water up several floors: and in 57 cases, the water supply was shared by three or more families, and several houses shared the same pump.

The 'hidden sore' of the 'submerged tenth' showed that 12 per cent to 15 per cent of poor families in Merseyside, Bristol, Sheffield and Southampton had only 4s a week to spend on food. Even the 'perfect housewife', when living below the poverty line, could not manage to pay for 'the bare essentials of rent, food, clothing, fire, light and cleaning materials necessary to keep her family in health.' Some women and girls were reported to wear no protection during menstruation (the Suffrage campaign had already reported that no provision was made for this in Holloway Prison), and some women used only wads of rough lavatory paper.

The book stressed that 75 per cent to 80 per cent of the poor managed nevertheless to live decently, and with the constant scrubbing of linen, uneven floors and walls, managed to keep such pests as lice and bedbugs under control. Other women, through lack of education, severe poverty and the burden of too many pregnancies in slum housing, now presented the more privileged and healthy countryside with problem families that no one knew how to handle.

The voluntary services were appalled by the unpreparedness for evacuation of the rural authorities. There was a desperate need for some sort of reception where children could be checked for disease and supplied with bedding and clothing. With subsequent evacuations these were set up by the WVS, and sickbays, dormitories or canteens were improvised in garage or chapel if necessary. But during the first weekend of war, the state of affairs was such that the WVS were obliged to make a thousand straw-stuffed mattresses. Lord Woolton from the Ministry of Supply (he was later Minister of Food from April 1940 until November 1943) broadcast an appeal for blankets, winter clothes and boots. Blankets were handed in at post offices. Girl Guides, Brownies and Cubs knitted patchwork squares from old sweaters, tailors relinquished their pattern books, and months later the WVS were still vigorously converting an American consignment of palliasse covers into sleeping bags. Mountains of boots, clothes and blankets arrived at the Salvation Army, Red Cross and WVS, donated gladly at the time, though later, with increasing shortages, remembered with pangs of regret.

From January 1939 mothers in towns and ports were under increasing pressure to consider evacuation in the event of war.

Two million people arranged private evacuation to hotels, friends or hired cottages, and during the summer months of 1939 thousands left for the USA. Some schools were evacuated intact. Wellington and many of its pupils crossed the Atlantic to spend most of the war in Kingston, Ontario, while at home, the boys of a small northern cathedral choir school, for example, ran blissfully wild for weeks through the grounds of a country house in East Lancashire before sufficient equipment and extra staff could be got together for school-work to be resumed. In the case of other larger schools, less happily relocated, the period of readjustment was a good deal more trying, for staff and children alike.

The official recommendation of the Anderson Committee on Evacuation was that all schoolchildren should be fostered to the country. (Billeting children was to be compulsory for country women even if childless and single.) Children under five should be accompanied by an adult, preferably their mother, although exceptions were later made. Children attending the few existing nursery schools could be boarded in the even fewer residential nurseries, and pregnant women were also advised to leave the danger zones.

Throughout the summer of 1939 broadcasts, newspapers and posters waxed lyrical about the advantages of a healthy, rustic life for the children, contrasting this with an urban life of shattered glass, falling buildings, disrupted schooling and a gnome-like existence under the stairs or in Anderson shelters at the bottom of the garden. Many mothers were persuaded by official exhortations to 'Give them a greater chance of safety and health' to take the unnatural step of letting their children be reared by an unknown woman while they themselves faced injury or death, possibly never to see their offspring again. Yet the decision to accompany the children was just as agonising. The wife who left husband and home to the horrors of air raids faced not only the expense of a family budget divided between two houses, but the unhappy prospect of loneliness and the abrupt interruption of sexual relations.

A less publicised reason for evacuation was the probability that an increasing number of women would be needed to work for war production. And with the prospect of thousands of men about to be killed, it was essential to preserve the lives of the next generation and mothers of child-bearing age. It was also vital to counter both low morale, which would ensue if too many mothers and children were killed in air raids, and mass hysteria if a rushed or disorganised exodus was to start after the air raids had begun.

Finally, on 31 August 1939, with only twenty-four hours' warning, came the announcement: 'The Government have ordered the evacuation of schoolchildren. If your children are registered for evacuation send them to their assembly point at once.'

Heavy-hearted mothers packed a change of underclothes, washing things, a sandwich lunch and gas mask, and attached luggage labels with names and addresses to their children's coats.

On Friday 1 September 1939, 17,000 members of the Women's Voluntary Service were ready at dawn to organise a million and a half people at each stage of their journey from cities and ports throughout the British Isles to safety from the expected bombs. For many, this was their first glimpse of serious poverty in Britain – and a considerable shock. The number included 827,000 unaccompanied children, 524,000 mothers and children under five years old, 13,000 pregnant women, 7,000 blind, crippled or handicapped people with 103,000 escorts. Teachers and helpers were also included among the evacuees. With banners, flags and armbands, helpers guided their labelled herd on to trains and buses, destination unknown.

48 per cent of schoolchildren were evacuated, and from 1–4 September nearly one and a half million people left the cities of Britain – London, Manchester, Birmingham, Salford, Coventry, Derby, Nottingham, Grimsby, Hull, Newcastle, Glasgow, Portsmouth, Southampton, Walsall, West Bromwich, Smethwick, Liverpool, Bootle, Wallasey, Birkenhead, Sheffield, Rotherham, Bradford, Leeds, West Hartlepool, Gateshead, South Shields, Middlesborough, Dundee, Edinburgh, Rosyth.

Some children carried buckets and spades, mistaking their mothers' tears for regret that they could not share the treat. The poorest children from the urban slums often presented a horrific sight, dirty, ill-shod and verminous. Some of the children were padded with brown paper and 'sewn up' for the winter months.

The journeys were a harrowing experience for all concerned. One in Scotland, which took twelve and a half hours was described by an escort as 'the most depressing, deplorable and disgusting journey I have ever had the misfortune to make'. Helpers did their best, singing 'Run Rabbit Run' and 'Ten Green Bottles' for the overexcited, sticky, tearful and dirty children. Many trains had no corridors or lavatories, with inevitable consequences. By the end even well-groomed children looked 'off-putting' and those from deprived districts looked 'horrifying'.

On arrival, kind-hearted helpers waiting at bus depots and stations often found that their group had been split up or deposited elsewhere. It was not unusual for mothers and children to be subjected to a cattle-market inspection by villagers naturally eager to find respectable evacuees. This invariably left all the rougher groups swearing, hungry and exhausted. One unexpectedly large party from Dagenham arrived by boat in East Anglia. 'No organisation existed for dealing with them. Schools and other buildings were opened, but blankets did not exist. Some slept for days on straw and under sacks with only apples, cheese and milk to eat.' Spaces were hastily improvised, often bleak village halls with camp beds and benches, the kindness of the women helpers making up in some

Millions of town children (note their gas masks) leave home wearing inadequate summer clothing. 'The fact that many were bedwetters and unwashed aroused more pity than anger. What really aroused the country woman's anger was the town mother's inability and lack of desire to train her children. Yet their anger was directed far more against the system which produced such ignorance than against the individual.'

part for the unwelcoming surroundings. Even wards of mental hospitals and workhouses were used.

Groups of heavily pregnant women arrived miles from maternity homes. One who arrived exhausted and unexpectedly at a WVS rest centre in an old chapel was aching for a bath. The woman in charge eventually improvised a tin bath with hot water in the pulpit! Elsewhere, children were thrust through rustic front doors late at night, and school parties which had crocodiled obediently on to the train were split up on arrival or found themselves at the wrong destination. And though all children had been issued with a postcard to write their new address to their parents, many of these had been lost, along with teddy bears, dolls and favourite books.

When accompanying mothers moved into the billets as well there was almost always tension. By November, country members of the Women's Institute were describing compulsory billeting as 'dictatorship to the housewife – and after all, we're supposed to be fighting a dictatorship.'

Although some effort was made to match billets and evacuees, some slum children found themselves in stately homes cared for by grumbling servants, while 'respectable' mothers and children might find themselves sharing a lowly cottage, daunted by earth closets, oil lamps and water pumps. Long-standing class rituals were under strain – what time to have supper, whether to eat together or not, what to eat, whether to wear best clothes on Sunday or to work, how often to bath and the difficulty of sharing rations were issues that quickly led to considerable tensions.

'Here we have Sunday dinner every day!' One boy gained 7lbs in one week. School dinners, along with the new milk and vitamin schemes increased multifold over the war years, resulting in a marked improvement in health especially among the children of the poor.

The complaints of evacuee mothers were understandable. Women were exhausted by carrying their small children everywhere, since prams were not available. One woman in Norfolk complained that her aristocratic host would only let her use the water pump at certain times to wash her baby's nappies, and that the maid obliged her to collect sticks for the fire when she asked for a cup of tea. Another complained about sharing meals. 'It's too posh for me. We'd rather have our meals in the kitchen. It's too clean. You can't be yourself here.' Or, 'We may be poor but we have our own little flats with gas rings to get tea quick.' Other women were unnerved by the silent distances of the countryside or, as the mother of a 'difficult' family billeted in West Cumberland described it, 'Them bloody 'ills drive me crackers every time I look at them.'

With two months' experience of evacu-ees, a member of the Women's Institute wrote to the editor of *Home and County* magazine in November 1939:

Hundreds of WI members listened recently to Mr Strong's broadcast story on the wireless. Our circle was silent at first, then someone snapped out, 'Propaganda of course, timed to prepare us for the next horde of evacuees.' After a full month's hard thinking, certain facts seemed to emerge:
1.   There is no criticism of the central idea that children should be protected.
2.   Indiscriminate billeting can be tolerated only as a very temporary emergency measure.
3.   The casting forth of mothers and children has been, in the main, a failure . . . Is the town mother in a danger zone to put her young children before her husband and home? Had they not better stand or fall together? In the wireless story, the acceptance by the men of the sacrifice of their home and comfort was suggested as right and proper. The weeping woman was considered hysterical because she could not see it like that . . . Are women

human first or women first? If human, theirs is the right to choose, but if their sex differentiation is their highest function, then, like children, they must be preserved.

The country woman was asked to provide facilities for her evacuees to bath, eat, and so on, but she was not obliged to sacrifice her sitting room, parlour or kitchen throughout the day. Even tactful evacuee mothers were soon resented, as villages and small towns became overcrowded. Shop queues lengthened, chips (when there were any) ran out at the fish and chip shop and favourite brands of goods disappeared. Homesick mothers reacted badly to the enforced intimacy and the supreme tact required of them. Some wandered aimlessly with children down lanes or to the village green, their lives completely disjointed and unreal. Many of the poorer families had never seen a field, a cow, a chicken or even an egg before, and longed to return to the swarming city. Others regarded evacuation as a holiday and expected to be waited on by their hostesses.

Clubs and social centres were quickly requisitioned by the wvs. In 'safe' towns and rural districts, anything from a shed to a large room was provided with makeshift toys and furniture, books and lectures; many were soon demolished by the rougher sections. The centres also attempted to feed evacuees at midday 'with no expenditure to fall upon the reception areas', but this became less necessary with the arrival of the Government's British Restaurants early in 1940 – the national guarantee of at least one good, coupon-free meal a day. (This was similar to government policy for school meals which expanded from 250,000 a day to 1,850,000 during the war years.) By 1944, British Restaurants numbered about 2,000, and served about half a million meals a day, providing enough meals for every family to eat a coupon-free meal once a month, at about 1s 2d for a three-course meal. For part-time working mothers, however, who sometimes wanted to seize the chance to save rations, shopping and cooking by eating out with the children, it

was still too expensive to use regularly.

Their new charges were an irritating source of amazement to foster mothers. Many of the poorer children had never seen fresh vegetables, chicken or meat and refused to eat them. Some had used neither knife nor fork before and came from dwellings where cooking was impossible with only a shared tap for a whole tenement and a slow burner to boil a kettle. They were used to a diet of sausages, fish and chips, or bread and scrape.

The children's attitudes varied. 'The country is a funny place,' one child was heard to say. 'They never tell you you can't have no more to eat, and under the bed is wasted.' Some Stepney Jewish children were overwhelmed by their new homes. 'Rose whispered for days. Everything was so clean in the room. We were given flannels and toothbrushes. We'd never cleaned our teeth up till then. And there was a lavatory upstairs, and carpets. And something called an eiderdown, and clean sheets, and all rather scary.' One child was staggered to discover that cows were bigger than dogs, having only seen them in books before. Others got confused between pigs and sheep, and a ten-year-old Cockney's essay was read on the nine o'clock news on 29 October 1939, to amuse listeners:

> The cow is a mamal [sic]. It has six sides, right, left and upper and below. At the back it has a tail, on which hangs a brush. With this it sends the flies away so they do not fall into the milk. The head is for the purpose of growing horns and so that the mouth can be somewhere. The horns are to butt with and the mouth is to moo with. Under the cow hangs the milk. It is arranged for milking. When people milk, the milk comes and there is never an end to the supply. How the cow does it I have not yet realised, but it makes more and more. The cow has a fine sense of smell, one can smell it far away. This is the reason for the fresh air in the country.
>
> The man cow is called an ox. It is not a mamal. The cow does not eat much, but what it eats it eats twice, so that it gets enough. When it is hungry it moos and when it says nothing it is because all the inside is full up with grass.

IT HAPPENED EVERY NIGHT

1. *I am secretary to the Managing Director of a big firm that evacuated to the country when the Blitz began. "Wonderful! Now for some peace and quiet," I thought.*

2. *Peace and quiet! The first week, the old banshee howled thirty-eight times, mostly at night. Up we'd have to get and trapes off to the shelter and sit around till the All-Clear.*

3. *After a bit we stayed in bed unless we heard something happening. That's when I began to feel terrible. I must have had one ear open for the siren even in my sleep.*

4. *My nerves went to pieces. So did my work. One morning, I took a long memorandum in shorthand and couldn't read it back. I'll never forget it. I actually cried in the office!*

5. *It was then that one of the older girls told me about the three sleep groups. "You'll never keep going unless you get 1st Group Sleep," she said, and she advised me to take Horlicks.*

6. *She seemed so sensible, I took her advice. That night and ever since I've had a lovely cup of hot Horlicks. What a difference in the way I feel when I waken up — and all day long!*

7. *All that horrid nerviness and depression has slipped away now. In fact, I feel so much better than I have for years, I believe it's 1st Group Sleep I've been missing all the time.*

THERE ARE THREE SLEEP GROUPS

SCIENTISTS divide us into 1st, 2nd and 3rd Group Sleepers. The last group are wakeful, can't get to sleep. Group No. 2 may sleep 8 or 9 hours, yet wake still tired. Group 1 sleepers get the deep, refreshing sleep we must have to keep going.

The great value of Horlicks is that it helps you to get 1st Group Sleep. Start taking Horlicks to-night and see how it helps you to take the second year of war in your stride. *Prices as before the war*: from 2/-. At chemists and grocers.

HORLICKS

A popular 1940 joke was of a child explaining to its visiting mother, 'This is spring, Mummy, and they have one down here every year.'

Many of the few rural day nurseries had closed temporarily for days or months, or been taken over for the war effort, as were most public buildings, leaving the evacuated mother with neither enough chores to occupy her in someone else's house nor the means to work. The foster mother, too, had no support in her care of the under fives. Although in November the Ministry of Health and the Board of Education strongly recommended nursery centres, they were rejected as too expensive.

On the whole the two worlds did not merge successfully. Within a few months, as the threatened bombs failed to materialise, mothers were tempted to recall their children. An official poster which showed a leering Hitler beckoning towards a war-torn city advised, 'Don't do it mother, leave the children where they are.' Yet by January 1940, 88 per cent of mothers and 86 per cent of child evacuees had returned home.

But this was only the end of the first phase in the chaotic experiment intended to save a civilian population from the horrors of aerial bombardment in a 'total war' which the experience of the Spanish Civil War had led everyone to fear. By September of 1940, less than three months after Dunkirk, the 'phoney war' was over on the home front too, beginning with the first large Blitz on London, and spreading rapidly in succeeding months to Birmingham, Coventry, Manchester, Sheffield, Portsmouth and the other provincial and manufacturing cities. Following each attack, a new wave of evacuees struggled out of the smoking cities into the countryside, where the situation was often as chaotic and disorganised as in London at the beginning of the Blitz. The provincial cities, with fewer ample outer suburbs to absorb the homeless, often suffered more acute and complicated rehousing problems.

Mass Observation reported that only a

small percentage of mothers were glad to be evacuated and discovered that the only reason that many remained was that their homes had been bombed. Of mothers who remained in towns to work, 42 per cent were found to be very unhappy without their children, 46 per cent had mixed feelings (ie. they did miss them but felt they were safer in the countryside), and only 11 per cent were glad.

The country woman who took in the children also had grave misgivings about evacuation:

> ... the incompatibility of town and country, the difficulty of adjusting richer to poorer, clean to unclean, etc... If we countrywomen are asked for a considered opinion, we shall probably stress the need for crèches or nursery schools as the solution. We shall then hear about prohibitive cost and we shall be conscious of our own unoccupied rooms... We learnt by actual contact that the other half appreciates us as little as we appreciate it. For the children, creches and camps seem to be the only acceptable solution. For the mothers, surely we must think again, giving them the decision as to how and where their duty lies ... It is tragic at the present time to see schoolchildren running wild in both town and country. The teachers are doing their best with a patchwork scheme, but wherever there are children, adequate schools should be speedily opened with proper shelters.

With the ending of large scale evacuation the need for nursery provision became urgent, and a centralised policy on this was essential. Mothers remonstrated at the impossibility of factory work if the shortage of nurseries for young children continued. The Nursery School Association protested: 'In many cases women have to take time off from work in the factories to look after their children. Sometimes women working on shifts all night have to take care of their children during the day.' One of these mothers, working in a clothing factory, reported: 'I feel very keenly the splitting up of homes caused by the evacuation of children: it is difficult to carry on work efficiently if one's mind is not at rest about the children. The Government should commandeer country houses, and nurses employed by rich women should be used to look after the children of women who are helping in war production.'

Even before the mobilisation of women in the spring of 1941, many mothers desperately wanted or needed to work, but the shortage of nurseries was acute. Only destitute children already in full-time nurseries were catered for in the evacuation to residential nurseries. A mere 104 day nurseries and 118 nursery schools were registered in the British Isles of 1938, and these accommodated a mere 13,795 children. Of the 55 day nurseries in Scotland, 38 were run voluntarily. A further 170,000 children were squeezed into elementary schools, only half their number organised into nursery classes. The remainder were cared for by 'a mums' rota', or by minders who charged about 6d a day, but they too were eventually mobilised.

Within days of the outbreak of war, others who had chosen not to evacuate their younger children found all familiar lifelines gone – husbands, neighbours, friends and eventually grandparents dispersed and all nursery schools in danger zones closed down, although a mother remembers that 'we all kept an eye on each other's children and they knew that they could go to a number of houses if the siren went.' The new 'social casualties' of war were mothers previously quite able to cope but now in a 'potentially precarious position', and particularly the two million wives of servicemen who now needed to work for more than patriotic reasons.

In fact it was not until June 1940 that the Ministry of Health began to recognise the social distress of families with children, and even then it was only finally moved by the urgent need for more woman power in the war factories and Civil Defence. In spite of a new Factory and Welfare Department of the Ministry of Labour, set up in June 1940 to help women, 'Action was still to be confined to specific districts where the Ministry of Labour reported an actual or potential shortage of women workers'.

This urgent need for woman power,

coupled with air-raids and more evacuations finally forced the slow growth of two kinds of day nurseries, with meals, milk, baths, regular sleep and stimulating play. Full-time nurseries were to be open for twelve to fifteen hours a day to allow full employment for the mother, and cared for babies from a few months old to five-year-olds for 1s a day. Part-time nurseries for 3d a day catered for two-to-five-year-olds during school hours, and were especially suitable for evacuee children or part-time working mothers.

Between October 1940 and March 1941, official day nursery costs were estimated at 25s a week. The Ministry of Health reimbursed 6s of the cost, the mother paid up to 12s and the rest was paid by local rates. By January the Ministry of Labour, worried that the high costs of these new nurseries would deter mothers from working, suggested that 6d a day should also be the rate for day nurseries, but the Treasury was strongly against this on grounds of increased costs, and the Ministry of Health supported it.

In November 1939 the *Daily Worker* reported some cases of mothers for whom the cost of evacuation was a real hardship.

8s. A WEEK

Mrs S. has three children, two of whom have been evacuated. Her income is £3 3s and she has a total weekly expense of £1 15s, leaving £1 8s for groceries and smaller items. Yet she still has to pay 8s a week for her two children in accordance with the official method of reckoning.

Mrs. W. stated that her total income was £3 2s, including 15s 2d, the wage of her 15-year-old son.

NO BALANCE

Out of this she pays £2 19s 0½d for the up-keep of her home, including groceries. From the remainder, 2s 11½d, she is still expected to pay 5s 6d for her one evacuated child.

These women are demanding that the whole official method of assessing capacity to pay should be revised.

They feel that it is entirely unfair that rents and fares are the only items of house expenditure allowable in the Government scale, and that the personal 'allowances' are completely inadequate.

But only after May 1941 did the turning point come as the Ministry of Health accepted the entire responsibility for the floating population of children. Even so, by November 1941 only 194 nursery centres were open, with another 493 either planned or about to open to care for 13,200 children. The Birmingham Day Nursery proved that in their district alone 300 nurseries were needed.

The first bombings resulted in the overcrowding of existing orphanages and government receiving centres as increasing numbers of children became parentless, either because of an ever-growing need for women to work, or through a mother's hospitalisation, or her death in an air raid. The under-fives panel of the wvs could no longer handle the increasing numbers of requests for full-time residential care of small children either in nursery or billet. Requests for help to the wvs alone rose from 264 in March to 1644 in June 1940. Receiving centres were set up in the countryside, but financial confusion set in at once. Were the new local authorities to foot the astronomical bills (between 28s and 35s a week per child in a residential nursery) or the district council the children had come from, which would leave voluntary and local authorities with too great a financial burden to finance the re-opening of town nurseries?

The Ministry of Health paid the official billeting allowance to residential nurseries as well as housewives, but was only prepared to pay for new residential nurseries if the children could be proved destitute. The 'recommending bodies' for evacuation were groups like the Borough Infant Welfare Officers, the London County Council Organisers, the Citizens Advice Bureau, hospital almoners, social workers, the Women's Institute, Women's Voluntary Service, Red Cross and the Salvation Army. The criteria laid down in March 1940 were strict.

Specimen Cases Suitable for Evacuation:

1. Father serving in Army, Navy or Civil Defence post which is, or would become, full-time in the event of air raids, mother dead, ill, or requiring to be removed to hospital (includes mental hospital); no relatives to whom the child could be sent in the country, no other responsible member of the family who could accompany and care for the child in the event of air raids.
2. Father working at wage insufficient to pay for care of child, mother dead or ill . . . other relatives in work of national importance.
3. Father on small wage, mother nearing confinement and able to show good reason why she has not accepted evacuation as expectant mother.
4. Parents with more than one child under five.
5. Father unemployed but looking for work, mother engaged on work of national importance.
6. No father (includes desertion), mother engaged in work of national importance . . . no grandparents, etc.
7. No father (includes desertion) with mother nearing confinement.
8. Father and mother both engaged on work of national importance but unable to pay for care of child or to arrange for its evacuation. Orphan child without father or mother, resident with aged or infirm grandparents.

These Happy Evacuees
came from crowded, smoky towns to an unfamiliar countryside. They were inclined to mope a bit at first and go off their food. But country air and country fare cured that. Now they're always ravenous. And you can be sure that H.P. Sauce did its share in restoring appetites and making meals the jolliest moments of the day.

With each terrifying wave of bombing the wvs under-fives department answered a deluge of renewed requests for residential help, helplessly: 'So few vacancies; no new nurseries are being opened . . . We will do our best, but . . .'

On 13 September 1940 the American Red Cross donated £78,000 for residential and convalescent nurseries, to be supplemented by the Ministry of Health. Nurseries catering for between five and fifty children were immediately set up in a variety of premises ranging from stately mansions to rooms over village shops and concrete huts supplied by the Ministry of Works. 'Baby buses' were laid on by the wvs to transport the infants from receiving centres to safe and distant nurseries. These receiving centres could only manage a turnover of 800 children a month, all cared for by volunteers. During their two days at the receiving centres, children had name tapes sewn on to their ankles, received a proper medical inspection, were deloused, bathed, given clothes, fed and reassured before the final stage of the journey, through air raids if necessary.

One such heavy air raid was reported by the receiving centre at Highgate after a land-mine had flattened an extension. It also broke the Matron's arm and gave her a black eye . . . The remaining eighteen children were carried amid falling bombs to another house in the grounds and went peacefully to sleep under the dresser, the kitchen table and the sink; but an hour later this house was also pronounced unsafe and the party had to move again. It was

I WISH TO MARK, BY THIS PERSONAL MESSAGE, my appreciation of the service you have rendered to your Country in 1939.

In the early days of the War you opened your door to strangers who were in need of shelter, & offered to share your home with them.

I know that to this unselfish task you have sacrificed much of your own comfort, & that it could not have been achieved without the loyal co-operation of all in your household.

By your sympathy you have earned the gratitude of those to whom you have shown hospitality, & by your readiness to serve you have helped the State in a work of great value.

Elizabeth R

Miss Bowker.

A tribute from the Queen.

28

imperative to move the children the next day, but although the new nurseries were staffed, neither cots nor equipment had arrived. An old van was floored with mattresses for the toddlers, and the remainder taken in a car to a nursery forty miles away, 'driven off as the night raid started. A frightened baby who had to be nursed all the way and a terrified four-year-old who kept on whispering: "We're getting safer now, aren't we?" completed the party.'

In the nurseries, former nannies and women who had completed the training for the emergency child care service took over, headed by state registered nurses until these too were needed for hospital service. The unnatural segregation of children from family life and men in particular was a constant problem and tradesmen were encouraged to come in with their goods 'to provide a much needed reminder that there was a Mr Noah as well as a Mrs in this Ark of Refuge'. Brownies who undertook a 'free' postal service for the older evacuees, collecting and delivering mail all over the country, also volunteered to take the little ones for walks, and bath or help feed them in an attempt to make nursery life more family-like. But in spite of these drawbacks the new nurseries were often far more acceptable to working mothers than the unfamiliarity of strangers' households.

In 1942, *Our Towns* strongly recommended that nurseries should have proper sanitation, 'not closets which are archaic, evil-smelling and unprovided with toilet paper', and that the chance should be seized to teach good eating and sleeping habits, bodily cleanliness and sanitary training as well as a sense of social responsibility. Regular dental and medical examinations should also take place. 'We cannot afford not to have the nursery school; it seems to be the only agency capable of cutting off the slum mind at the root', she wrote. By the autumn of 1944, almost at the end of the war, 106,000 children were at last receiving day-time nursery care.

Some children evacuated for the whole war adapted completely to their foster home or war nursery and became closely attached to their substitute parents. But this too could create problems. At the end of the war a book, *Living Together Again*, published to help women reunite their families, describes how mothers with children in out-of-the-way billets, perhaps on the other side of Britain, could only rarely make the journey for a visit because of travel restrictions. Many arrived, footsore, to a tense and disturbing welcome. It was hardly a natural occasion – perched on someone else's sofa and longing for some sort of intimacy, or wandering around the village on a Sunday with everything closed. 'The grown-ups had come laden with small gifts, special food as a treat, carefully stored aside from rations ... The short visit has been too full of emotional excitement to allow any ordinary function.' The fact that children were often confused between Mum, the visitor, and 'Auntie', the comforter and provider, was an added strain.

For parents, foster parents and evacuees alike evacuation was a problematic and frequently distressing experience. Homesickness was agonising and, however kindly meant, 'understanding and sympathy' were simply not sufficient to comfort the ten-year-old suddenly transplanted from the familiar city street to the awful peace and quiet of a pretty village in the remote countryside. One mother in a Mass Observation survey perhaps summed up the feelings of many whose families were broken up when she commented that they might just as well have 'died a normal death', so awful was the separation.

WOMEN OF BRITAIN

COME INTO
THE FACTORIES

ASK AT ANY EMPLOYMENT EXCHANGE FOR ADVICE AND FULL DETAILS

Glossy image of 'heroic' life in a factory, making aeroplanes and tanks.

2. Women of Britain – Go to it!

INTO THE FACTORIES

Go to it! Go to it!
That's the way to it!
Put your back into it,
Show the world you're feeling strong.

You've got to climb up high
Just like the lark
And if the whole darn sky
Is grey and dark
The sun will show thro' it
If you go to it with a cheery song.

During the First World War women were urged to go into industry, agriculture and transport, which they did gladly to 'help the boys'. But when women in depressed areas needed work after the war, their bosses 'employed them on hard monotonous work at low wages and used them wherever possible to replace skilled men at semi- or un-skilled rates of pay. The trade unions made little effort to organise them.'

During the Second World War, with rising inflation and husbands away, many women, desperate for more income, were again forced to accept low wages and bad conditions. They had no alternative.

The Control of Employment Orders of 1939 and 1943 which could mobilise groups of workers whenever they were needed, directed women into engineering, shipyards, building yards, railways and electrical works and Royal Ordnance factories as well as hospitals. Women were exempt only if they were pregnant or had children under the age of fourteen or other serious domestic responsibilities. If women did not qualify for exemption they had little choice over work. Control of the Essential Work Order was so tight at the Ministry of Labour that the termination of any job was strictly recorded. 'In this way the Ministry is able to secure that workers who leave their jobs take up, without undue delay, fresh work which it is in the national interest for them to do.' The 'national interest' encompassed production of trench mortar bombs, air-sea rescue launches, tank guns and gun mountings, ship-building, fighter planes and sewing seventy feet of wingspan by hand a day, as well as riveting and welding. All the materials of war were somehow produced, from parachutes and camouflage nets to enormous bombs and minutely complicated radio equipment.

Until April 1941 (when they had to register for work) women had offered their services freely. Once registered, women aged 16-49 'not fully employed to their best personal advantage could be compulsorily directed to other full-time civilian employment and [from] May 1943 to part-time work also.' Thousands of 'immobilised' women too were ready and willing to enter factories on a part-time basis. *Women in War Jobs* described the success of a new scheme in London: 'In one such factory the women are working from 8.0 am to 12.30 pm and from 12.30 to 5. pm. There is already a waiting list of 300, and in ten weeks the bonus percentage has increased, absenteeism has dropped and there are no fatigue, shopping or transport problems, even though part-time wages are "ridiculously low".' After December 1941, women and widows (not recently widowed) without children could be conscripted, under the National Service Acts, for the Armed Forces. The only women not required to register for employment in April 1941 were those already doing essential jobs: the Nursing Services, the Women's Land Army or factory work, for example. The only 'mobile' women exempted from transfer away from home were those living with their husbands, or married to servicemen. Women could appeal to the Women's Advisory Panel if domestic circumstances were too demanding, but if a 'mobile' woman refused her transfer she could be 'formally directed' under the (Defence) Regulation 58A.

Munitions factories were often in remote districts for security reasons. Many eligible women were sent to these – in the words of the regulations, 'to districts where labour is scarce in relation to demands for the war factories'.

Defence Regulations 1941 stated that anybody who tried to avoid direction, or left a job for a more congenial one, could be fined up to £5 a day 'while the default continued'. Fines and imprisonment for conscientious objectors were imposed with severity by the courts, as several hundred pacifists discovered to their cost.

In January 1942 Constance Bolan, a housemaid, was the first woman to be sent to prison. She announced forcibly in court that she disagreed with war in any shape or form and, but for the war, she would not have been asked to work in a hospital which was for the better organisation of the war effort. During her month's imprisonment, she refused to knit socks for the army and was given no alternative employment.

Meanwhile women were subjected to a series of very successful and highly emotional propaganda campaigns in favour of war work.

The Mass Observation Survey observed that the search for more woman power had nowhere found any appreciable number of unoccupied women. But they recommended serious propaganda on the issue of precious war-effort time spent on housework.

If they are to keep up their present standards of houseproudness and the social prestige that is won by an elaborately kept home, then it is a full-time job keeping the house up to this standard. Definite constructive propaganda about simplifying home life might do something to remedy this – and such propaganda should be addressed quite as much to men as to women; for a great deal of the inessential trouble women spend on their homes is to win the husbands' appreciation.

Patriotic propaganda conditioned people to accept that it was 'not done' to slink away for a weekend with the enemy at the door and men at the front dying daily. What did minor privations matter in the midst of all this suffering?

Did you know that over 10,000 women are doing men's work on one British railway alone, acting as platelayers, and permanent way labourers, helping with maintenance work, clerks, ticket collectors, porters, etc?
Go to it!
Want a job to stick to? Then try billposting!
Bravo, the women flight mechanics!
Ever thought of yourself as an electrician?
Be a welder.
Come into the factories!

And so on. These were the sort of appeals that bombarded women from hoardings, the pages of magazines and on the wireless. Diana Thomas broadcast on the Home Service of the BBC in May 1941:

Today we are calling all women. Every woman in the country is needed to pull her weight to the utmost – to consider carefully where her services would help most and then let nothing stand in the way of rendering such services. Like her, many women have made their sacrifices already and are doing their utmost to help win this war. But to those thousands who have not yet come forward I would say that here and now *every one of us* are needed. It's no longer a question of what is the most comfortable arrangement for each family. We are fighting for our lives – for our freedom and our future. We are *all* in it together, and what is already being done by other women *you* can do. Don't be afraid of being alone in your sacrifice – however great it may be; all round you you will find that your burdens and perplexities are shared. All those little things that are so important in every woman's life – we treasure them and cling to them, they are our life-blood. And now we have got to fight for them. Isn't it worth it? Together, yes it is.

Women accordingly enrolled for work until almost all were doing war work of some kind. By 1943 90 per cent of single women and 80 per cent of married women with children over fourteen were working. Such was the climate of opinion that many of the remainder volunteered to work from home at night, without pay if necessary.

By 1942, when many women had taken on more than one job, the journal *Woman's World*, announced: 'Hurrah for the Sunday Volunteers! In certain districts, office girls are volunteering to keep factory machines going while the usual workers take a Sunday off.'

The conversion of peacetime factories to war industry was brought home to customers by a Board of Trade announcement sent to shopkeepers.

> IN WARTIME, production must be for war and not for peace. Here are examples of the changeover from peacetime products to wartime necessities:
>
> CORSETS become Parachutes and Chinstraps;
> LACE CURTAINS become Sand-fly netting;
> CARPETS become Webbing Equipment;
> TOILET PREPARATIONS become Anti-Gas Ointments;
> GOLF BALLS become Gas Masks;
> MATTRESSES become Life Jackets;
> SAUCEPANS become Steel Helmets;
> COMBS become Eyeshields.

The munitions and aeroplane factories were the most voracious in their appetite for ever more female labour to replace the men who were constantly sent away to fight in the Forces or into other essential work. In 1938 the production of 12,000 military aircraft within two years had been planned by the Air Ministry for a Britain that was virtually unarmed. All available military equipment was used up by the time of the evacuation of Dunkirk, and by mid 1940, with invasion apparently imminent after the fall of France, little more than the British Channel defended our front line. This was the moment when Churchill announced, 'We shall defend our island whatever the cost may be, we shall fight on the beaches, we shall fight on the landing grounds, we shall fight in the fields and in the streets, we shall fight in the hills.'

The 'Dunkirk spirit' immediately took over the factory benches. Output doubled in many cases and a normal working day was extended to 11 hours, from 8am to 7pm, with night shifts as

'They make the guns we need'. A munition worker putting together the intricate mechanism of a field gun.

33

well, especially in the fighter plane industry. 'But almost every worker exceeded them, and many kept going till midnight nodding over their machines, and then slept on couches in the office or on sacks in a corner of the toolroom.'

The State-owned Royal Ordnance Factories adapted to their new role of super-production. Conditions were often improvised and inadequate as machines were moved about or discarded and new ones set up within hours. Other factories adapted overnight from making gloves to sandbags, from bicycles to tank parts. A hasty building programme that lasted until the end of 1941 threw up factories (as well as hospitals, camps and hostels) in strategic parts of the countryside, though this usually meant a very awkward journey for the worker and often poor sanitary and safety conditions. 'Sanitation for 250 workers in our shop is ten washbowls and six lavatories and there is a very bad supply of hot water. We are given five minutes for 250 people to wash and use the lavatories.'

The dawn queue for the factory bus included increasingly more women. By 1943 57 per cent of the workers were female and represented all sections of society. Over a million maids, cooks, nannies and 'dailies' were directed away from their work, often to their great relief, with tripled wages and some real independence. Young girls left home, tempted by a wartime excitement that introduced them to hostel life, cosmopolitan dances and financial freedom. Women of all trades between twenty and thirty years old could be directed, after brief training courses, to factories. In peacetime these women would have worked as shop assistants, clerical workers, typists, dressmakers, book-keepers, waitresses, manicurists or hairdressers. Suddenly they were working at welding, shipbuilding, portering, unloading at docks, maintaining engines, inspecting and mending gas fittings. In one electrical engineering firm in the South of England 75 per cent of the workers were women, translating working drawings into metal: 'They strip down, test and repair radio sets reclaimed from the sea. Women carry out all the processes from the initial marking out to the final riveting and welding.' A Welsh factory, where women performed all work except heavy forging, delivered in April 1943 its seven millionth trench mortar bomb. Examples of record production by women were supplied by the Ministry of Information in 1943. One of six women employed on the electric welding section of a shipbuilding firm produced 'thirty feet more than a man on similar work.' Since this was piecework she earned £9 18s in one week. 'A woman in a North-Eastern munitions factory broke all known records for her type of work in mid-1943. She turned out 120 pieces for machine tools every day, the average for other factories being 100.'

Housebound women and elderly relatives assembled parts of aeroplanes or guns, or anything that could be made with small tools like screwdrivers and pliers, in the sitting room. Small groups would work together not just for the company, but also to economise on light bulbs and fuel. One firm, reported by the Ministry of Information, was able to save 1,800 factory hours in three weeks in this way. It was asked to double its output by January 1943 and in March to treble it. 'Every woman within reach of the factory had been pressed into service and mobile women imported until living accommodation was strained to its utmost capacity.' Women out-workers in surrounding villages managed to reach the astounding triple production level by May. By 1943, even groups classified 'immobile' (ie. those born before 1893 or those with children under fourteen) were exhorted to join the factories for a part-time week of up to thirty hours, and eventually even those in wheelchairs, the deaf, the blind and the old were being given work they could manage.

The advertisements that persuaded women into dungarees presented a picture of working conditions for the woman factory worker very different from the reality:

Women cleaning the wheels of a railway engine.

Women painting the wings of a giant bomber in response to appeals for more workers in December 1940.

'If you are working for export you are working for victory.' Newspapers, posters, magazines, films and even comics cheered women on. As *Woman's World* enthusiastically exclaimed on 7 March 1942: 'It must have been encouraging for the factory workers who recently saw a film showing the tanks they make in action against the enemy. What a thrill to know we have earned a place in the march to Victory!'

A more down-to-earth picture was drawn by the personnel manager of a war factory:

> They had been told stories of nice clean factories with everything up to date and all modern amenities... I am genuinely sorry for these girls who emphasise some of the facilities which should be provided for them. Our canteen is not so good... Lavatory accommodation will revolt these girls.

A day earlier he had written about the insensitivity of directed work: 'A young girl came into my office in tears almost. The noise and smell of oil coupled with nervous and emotional strain had got her down. This girl was a trained masseuse and would have been better suited to hospital duty.'

Even the Ministry of Information complained, officially, about working conditions. Blacked-out windows not only increased noise in factories but prevented any circulation of air. This was a particularly bad problem in steelworks or hot factories with blast furnaces and coke ovens. Women had to put up with a 'psychological impression of stuffiness' as well as the grinding, often deafening noise of machinery. Norman Longmate cites girls from an Andover factory who longed for the evenings of their sixty-hour week when they could go dancing and forget the monotony. One woman remembered:

> Working in factories is not fun. To be shut in for hours on end without even a window to see daylight was grim. The noise was terrific and at night when you shut your eyes to sleep all the noise would start again in your head. Night shifts were the worst... The work was very often monotonous. I think boredom was our worst enemy.

The monotony was considered even more wearing than the pressure of the long hours. A young woman on a twelve-hour day shift reported a typical working day for Mass Observation:

> The room is about forty yards long by twenty broad, and lit by thirty high powered lights in the ceiling. There are three benches of small machines (mostly drilling and tapping) and a few large machines standing on the floor. At a long bench running lengthways down the side of the room are about fifteen girls engaged on filing by hand. Altogether there are about forty women and girls and about a dozen men.
>
> My machine is a drilling one, and I am given a heap of small brass plates to drill holes in . . . It is quite dark when we come out – which strikes one with a curious shock of surprise. For one feels not so much tired, rather as if one had missed the day altogether.

In order to relieve the boredom 'Music While You Work' was introduced by the BBC in June 1940, but this was only for two half hours a day, at 10.30am and 3.30pm, times at which it was found that production flagged. At other times women used to sing their own songs, like this one:

> *I'm only a wartime working girl,*
> *The machine shop makes me deaf,*
> *I have no prospects after the war*
> *And my young man is in the* RAF
> *K for Kitty calling P for Prue . . .*
> *Bomb Doors Open*
> *Over to you.*
>
> *Night after night as he passes by*
> *I wonder what he's gone to bomb*
> *And I fancy in the jabber of the mad machines*
> *That I hear him talking on the intercom*
> *K for Kitty calling P for Prue*
> *Bomb Doors Open*
> *Over to You.*

'Music While You Work' was so successful that it continued until 1967. Another morale-boosting effort was Ernest Bevin's ENSA – Entertainments National Service Association – which offered a range of entertainers, from Sybil Thorndike to George Formby, to factory workers in their lunch break as well as to the troops and to the civilians in Underground shelters.

Women's dissatisfaction with their working conditions was summed up by the Labour Research Department in 1942: 'Thousands of women who want to volunteer find it difficult or impossible for them to undertake a war job. The most important reasons are: low wages, insufficient day nurseries, long working hours and consequent shopping difficulties, bad canteens and inadequate transport.'

In 1940 the London Women's Parliament was organised by Mary Corsellis as 'a means whereby women can come together to discuss their many problems' – about wages, safety at work, nurseries, canteen conditions and overlong hours. 346 women represented 90,300 others from 179 organisations – factories, trades unions, education committees, women's guilds, hospitals, housewives' associations, and other political groups. The result was a bill presented to the Minister of Labour. But the response to their simple demands was very slow. Women's wages lagged far behind men's. (Even in engineering they were 75 per cent or less of a man's wage – a starting rate of 43s rising to 47s, compared to 22s 6d a week more for men.) They had to fight for adequate bomb-proof shelters, and for the right for all workers to go to them when the sirens sounded. They also demanded that at least one meal should be provided at popular prices, with proper tea breaks on day and night shifts. Overalls should be provided without using precious coupons and there should be cheap laundry facilities for women who, of course, had to return home to their second shift of household chores.

Although canteen facilities in larger factories (with over 250 employees) were slowly increasing, organised communal feeding was negligible for the first years of war. British Restaurants were eventually provided as one solution.

By 1942, 1,688,000 women were members of the Trades Union Council although they were sorely under-represented in its higher levels. A woman shop steward protested in 1941:

Women head for the recruiting van to protest at the lack of nurseries.

We have no objection to working in the factories but we do object to the conditions we have to work under. Women in industry today are called upon to bear burdens that are beyond imagination. Many are soldiers' wives who are obliged to go to work to keep their homes together as their allowances are so inadequate... Our hours are ordinarily an eight and a half hour day but with overtime this is often brought up to ten hours.

In the morning we feel fresh and do a good amount of work but the ventilation is so bad that by the afternoon we get weary. Then down goes output... A man is employed to do lifting, maybe only small trays, but this prevents the women from earning a man's wages.

In July 1943 a Ministry of Labour survey on wages illustrated the inequality of earnings, including overtime work, among six million women and men;

Men over 21 years:	121s 4d
Men under 21 years:	47s 1d
Women over 18 years:	62s 11d
Women part-time workers:	29s 0d
Women under 18 years:	·33s 11d

Women protested further as they discovered that the compensation for the loss of a male limb was worth more than their own, whether through bombing or industrial accidents. With so many women grappling with unfamiliar machinery the accident rate was bound to rise, and it did. As early as 1939 the National Women's Citizen Association (formed in 1918 to teach women how to use their vote) had allied itself with the peace organisation the Soroptimists and the National Federation of Business and Professional Women's Clubs to protest about this. Not until 1943, however, was their complaint recognised and changed under the Personal Injuries (Civilians) Scheme although the amount paid still varied according to women's wages, not their injury.

Another problem was the cost of hostel life for women lured or directed away from home. 'Girls... have to find 25s to 30s a week for lodgings, out of wages which may be even lower (about £2 at eighteen years in many cases). How can they send money home or save the fare for the occasional visit?' An added difficulty for women with husbands or children was the lack of transport. Buses and trains were reduced to a minimum – 'Is your journey really necessary?' asked the posters. Dutiful to the atmosphere of war, women queued in their lunch breaks at the single shop where their ration book was registered. Factory hours made normal shopping impossible and often many of the goods were already snapped up. Munitions factories especially were tucked away in 'safe' places in case of explosion. Travelling time of three hours a day was not uncommon, with queues at both bus stop and shop, and then perhaps a further journey to the child minder or nursery before returning home to the housework. In households without an alarm clock there was the daily problem of getting the early risers out of bed and off to work. Clocks were considered 'inessential' at the start of the war and only three years later was a Utility version finally produced.

A Mass Observation survey on housework revealed the kind of chaos that must have been hard for formerly houseproud women to adjust to. It typifies the memories many women have of a home life lived between shift work. The reporter recorded his interview with Mrs B., a woman chosen at random from the factory. She had no

time to stop, having a husband on shift work, two children at school and two in war work, but she invited him home while she 'straightened up'.

> When I arrive the whole house is a complete mess. Two days' washing-up is piled in the sink, a great bundle of washed but unironed clothes lie on the floor; odd shoes and socks belonging to the children are scattered on chairs and the table is a mass of crumbs and dirty crockery.

The interviewer describes Mrs B. attempting the washing up, the laundry pile, the vegetables and the neck of mutton for supper, 'but even with us helping it is not nearly half done before she has to rush back to the factory'. Norman Longmate describes another typical case discussed in the House of Commons where a man got official permission to start work at 8am instead of 7am. 'He could not arrive any earlier since his wife had to be at another factory at seven, and he had to take their child to its grandmother who did not come back from her night shift until seven o'clock.'

It is hard now to imagine the total upheaval of family life through the mobilisation of so many women. But there were three consoling factors. First there was the reward of higher war wages which meant some financial independence for women. Second, there was the humour and kindness which people displayed in times of great danger, the intimacy of sharing the strain of an air raid, the understanding and sympathy shown in times of bereavement or distress. Third, the feeling that they were doing something to win the war became a serious consideration for the majority of women. The more military the work the greater their commitment to it. Many women felt happier doing the dreary and physically monotonous work of making bombs or life-jackets than looking after the children at home, though this last was portrayed by the government as 'its own form of National Service'.

As for men's attitudes, the men workers

(43 per cent) retained in these essential jobs for their particular skills at first accepted their new co-workers with suspicion. The idea of women, clothed in dungarees to protect them from oil, turbaned to prevent their hair getting caught in dangerous machinery and often with delicately painted fingernails (one of the few remaining ways to show a degree of femininity), was at first doubtfully received by men in both light and heavy industry. These attitudes were reflected in wages – even by 1944 women metal workers were still only earning half as much as the men (£3 10s compared with the men's £7). Nevertheless, during the war the inroads they made into a man's world soon won respect and admiration. In September 1942 Clement Attlee declared, 'The work that women are performing in munitions factories has to be seen to be believed. Precision engineering which a few years ago would have made a skilled turner's hair stand on end is now being performed with dead accuracy by girls who had no industrial experience!' Churchill, who in 1944 denounced the claim of women teachers for equal pay as 'impertinence', only a few months earlier had announced magnanimously: 'This war effort could not have been achieved if the women had not marched forward in millions and undertaken all kinds of tasks and work.' Nevertheless, with the Control of Employment Act of 1945, demobilised women took second place at the Labour Exchange, despite the fact that many of them wanted to continue to work and retain their hard-won independence.

Women ferry pilots in the Air Transport Auxiliary Service take over the delivery of planes at an aerodrome.

3. This is the Army, Mrs Jones

Women up to the age of forty-five had *volunteered* for the armed service of their choice until April 1941, when the Registration of Employment Order compelled women to 'sign up' with particulars of the work they were or were not doing. Thus classified, general powers were taken to *enforce* the conscription into particular services of childless, single women between the ages of nineteen and thirty. This meant that a woman not already occupied in work 'essential to the war effort' could be mobilised into the ATS (Auxiliary Territorial Service), the WAAFs (Women's Auxiliary Air Force) or the WRNS (Women's Royal Naval Service) unless she chose (which about a third did) to work in a factory instead. Women were not put on active combat duty, but only assisted at close quarters, ie. at anti-aircraft sites they serviced and loaded the guns but did not fire them.

Women in the Auxiliary Services were seen by many civilians as leading a comparatively comfortable life. They were fed on far better rations than the families at home. Two pairs of shoes and a 'glamorous' though often ill-fitting uniform were provided. They had three weeks' paid leave a year with free travel warrants, free medical attention, shoe repairs and lodging. Above all, the majority could count on the security of following orders in nightmarish situations, while civilians faced constant uncertainty and improvisation not only when the bombs started to fall, but in the shops, the home, the air-raid shelter and at work. And women in the services had lovely dances laid on for them with foreign soldiers!

In exchange for these comforts, however, women of the armed forces worked extremely hard (often with only two and a half hours' sleep during 'uneventful' night duty) and faced real danger alongside the troops. Pay was a pitiful 2s a day for the lower ranks, the same as for their male counterparts.

Although official numbers of serving women were kept 'hush-hush' throughout the war, morale-boosting articles in women's magazines announced in March 1942 that 10,000 women a month were joining the ATS. In fact, by 1943, 443,000 women staffed the ATS, the WRNS, and the WAAFs. By the end of the war, of the 74,000 WRNS, 102 were killed and 22 wounded; of the 198,000 ATS members 335 were killed, 302 wounded, 94 missing and 22 taken prisoners of war; and of 171,200 WAAFs, 187 were killed, 420 wounded and 4 were missing. Smaller ancillary service units of women worked closely with those in the three major armed services in order, it was constantly stressed, to release men as far as possible for combat duty. The smaller groups included the FANYS (the Women's Transport Service) and the Royal Observer Corps, who manned isolated lookout posts day and night. The VAD nurses (Voluntary Aid Detachment) worked in military hospitals or on Thames barges converted to ambulance hospitals. Nursing reserves, attached to each branch of the Forces, often endured the same hardships as the men, like being adrift at sea in open boats after being torpedoed. Others nursed men at the Front. In the Far East nurses suffered long marches, close to starvation, after capture, or died in brutal prisoner-of-war camps. Some flew aircraft and others parachuted medical supplies into places where they were needed.

Women who chose to nurse with the Forces joined Queen Alexandra's Royal Naval Nursing Service, Queen Alexandra's Imperial Military Nursing Service or Princess Mary's Royal Air Force Nursing Service. They earned a starting wage of £95 a year or about £1 17s a week. Their strenuous duties included medical care of the mutilated bodies of young men, their lives often shattered by their injuries. Overcrowded operating theatres required a clear head, often when the nurses were dog-tired. And they often had to do arduous and unsavoury cleaning work as well.

A nurse, Kate Phipps, recorded her first impression of troops arriving after the evacuation of Dunkirk. Some wounded men refused stretchers. They had swum to the rescue boats under fire. Some had sunk and the men had had to swim to another boat, often standing packed like sardines all the way across the Channel.

> I was glad Sister had warned us about the stench of dried blood. We wanted to smile a welcome but felt nearer crying. What little uniform they had was in a bad state. We had to cut it off in most cases. 'Down the seams nurse. It may have to be used again!' We found some of the wounds had field dressing still on that stuck and had to be soaked off. Their feet were in a bad state from marching and their socks too had to be cut off. My scissors got so blunt in cutting through all the heavy khaki that in the end it was more like sawing but somehow we got them undressed. The men seemed dead tired and we had to wash many asleep . . . I could not help thinking of those wounded who had not been collected, lying out in fields or ditches with no help at hand.

Besides being subjected to the tensions and emergencies of military life these women were also sworn to secrecy so that off-duty pastimes like chatting about work, taking photographs of friends in the Forces or writing home about their life were forbidden. Discipline was rigorous. A young woman in the WRAF remembered the shock of the first few weeks – of having 'to be made into what you were not in a very short time'. She had volunteered, but remem-

bered feeling sympathy for the conscripted recruits who were drafted in 1941, and especially for the country girls: 'The excitement of leaving home to serve your country didn't sustain the alarm we all felt at times through not being able to leave until the end of the war.'

In the first week of training no one was allowed to leave the camp. Lectures on the King's Regulations took place in huge hangars. 'Our kitting was standing in line with clothes either small, medium or large being thrown at you. If the jacket of the uniform sort of fitted then you got the skirt.' The kit consisted of 3 vests, 6 pairs of winter and summer knickers, 3 pairs of duty stockings, 2 pairs of identical lace-up marching shoes, 3 shirts, 6 collars, 1 pullover, 2 uniforms (one for best), 1 greatcoat, 1 groundsheet and a gas mask. The kitbag also contained a set of irons (knife, spoon and fork), a 'housewife' of sewing things (pronounced hussif), a button-polishing kit, and shoe brushes and polish.

At first it was seriously doubted whether women would be able to handle the 'man's job' of getting the heavy barrage balloons up and down.

" Shall we join the gentlemen ? "

45

Civilian recruits get their first taste of the WAAF *as they march towards Castle Station in Lancaster (March 1942).*

A WAAF girl in her twenties remembered that they were only allowed to report for sick duty if they could no longer stand. Their unheated dormitory huts, she recalled, were freezing in winter. After an eight-hour day or night shift in the underground head-quarters of Bomber Command Head-quarters, where they plotted the precise advance of enemy attacks, WRAFs used to collapse onto their horsehair pillows and 'biscuits' (the nickname for the official mattress of three rock-hard straw-packed cushions).

> We were often too tired to eat after those shifts of plotting, where any mistake in the precise movement of the enemy would have meant a disaster. First thing in the morning we managed, though half asleep, the rigours of button polishing, toothbrush inspection and kit check. Everything had to be laid out just right with even the toothbrush facing a certain direction. They would have got us to polish the coal if they could!

After meals, which included bromide-flavoured tea 'to quell our passions', their 'irons' always had to be washed in the canteen bucket and 'we tipped mounds of unwanted food from our plates into the pig buckets' before queueing to leave. It was not a world for home-lovers nor for the shy or sensitive. Confidences as well as baths were shared. A white-painted line usually showed the exact limit of the five permitted inches of water. 'With three of us in we were often tempted to make it fifteen, but we never did!'

In all sections of the armed forces wages rose according to skills, and women undertook training which varied from one week to six months. Some of the more dramatic courses in the WRNS trained women to overhaul torpedoes, depth charges, fire control and gun circuits, and taught them how to perform electrical repairs on mine-sweepers and coastal force craft. Some became ships' mechanics and rebuilt light engines, or made new parts for submarines and landing craft. Other technical work included plotting the routes of enemy and allied aircraft and ships, as well as working in all branches of communications from morse code to teleprinting. Women cypher officers maintained contact with ships at sea or worked from the warships themselves. Wren officers were able to replace paymaster lieutenants in admirals' secretariats. The remainder, as in the other forces, undertook all domestic and mess duties as well as coping with mountains of clerical work.

WRAF work included staffing the barrage balloon posts where 47 per cent of the personnel were women from January 1941. When the first balloons went up in 1939 they caused much rumour and conjecture, but by the time women were managing the ponderous winches and the heavy swaying balloons, subject to the least breath of wind, most people had realised that they were simply meant to act as a deterrent to low-flying dive bombers. Operating the whale-like 'Blimps' needed so much sheer physical strength that at first it was doubted if women could manage. But they did – and almost halved the manpower required. An

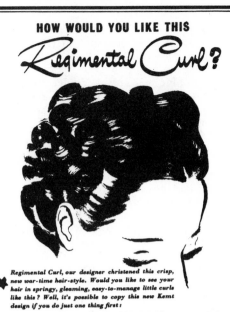

enemy plane was occasionally brought down and one such was recorded in the North East in 1942.

> You can't hit back at 'em. You've just got to sit and take it . . . the noise of the plane changed to a whine. It seemed just as if it was diving right down on top of us.
> '* * * *,' says one of our airmen. 'He's going to machine gun us.'
> 'He isn't,' says I. 'He's going to hit the cable.'
> And he did. He went smack into it. There was a crash and the cable sawed through the wing just like a grocer's wire goes through cheese . . . We celebrated our first Jerry with a nice cup of tea. Then of course we realised we'd have to put up *another* in place of Annie.

Women volunteers from the ATS were first trained to work in mixed batteries on the anti-aircraft guns in the spring of 1940. 'The men were newly joined recruits, the point being that men who had known no other army life would not find the atmosphere of a mixed battery so hysterically unorthodox.' Not surprisingly 'there was none of the musical-comedy-chorus atmosphere which had been anticipated'. Soldiers are trained to live hard and it was doubted whether the women could remain 'tense and cool'. But the officers in charge of the first battery to shoot down a German plane expressed

> without hesitation a preference for a mixed battery. The girls cannot be beaten in action, and in my opinion they are definitely better than the men on the instruments they are manning . . . They are amazingly keen at going into action, and although they are not supposed to learn to use the rifle they are as keen as anything to do so.

Churchill was at first adamant that conscripted women should not have to do military combat. His suspicion that fighting women would have a demoralising effect on the nation was probably wrong. Some women taught themselves to shoot. One woman working at the Home Office took Churchill's attitude to be a token one, since women already undertook extremely dangerous work: 'Anyway, a fit woman can fire a rifle better than an unhealthy man, and what could be more military than managing the ack-ack guns?'

Serving women had to be careful about being photographed for 'reasons of national security'.

However, by October 1941, Churchill had visited the Richmond Anti-Aircraft Mixed Battery, and discovered discrimination in the form of 'no *esprit de corps*. This is very wounding to the (Women's) Auxiliary Territorial Service, who have been deprived of badges, lanyards, etc.' He announced that the women should be called 'Gunners'. On 29 October 1941, he admitted the 'immense importance' of having a large number of women in the AA (ack-ack) batteries in order to keep 'the maintenance of a larger number of batteries with a smaller number of men'.

Other jobs for women at the ack-ack posts included sentry work (armed with a pick-helve), driving and servicing the trucks, dispatch-riding on motorcycles, and always the same marching, eating and drilling routines as the men.

By April 1941, 54 ATS recruits, aged between 19 and 35 were trained to manage searchlights, a dangerous job since they became instant targets themselves. After a month's training in aircraft recognition, map-reading, route marches, drill, physical training and anti-gas precautions to prepare them for a tough outdoor life 'the standard reached was higher than that of most men'. Other jobs at the searchlights included the shifting of tons of earth to make paths, filling and laying sandbags, renovating derelict sites, logging all aircraft and transmitting messages between the command post and the gun operations room. After perhaps hours of silence, a frenzy of Morse code would bombard the telephonist, 'and if one miscounts the pips it means a wrong plot being made, and perhaps a target being missed'.

Many forms of communication were taken over by the ATS military convoys. Military supplies and food had to be transported to troops or the scenes of emergencies, often without signposts, by secret routes at night. *Woman's World* advertised in 1942 for women to drive lorries in the road convoys: 'some knowledge of driving is necessary to start with but after that, what

'Enrolment is for the duration'.

you don't know you'll very soon learn, not only in the lorries but under them.' Women drivers in the services were completely responsible for the maintenance of their vehicles, whether motor-bike, jeep or lorry. A training course in mechanics automatically qualified them within weeks. Mass Observation reported on the women working in the RAF maintenance units: 'The men down tools promptly on time but the new women work jolly well. We often have to tell them to knock off as they work so damned hard.'

Emergency field kitchens were always on standby, staffed by the ATS, to feed troops in isolated posts or civilians after air raids. Working closely with the Red Cross and Women's Voluntary Service, helped perhaps by Girl Guides, the Sea Rangers or Home Guard, they supplied improvised meals. However the work demanded not just the ability to prepare food amidst chaos, but also the sympathy and toughness to cope with homeless and bereaved people, often in a state of bewildered shock. In comparison, getting food to troops stationed in deserted parts of the countryside was straightforward, although it did sometimes involve sleeping rough.

In the field of intelligence, top-secret work on radar control was furthered with the help of women scientists. At the Bletchley headquarters, where successful codebreaking meant many enemy plans were reported to Churchill as soon as they were issued, a young woman remembered shifts so long and concentrated that she worked pencils down to the butt at the rate of three an hour. Unlike the factory women she had no time to ponder on monotony but used to reckon to 'look at the clock when I've finished two more pencils'. Security was so strict that one of her jobs was to burn the contents of the waste-paper baskets before the cleaners arrived. The mental tension was astounding, but she recalled that for relaxation 'the minds of people working there were so brilliant that they used to play chess and card games without pieces. The strain of keeping up was quite a challenge.'

At times of particular crisis, when a German invasion of Britain was feared, many women in and out of the Forces were prepared to take up arms even though they were officially discouraged from doing so. But official attempts to woo new women recruits continued and an Air Ministry advertisement in *Woman's World* (16 May 1942) presented some picture of the range of jobs and training open to women serving in the Forces:

> If you're hoping to join the WAAF you'll be interested to hear about jobs: dental clerk orderly (over 18), nursing orderly (over 23), radio operator (not over 36), radiographer, masseuse, pigeon keeper, cine-projectionist, bomb-plotter, batwoman, shoe-repairer, parachute repairer, tailor, photographer, flight mechanic, telephone operator, waitress, cook, radio mechanic, and that's not the whole list!

Although women undertook extremely dangerous work in wartime, Churchill considered that morale would suffer if they used firearms. In spite of women's own wish to join the Home Guard and defend their own homes, parliamentary opinion wavered. In the end thousands of women took matters into their own hands and formed the Women's Home Defence Movement. Here, Sergeant Tearne is teaching women how to fire a revolver in the Kensington Unit.

4. Your gas mask will take care of you

WOMEN IN CIVIL DEFENCE

'I think it is well for the man in the street to realise that there is no power on earth that can prevent him from being bombed. Whatever people may tell him, the bomber will always get through . . . The only defence is offence which means that you have to kill women and children more quickly than the enemy if you want to save yourselves.'

On the subject of civilian populations in wartime the House of Commons heard this warning from Stanley Baldwin as early as 1932. Seven years later the people of Britain were told: 'If this island is invaded by sea or air, everyone who is not under orders must stay where he or she is. If you do not stay put you will stand a very good chance of being killed. The enemy may machine-gun you from the air in order to increase panic, or you may run into enemy forces which have landed behind you.'

The inevitable intensification of the war which followed the surrender of Belgium in May 1940 and France in June left the armed forces with such a dearth of men and munitions that the Manpower Requirements Committee, headed by William Beveridge, estimated that the Civil Defence and the Forces alone would need one and three-quarter million men and 84,000 women within a year. Half a million men were drafted from the munitions industries, which already employed three and a half million workers but desperately needed a further million and a half. With increasing strictness Civil Defence Regulations could direct any person in the United Kingdom to perform such services which in the opinion of the Minister of Labour the person directed was capable of performing.

The problem was two-fold: how to defend the Home Front (since the army requested 357,000 more recruits by March 1941 with a further 100,000 a month thereafter) and how to keep the defence industries supplied with labour. The only answer, as always in times of national crisis, was to register women compulsorily from April 1941 for the necessary work and defence forces. By September 1941 the 'grannies', born after 1893, were also included.

Many women were angered that their earlier offers of active support had been rejected, especially in the field of CD (Civil Defence) which many women felt was the most positive way to defend their homes. Barbara Nixon recalls how in December 1939 she had experienced typical difficulties enrolling as an Air Raid Warden when 'the Town Hall . . . had objections. First they said they did not want any more women, then, when that argument was disposed of, they said they would not employ married women, and asked me WHY I wanted to work when I was married . . . at length after four or five weeks they agreed to appoint me.' But by 1942, women in civil defence numbered 19,400 full timers and 127,000 part-timers, rising in 1944 to 179,800 – almost all in unpaid work.

But Goering's 'armed reconnaissance' of the London docks in July 1940 had resulted in a hasty and disorganised CD, to be augmented by women. By 1943 one in four CD workers were women – working as air-raid wardens, fire-guard duty personnel, emergency messengers and staff at the emergency control centres. Women were found in strength in the auxiliary medical services, at first-aid posts, in shelters and rest centres, driving ambulances and helping rescue parties. They often provided or organised help where it would not otherwise have existed,

This is one of the fifty units of the Women's Home Defence in action by February 1942. Women could join what must have been one of the only wartime organisations without any red tape, forms, regulations or uniforms.

and with each fresh crisis they learned a little more about how to deal with the tragic disruption of the war, and the devastation caused by the Blitz which lasted from September 1940 to May 1941. Increasing numbers of women complained bitterly at the lack of facilities, such as nurseries, which would enable them to take an active part in defending their families. Family life was already devastated but as the bombings spread to all major towns, ports and docks in 1941, the full horror of civilian casualties dawned.

For the first few nights of the Blitz people reacted variously. Sheer horror, terror, misery and bad temper in the shelters (to which some trekked daily with small chairs, bedding and food) were common. Some tried to sing, others cried, fearful for their homes and families. The Mass Observation Survey reported some of the reactions to the first tremendous crashes and sounds of gunfire. Women screamed and huddled together, waiting:

Then suddenly a woman of 25 shouts at a younger girl: 'Stop leaning against that wall you bloody fool! Like a bleeding lot of children! Get off it, you bastard . . . do you hear? Come off it . . . my God, We're going mad!' People began shouting at one another. Sophie, 30, screams at her mother: 'Oh you get on my nerves, you do! You get on my nerves! Oh shut up, you get on my nerves!' Here the ARP helper tries once again to start some singing. 'Roll out the . . .' she begins. 'Shut your bleedin' row!' shouts a man of 50. 'We got enough noise without you.'

'Male armchair critics may laugh at the idea of women learning how to use firearms, but that doesn't discourage the women.' A member of the Women's Home Defence Unit learns how to aim a rifle.

In the morning screams of horror greeted the devastation as people scrambled out shouting or weeping for relations. After several weeks of working by day and sleeping in the shelters at night, most people adapted to the tension. Some who had been unaffected at the start later spent their days in dread of the night. One woman who could talk of nothing but the raids would dash to the lavatory frequently as the time for the sirens approached, and when they sounded would urinate on the floor and burst into tears.

Others in ARP (Air Raid Precautions) work were positively exhilarated at first by the excitement but only if they were outside the shelters: facing danger and doing something to help was often an easier way to cope than enduring the controlled strain underground.

Dr. Edith Summerskill, on the left, founder of the Women's Home Defence Unit. Here, volunteers are signing on for service.

With the fear of invasion, women were forced to consider how they would deal with Nazis at the front door. Might it not be better to die with the children before they arrived, rather than face a massacre or a fascist regime? But frustration and anger caused most to join the fight, however dangerous, however dull, and however 'immobile' they were considered by the Ministry of Labour.

For some the response was to set up private women's armies like the Amazon Defence Corps, but these were all refused an official supply of arms. In the case of the Women's Voluntary Service, formed in 1939, groups of women made Molotov cocktails 'for a weaponless army manning the last defence line for liberty', so dire was

the shortage of ammunition at the Home Front. (The Local Defence Volunteers, the Home Guard, during the first year of war still had little more than pitchforks, broom handles and chair legs for their exercises until supplies were sent from the USA in 1941.) By 1942, branches of the Women's Home Defence Corps were springing up in many districts to teach women how to handle rifles and grenades. 'In one unit alone there are over 100 members between 18–60. We don't want to fight, but if it comes to it, we might as well know how to defend ourselves and our homes.' Especially when the Ministry of Home Security reminded them that 'Invasion conditions differ from blitz conditions in that military labour will not be available for civil purposes.'

Civil Defence was an alternative. Since it was based on the idea that each neighbourhood could best help itself without an outside force of neo-military workers and since the majority of air raids were by night, it was a little more suitable for women at home, though it often meant waiting for work-weary neighbours to return to baby-sit. Many thousands of working women returned home to cook before changing their hats, so to speak, for the tin helmet of their night-time role as warden, fire watcher, shelter attendant, dispatch or ambulance driver. Many were already well-informed or well-practised in the disposal of small bombs, and demonstrations with stirrup pumps took place all over the country. They might have spent all day unloading cargo at the docks, repairing and maintaining engines, standing on the buses or carrying luggage as porters, and their night-time Civil Defence work was on the whole unpaid and of the most dangerous nature. Of the Civil Defence's million and a quarter workers, only a fifth were full-time paid workers, earning on average £1 1s a week from the age of 16 to £2 15s at 20, though full-time workers in the Fire Service earned at least £3 2s a week. 47,000 women enrolled as part-time and unpaid workers in the fire service. The remaining 2,600 full-time workers were the best-paid in Civil Defence. The part-timers could receive 'remunerative benefit' if they missed time at work through their duties as firewomen during emergencies, but only 'whole-time personnel performing continuous duty for 12 hours or more in circumstances which prevent their obtaining a meal at home may receive a free meal to the value of 1s.'

From January 1939, and with increasing fervour, Civil Defence Acts had encouraged men and women to form such a civilian army. In May 1940, Anthony Eden broadcast a fresh appeal for half a million people between forty and sixty-five to be known as the LDVs (Local Defence Volunteers) and later the Home Guard. From 1 April 1941, full-time workers, and later unpaid volunteers, were restricted from leaving their jobs without official consent. On 16 March 1942 they had to register their qualifications by an order of the Minister of Labour and National Service. In April this information was used to make all Civil Defence personnel interchangeable if so needed. Refusal could result in a £10 fine or a month in prison, particularly hard for conscientious objectors who hoped to be stretcher bearers but could now be transferred to non-pacifist work like constructing Civil Defence posts.

Voluntary Civil Defence work was eventually made compulsory in 1943 and subject to fines from £2 to fifty guineas or imprisonment if workers refused to 'volunteer', much to the chagrin of those already doing more than they could endure before the return to factory bench or children the next morning.

By 1943, 375,000 women had joined the Civil Defence as wardens (one in six were women), as members of the decontamination squads for those suffering from gas injuries, the police force and first aid posts. They drove ambulances and sometimes fire engines. They also staffed the control centres which linked each tragedy to the emergency services, waiting hours for news and then, with the warden's first telephone call, passing on details of death and damage with calm self-control amid a frenzy of activity. Even when the control centres themselves were hit, as at Clydebank in March 1941, women knew that they had to carry on, and did so with 'remarkable calmness'. 'The building shook and the dust of ages came down on us. The lights went out and we did not know whether we were going to Kingdom Come.' Once the lights were reconnected, 'the Control Centre continued to do fully efficient work for the rest of the night . . . its 90 messenger lads, boys of 16 and 17, the eyes and ears of the Control, coolly went their rounds among the bombs and wreckage.'

A further 130,000 women in the Post Office included in their numbers those whose job was to maintain communication and convey messages at all costs. Tin-hatted, they would motor-cycle, bicycle or run and scramble through air raids, over fallen masonry and torn bodies, groping their way to their destination. Others made the same journey to repair telegraph or telephone cables by the 'glare of bombs, if you were lucky'.

Once the air raid sirens had sounded, the only official population above ground were the wardens, the fire guards and the police force (340 of whom were women recruited expressly for their delicacy in dealing with 'the special problems of war', namely the devastation of home and family). The wardens' job was to patrol the locality, and as soon as a bomb fell to go to the scene at once and estimate the damage before alerting the emergency services. Their duty then was to guide, advise, and soothe and help the survivors, quelling any panic (which was rare) and dealing with those in a state of shock. It was local wardens who could best guide fire engines, ambulances and mobile medical teams through blocked streets and lead the walking injured to the first aid post and the destitute to the rest centre. Then they would return to help the rescue parties to dig for bodies, alive or dead. The rescue men (usually builders reserved from the services for their knowledge of house struc-

Maternity nurses from the Salvation Army visit a Blitz District. Many women remember the horrors of giving birth during air raids. According to official policy, they should have been evacuated, but many preferred to stay at home, knowing full well that any ambulances during an 'incident' would be busy collecting air raid casualties.

ture) relied on the warden to know exactly who might be buried in the debris of each house – whether the old auntie was or was not at No. 34, or the Smiths who slept in the Anderson shelter – though when public buildings like the Café de Paris and the Hammersmith Palais were blitzed it was impossible to gauge the numbers or identify the bodies under the debris.

The lull between the sirens and the first bomb explosion (if there was one) was, a woman recalled, a looter's paradise, the twilight hour when the blackout assisted the Black Market. A notice in London read: 'Looting from premises which have been damaged by, or vacated by reason of, War Operations is punishable by death or penal servitude for life.' A twenty-year-old Red Cross nurse, in charge of seven public shelters, remembers

> the fear of walking in empty dark silent streets, knowing not a soul was in the tall buildings on either side, the extraordinarily loud sound of one's own footsteps when guns were silent, and the memory of kind, willing old Charlie (an air-raid warden) so recently and horribly knifed, and the light-hearted prostitute I walked with one evening, of whom people in the shelters said 'Serve her right', when she was murdered. Another woman who returned from the shelter to fetch her purse was stabbed on the doorstep for a few shillings.

But others had different experiences.

> There was great camaraderie – I cannot recall ever being nervous of fellow human beings in the blackout. Once I was accosted by a soldier – he sounded very young. I said 'Have you a torch?' 'Yes,' he said. 'Then shine it on my face and you will see that I'm old enough to be your mother.' He didn't and faded away.

Warden Mrs B. was present at the birth of three babies during heavy attacks on her town. The third was entirely in her charge since neither doctor nor nurse could get there – 'But I know it all backwards.' Immediately the baby was born, the roof of the house fell in. The mother refused to be moved, and Mrs B. spent the rest of the night sitting at her side under a tarpaulin hoisted on furniture and broken joists. She

became the baby's godmother. Since pregnancy was called the 'prevailing disease of war conditions', these sorts of births were not uncommon, though often badly traumatic for the mother, who might find it impossible to relax or breastfeed.

Even when wardens had to report an unexploded bomb in their own street, or that their own homes had been bombed, they stuck to their posts. On one night alone in Hull, 200 wardens' houses were bombed, but they carried on their heroic work regardless. Many developed an uncanny sense of imminent danger. A warden in charge of 25,000 people and 250 other wardens, 'whose children must find her a very gentle mother', admitted that her insides turned over whenever a bomb fell, but one night began to carry an incendiary bomb to the nearest police station. Someone offered to take it for her. She handed it over (for she had other things to do) explaining carefully and at some length just where it should be held and the importance of not knocking it. Not until breakfast the next morning did she learn that the helper had been her husband!

Throughout the autumn of 1940 and with each subsequent Blitz, up to a thousand fires a night were starting in any major town on any one night. Liverpool, Hull, Portsmouth, Glasgow, Plymouth, Manchester, Birmingham, Coventry, Exeter, Leeds, London and all the important ports were badly blitzed. Any unfortunate village near an aerodrome, power station or arms town might be hit, while the enemy emptied surplus bombs over farms, seaside towns or fishing boats in 'tip and run' raids on their return journey. Conflagrations were common, especially when docks and warehouses were shelled and boiling paint, sugar, cheese or oil would explode over neighbouring houses in a spreading mass of flames. Firemen slumped on their hoses for hours on end, watching red-eyed and helpless as mates were tossed bodily into the air by new blasts. Smoke-choked and exhausted, their efforts were sometimes to no avail.

Health *and* Efficiency

MUST BE

Maintained!

that is why you need Ovaltine –

In the Workshop–

Each high-explosive bomb brought its own chaos in terms of injuries, districts cut off by flames or a crowded shelter bombed. It was worst when the water supply failed, with hydrants buried under the debris or water mains blitzed. During a raid, up to ten miles of pipe might be led in the darkness to the nearest canal or river, sometimes only to be burnt through by flying embers – and the whole nightmarish job would begin again.

By February 1942 the fire service was busy recruiting women as drivers, mechanics, dispatch riders, wireless operators, hose repairers, cooks and control room staff. An advertisement in *Woman's World* announced: 'Maybe you're eligible for the National Fire Service which is asking for recruits and offers wages from 47 s a week.' The advertisement concluded: 'There are no extra coupons for weddings, so it may help brides to know that rationed goods may be hired for a special occasion without the surrender of coupons.'

On a London Transport poster encouraging women to become drivers in the fire service, there were A.P. Herbert's famous words:

> *Thank you fire fighters harnessing your hoses*
> *Busy at your pumps or patiently at play*
> *Once upon a time we used to throw you roses*
> *You don't see quite such a cloud of them today.*
> *Some of us remember the blitz and the burning*
> *The black-faced force in the red and the blue*
> *St Paul's in peril and the Hun returning*
> *The tanks all day and the night half through*
> *When they sound the sirens, some of us are sleeping*
> *Some of us turn over, some of us complain*
> *But you are at your job still, we are in your keeping*
> *And one fine night, we'll be glad of you again*

25 firewomen died during the war, and 793 firemen; 7,000 were injured, many were blinded by heat or sparks. Almost all suffered ill health 'from the extremes of heat and cold, from exorbitant hours, from the lack of regular meals and the constant physical and nervous strain.'

As in other branches of Civil Defence, from August 1942 women who had already volunteered could be compelled to do fire-watching duty for a minimum of forty-eight hours a month, regardless of the strain they were already under, and from September in the same year women working at business premises were liable for compulsory duty there.

Of essential help too to the fire service was the Supplementary Fire Party of fire-watchers who aimed to catch and extinguish fires and bombs before the blaze grew too great. Women formed a large part of the four and a half million householders who volunteered to take every precaution against incendiary bombs setting fire where they landed. As they fell by the hundred, this was no mean task. Usually armed only with a bucket of sand and a dimmed torch they would stalk the lonely dangers of the blackout for the first sign of glare from moorland or deserted street. Only the luckier recruits had tin helmets and armbands marked SFP. They were trained to use wheelbarrows, stirrup pumps or light trailer pumps if necessary, though more often the official *Fire Party Handbook* recommended 'sand, a tin helmet or even a saucepan' for the smaller bombs. Others could be pushed with a spade into non-inflammable gutters before it became necessary to summon the overworked fire service. The handbook familiarised a catechism of procedure in case of domestic fire:

Question: What materials may be used to prevent such a bomb from burning through the floorboards of an attic, etc. and falling to the room below?
Answer: The floor may be reinforced by any of the following:
1. Dry sand, 2" thick.
2. Foamed slag, 2" thick.
3. Dry earth, 2" thick, etc. etc.
Question: Why could not the hose be simply attached to a domestic tap?
Answer:
1. The pressure from a bathroom or other upstairs tap would often be insufficient.
2. In any case, it is very unlikely that any water would be available during or just after an air raid as fire brigade appliances will most probably need the whole supply.

And so on, for sixteen pages.

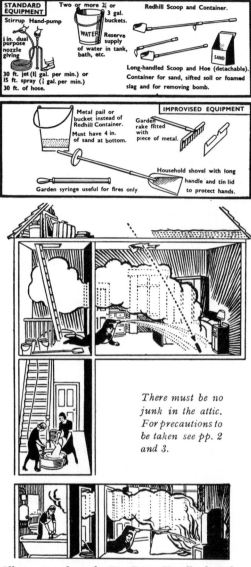

There must be no junk in the attic. For precautions to be taken see pp. 2 and 3.

Illustrations from the Fire Party Handbook. Others included pictorial advice for women on their own, and how to put out a fire-bomb in eight simple stages. Women's magazines were full of advice on how to patch up the roof etc.

But regulations, inevitably, were hard to keep. One empty-handed warden broke into a house and found an incendiary bomb burning the carpet and curtains. 'I looked around for something to throw on it and the first thing I saw was two dozen eggs in a bowl on the sideboard. I got it out with eighteen!'

Often a single incident during the blitz

would incur hours of hard physical exertion running from bomb blast, guiding the homeless, digging for and finding parts of bodies among burning debris, often under a spray of water and with crashing walls and explosions all around. Women found that the evening work they had volunteered for would stretch into long, distressing hours of night-time labour. In contrast to their peacetime routines, these 'ordinary' women were battered by shock after shock, night after night as they handled the human muddles which no authority could predict or cater for. A woman ambulance driver records one such night:

> A warden brought in a basket and said, 'You're to have these'. Well, we asked what it was and he took the paper off and it was all fingers and toes.
> 'The hospital won't take it because it's not a casualty and the mortuary won't take it because it's not a corpse. So it's yours to do what you like with.' Well, talk about red tape! The basket was there for two days. Eventually an ambulance driver buried it on the common.

Most of these ambulance drivers were women. As in the fire services, any suitable vehicle was used – taxis, private cars with the back sawn off or Fyffe's banana vans crudely adapted to take six or eight stretchers. On the Thames, VAD nurses used barges to transport casualties when the road was blocked.

'We took what we were given and quite often they were dead on arrival.' An even more unpleasant job was that of driving the 'corpse wagons', which at times drivers found scandalous and 'unfair on their relatives' since the bodies often had to be folded and on occasion fell out into the road from the makeshift vehicles, the back doors tied with string.

Nurses, like hospital beds, coffins, blood banks and bandages, were in short supply in 1939 when the Civil Nursing Reserve registered only 15,000 trained nurses and 46,000 assistant and auxiliary nurses. In anticipating 50 deaths per ton of bombs (estimated by the Air Staff in 1937) and

3,500 tons on the first day and night (1938) with 700 tons a day thereafter, the Ministry of Health thought that 2,800,000 hospital beds would be needed. Happily these figures were grossly exaggerated, but the shortage of nurses was nevertheless acute.

By the last year of war, 106,000 State Registered Nurses were working in hospitals, factories, nurseries, aeroplanes, battleships and in air-raid shelters and emergency first-aid posts. Nurses often made their own bandages until the WVS came to their rescue with yards of bandage and medicaments in well-scrubbed jam jars. A first aid post in a rest centre might be supplied with little more than disinfectant, aspirins, cough medicine and strips of cloth laid out on a bench. Many nurses had had only a few weeks' emergency training with the Red Cross, St John's Ambulance Brigade or the Civil Nursing Reserve and they often had to dig out their patients before administering morphine to whichever part of the body appeared first. One woman who was severely injured in the face and spent four months at a plastic surgery unit recalls hearing one doctor say 'she was lucky that the first aiders didn't get her!' A twenty-year-old nurse remembers spending more time digging than nursing. People might have been buried for days before the rubble was cleared, perhaps lying crushed but fully conscious beside a disembowelled relative. *Women in Green* records the case of a girl buried for 102 hours.

> [She] was lying with her head on the cellar step with the entire debris of the house actually covering her. There was no one to raise it from her. Her mother, sister and the sister's two children were dead under the ruins. She herself was holding one dead child in her arms. Both her arms and legs were temporarily paralysed but she was still quite bright. She had calculated the time almost precisely by 'Jerry coming over every twenty four hours'.

Rescue and medical teams helped by wardens or anxious neighbours would 'strain their ears for a muffled cry, even the sound of breathing. As they drew nearer they might be able to talk to their "patient" perhaps for the hours it took to get through those last impenetrable feet.' Once the teams knew people were buried, they preferred to see the job through, even if they knew there would only be mangled remains among the rubble.

Other victims were able to shout out from cellars with the news that neighbours were buried next door. Once close enough, a rubber tube might be passed through to help with breathing, or to give water or tea. Medical instructions were hard to follow and people had to be resourceful: many considered that their first-aid training, if followed too conscientiously, could actually lead to loss of life. In the absence of bandages, casualties were sometimes treated with whatever came to hand. A window frame for a splint or a sooty piece of skirt for a bleeding stump were sometimes the only life-saving solutions.

Conditions were little better at the hospital. Often several operations took place in the same theatre. When water supplies failed, a bowl of disinfected water was used, in which all the nurses washed their hands; it looked 'more like a bowl of soup by the end of the day'.

When the upper storeys at St Thomas's Hospital were evacuated to the country, surgeons asked for volunteer nurses to stay behind and run the air-raid casualty wards. So many volunteered, said the surgeon, 'that we had to draw lots. The lucky ones stayed and the others grumbled. They said that leaving London was like leaving a sick child with a high temperature.'

Nurses then, as now, received only minimal wages – about 25s a week, the same as the Land Girls and certainly not enough to live on. Many worked on night shifts, with a great deal of responsibility. It was not uncommon for them to have only one night in every two weeks asleep in a bed. Grim billets were their temporary homes and one nurse remembers that they were so tired that they were liable to sleep through air raids. They had an official notice to hang on the door handle if they wished to be called to go to the shelters, but many preferred to sleep. One nurse remembers waking up in a room full of shattered glass with a gaping hole in the wall after sleeping through a raid.

When the London Women's Parliament met in 1941 the working conditions of women in Civil Defence were among the subjects discussed. They complained that while women shared equally with men in the 'responsibilities and duties, they do not receive equal treatment.' Once Civil Defence work was made compulsory in 1943 the Women's Parliament reacted decisively, demanding equal pay for full-timers. Their demands illustrate how bad their conditions were. Among other mild requests they wanted uniforms which gave 'adequate protection', facilities for baths and disinfecting of clothing, bunks, stretchers or mattresses at all posts, adequate meals, time to shop and twelve days' holiday a year. Before 1943, as in the factories, compensation for injury 'as a result of enemy action' was far lower for women than for men. Before then, any 'non-gainfully employed' woman (ie. one who was not a wage-earner, and the very stuff of which the female Civil Defence Corps was made up) would only receive 16s 4d a week by way of compensation.

Although angered by this treatment of their selfless work, women went on courageously, inspired more by the attitude of the people than by rewards from the authorities. The journalist Hilda Marchant, in her angry account of the family under bombardment, *Women and Children Last*, records her meeting with a soldier while on a lonely patrol by the Embankment during a raid:

He asked me where I was going. I told him Fleet Street and he said he would like to come along with me for the guns were going and planes kept passing over the river. We talked of many things – how much he wanted to see his wife in Lancashire, how the raids on London only seemed to emphasise the Army's inactivity. 'We feel a bit ashamed of ourselves when we see it's the women and kids fighting the war for us.'

WVS *members prepared thousands of meals for the victims of air raids like this one in April 1941. These field kitchens were part of the sophisticated Food Convoy system, but other women made sandwiches or cooked on wood rescued from the rubble.*

5. Over to you!

BEHIND THE SCENES: THE VOLUNTARY GROUPS

The intensity of the first few months of the Blitz was quite unlike anything that was to follow. The enemy's aim was to destroy London in one great 'knockout blow' by devastating docks, power stations, transport centres and aerodromes, and, for the first time in history, civilian homes on a huge scale. The Germans hoped that destruction of the capital would create such demoralising chaos that the government would be forced by their despairing citizens to capitulate. (In fact London could have been brought to a standstill within three days by destroying the sewage system and the water supply, without any casualties at all.)

From 23 August 1940, when the first all-night air raid on London occurred, between two and four hundred enemy bombers dropped high explosives night after night for the next nine months, and more intermittently till the end of the war. Not counting the thousands of small incendiary bombs that women and householders often swept off roofs and doormats, over 50,000 high explosive bombs fell on London between September 1940 and May 1941. The September 1940 raids alone caused the temporary or permanent loss of homes of 40,000 to 50,000 people a week. By December 1940 the death toll from bombing in London was 12,696, with 20,000 seriously wounded. By May 1941 over 1,400,000 people in London had been made homeless and 1,150,000 houses damaged.

The housing situation had been bad enough before the war. In 1939 only a tenth of houses in Stepney had baths, half in Glasgow and two-thirds in Birmingham and Hull. Ten or more houses might share a lavatory, more often outside than in, while in Victorian Peabody flats four families might have to make do with a butler sink on the landing. When war started the government's housing projects ceased at once as 1,153,000 builders and engineers were set to build essential factories, camps and hostels (though not relief centres for the homeless). With the massive air raids of 1940–1 the situation became desperate. By May 1941 in London alone at least one in every six households faced the despair of homelessness. In Plymouth it was one household in four, not counting those 'temporarily unusable'. In fact the number of bomb hits exceeded the number of houses, since many were hit more than once. In Clydebank only 7 out of 12,000 houses were left intact: 35,000 were made homeless and took to the countryside – anything to get away from the hail of bombs.

After weeks of this bombing, although there was no capitulation, the civilian chaos that the Germans had planned arrived. All the requirements of a normal life disappeared. Gas, electricity, telephones, buses, houses, water and food were drastically reduced or disappeared altogether. By 18 September 1940, less than a month after the first all-night raid on London, German-controlled French wireless announced: 'The legend of British self-control and phlegm is being destroyed. All reports from London concur that the population is being seized by fear – hair-raising fear. The 7,000,000 Londoners run aimlessly about the streets and are the victims of bursting shells.'

In fact, the reverse was true. The British, thrown together by tragedy, became more united. As the sirens sounded, people urged each other to continue the fight. People hurrying to the shelters called out cheerfully 'I'll meet you tomorrow, same time, same sand bag.' A woman looking for her dentures was jovially scolded, 'Listen you, they're dropping doodle-bugs, not sandwiches.' Young and old declared that if Hitler thought he was going to let it get them down 'He had another think coming.' A song recalled by a woman factory worker, lonely and billeted, may not, forty years later, be completely accurate, but reflects some of the humorous refusal to be 'got down by it all'.

> I've got a cosy flat,
> There's a place for your hat,
> An alarm clock that won't let you down.
> And even way down here
> You can hear the all-clear,
> I've got the deepest shelter in town.

Not a single shop from Oxford Circus to Tottenham Court Road was left unbombed. Many displayed humorous signs – 'More open than usual', or in the case of the police station, 'Be good, we're still open.'

Between September 1940 and May 1941, with each fresh air raid, women took their belongings in bundles and perambulators at dusk to queue for the shelters, never knowing whether their homes might not be a mass of black smoky rubble in the morning. Many chose to sleep in the shelters every night rather than risk being buried alive.

With millions of homes either flattened into rubble or temporarily unusable all over Britain, the possibilities open to the homeless were limited to squashing up with neighbours, taking over a less damaged house or moving into one of the huge public shelters, where life was reduced to sandwiches, blankets, deckchairs and buckets for sanitation, at least for the worst part of the first Blitz.

Life was often further complicated by having to re-register with ration books at new shops if moving to a new district, or if a shop was bombed. Food offices handed out temporary ration books if necessary, and directed tired women with bundles, prams and children to alternative shops where the basics for these temporary living arrangements could be bought – if you were lucky. Women managed as best they could, either individually or in voluntary groups, to help each other.

Rest centres, supposed to house families for no more than a few days after bombing while they found new homes, often overflowed within a month with the completely homeless. Only in October 1940 was 'Red Ellen', Miss Ellen Wilkinson, appointed as Joint Parliamentary Secretary to Herbert Morrison, the Minister of Homes Security, to sort out shelterers' problems.

At last bunks, heat, light, lavatories and canteens were officially recognised as essential to those temporarily or permanently living in the larger shelters. London's rest centres (as opposed to shelters) were more organised than in the provinces, where 'nervy' families, many of whom had been bombed out more than once, sometimes packed up their bedding in the afternoons to spend the night on the moors, such as Dartmoor and the Yorkshire moors, rather than face the horrors again. Often further evacuation was almost impossible to arrange, with country billets already full to the brim, unless it was managed privately.

By November 1940 a census showed that 40 per cent of the population were sleeping in public shelters, at which they queued for admittance from 4 pm, and 27 per cent in back-garden Anderson shelters. In London over 177,000 men, women and children were sleeping in the tube stations alone every night. As there were a mere 22,000 bunks, they slept in waves of bodies with train passengers stepping over them, while sanitation consisted of overflowing buckets. Over 24,000 were in temporary rest centres which were often school buildings, without bedding or mattresses and only equipped for a few hours' shelter at a time, the official policy being simply that people in these centres would 'look after each other'. And many did, but thousands more drifted into inadequate public shelters to sleep and live – cellars, cinemas and vaults. The most infamous of all these was the Tilbury ware-

house, which 'housed' up to 16,000 people on some nights, with sanitation for only a handful. Other people worked on night shifts at factories, stations or with the emergency services, or made improvised shelters in their home with gas masks, sandwiches and thermos flasks near to hand.

Inside the shelters, few people had night-gowns, but many wore dressing gowns over daytime clothes for warmth. A few brought eiderdowns and mattresses, or just blankets, after turning off gas, electricity and water supplies at home and remembering to leave sand buckets, sand bags or stirrup pumps on the doorstep in case of fire. One habituee said, 'There was no undressing on the whole, and a lot of indignation when a portly French-woman insisted on taking off her stays: per-haps a little disrobing after lights out at 11 pm, but that was all.' Fights and quarrels were rare but more likely on Saturday nights when drunken vomit was added to the often already unbearable smells. Women in uni-form of any sort assumed a spontaneous

Families and helpers living in the Chislehurst Caves. Others slept on the escalators or in cinemas if they had been bombed out or had inadequate shelter. Many started their 'trek' in mid-afternoon with sandwiches and eiderdowns to survive the night's air raids.

authority on these occasions, dispersing troublemakers to their corners.

Trench shelters in public gardens, sometimes lined with concrete or steel but often hard to keep waterproof, are recalled with more shudders than most – 'hollowed out winding narrow caverns, sometimes with benches but nothing more. I can recall the smell to this day, and have not eaten fish and chips since!'

Yet in the shelters and rest centres after an air raid 'everyone was dirty, and everyone was kind'. Neighbours and strangers comforted each other and encouraged each other 'back to life'. 'At least there's something to be said for the Blitz – it does take your mind off the blackout!' as one old woman optimistically put it. Those thousands who 'lived' in the dismal bug-ridden public shelters could not have survived without a sense of humour. Many found the life oddly elating as accordions and pianos played louder and louder with the din of the air raid outside.

Bureaucrats declaimed against those wardens who complained of the conditions, as Barbara Nixon in her book *Raiders Overhead* remembered of her fellow 'bombing partner'.

> The Town Hall called him a communist because he had made a fuss about the shelters. Spacious, dry shelters under offices and private firms had been kept locked while people had to queue in the streets long after the sirens had gone before they could be squeezed into the overcrowded public ones.

A shelter nurse, remembering the filth and smell made worse by constant flooding of a large North London shelter under a bread factory marvelled that no great plague followed the second fire of London. Nurses dealt with boils, lice, fleas, impetigo, scabies, hysteria, shock and wounds as best they could.

By March 1941, 'when the smell of the shelters had penetrated even the nostrils of Whitehall', the shelters slowly improved. 'There is that sweet smell of disinfectant, there are decent latrines, proper feeding

arrangements and, usually, bunks to sleep in.' Even so the bunks took up more room than bodies and people squashed in head to toe. 'Children slept curled up round their mothers or rolled in tight balls . . . I heard a thin young Yorkshire voice saying "Mum, me bum's numb". He was sleeping on a thin blanket spread over bumpy cobbles.' All the official posters could advise was: 'Be a man – give up your place in the shelters to a woman', a policy which forced families even further apart.

Those who emerged from their shelters the morning after a raid, to find their street a mass of mud, rubble and charred wood with flaming gas jets and water showering over crushed possessions, cursed both Hitler and the authorities that had made no provision for their future. Although massive casualty figures had already been calculated (based on the experience of the Spanish Civil War), no post-raid welfare scheme existed for the human chaos that was bound to follow. The only choice for women was to help each other with support, kindness and humour. There was only improvisation to see them through. By 1942 most 'immobile' women were working for the war effort. But millions of women who wanted to help after raids, for a few hours whenever they could, joined voluntary organisations.

The wvs (Women's Voluntary Service) formed by Lady Reading to prepare women for wartime emergencies was the largest group of volunteer women. Many were over the 'mobile' age limit, many had jobs already and many had children. Thousands of women, from the very old to the very young, and even the infirm, joined other voluntary groups too – like the Women's Institutes, Townswomen's Guilds, the Co-operative Women's Guilds, the ymca and ywca and the Red Cross. All were hampered in their attempts to adapt their peacetime range of skills to those of war by the lack of official finance. Added to this, these groups also ran substantial fund-raising groups to finance the military side of war. All were appalled at the social misery of the blitzed and at the lack of organisation for the resulting problems. Women in the voluntary groups managed to help where and how they could, some with only a few hours a week to spare to scrub out a damaged building for use as a rest centre, or organise a clothing exchange for those who had lost everything or a food centre or enquiry post.

Mobile laundries were set up, washing fluttering among black ruins, and mobile water supplies. Since no welfare system existed for the homeless, it was these women who filled the breach wherever they could, helping those too numbed by bombs to think, or those unable to read the bureaucratic notices about emergency food tickets, insurance, money loans or injury benefits. Meanwhile they continually demanded better support from their local authorities. Official CABS (Citizens Advice Bureaux) were at last set up by the National Council of Social Service so that the destitute could get sensible and practical support. 90 per cent were volunteers, each giving about 9 hours' help a week until by 1944 1,064 Bureaux had opened. When the CAB in Coventry was bombed, a single helper continued to give advice from the gutter outside the Town Hall.

Women in the voluntary services stepped into the breach so efficiently that even the official answer to queries became, 'Ask the WVS.' Coping with the most appalling conditions of poverty and loss, they still managed to follow official advice: '*Your* image, *your* cheerfulness, *your* resolution WILL BRING US VICTORY.' Wherever people were bombed out, the WVS would try and be there, with tea urns and sandwiches, sometimes setting up tarpaulins while the rubble was cleared.

As the newly blitzed arrived at the shelters or rest centres, many were in a state of numb shock. Most arrived in their night clothes, some naked, except for their shoes – their clothes literally blasted off them. Most had no means of tracing relations and friends (were they in the debris, or at the hospital or morgue?) until incident enquiry posts were organised by volunteers and lists made of those passing through the rest centres before they were settled in billets. One answer to a question about the whereabouts of a husband was, 'In Libya, the bloody coward!'

Typical of the way women helped each other was a young mother who had already organised WVS Housewives services in her street of 80 houses so that people could take over during an alert, or get first aid. (She also helped with school meals and worked at an Infant Welfare Centre, 'lousespotting'.) She described her work in a Rest centre immediately after their houses were hit.

Many women and children came uninjured but often very shocked. We ran a sort of 'advice centre' and tried to get the women to write to their husbands to say they were alright. Some did not know how to. I'd suggest, 'Tell him what you and the children are doing now' 'It sounds so soppy,' was a typical reply. This lack of ability to communicate seemed to me one of my saddest war-time experiences.

The newly homeless had to be dealt with kindly but firmly, so that people could somehow pick up the pieces and force themselves to carry on. People whose homes were in ruins were sometimes excessively distressed by the loss of a photograph album, a ration book, the disappearance of a pet or, for more obvious reasons, the disappearance of the savings under the floorboards. Women with little or no training had to handle these cases with delicacy – the child who laughed hysterically on hearing that both her parents had been killed, the woman among the huddled families who cried all day after her husband, daughter and son-in-law had all been killed. One old woman who had lost everything could not speak for hours, but eventually signalled for a pencil and paper. On it she wrote, 'To the newsvendor on the corner. I shan't be needing my paper today.'

For the homeless an immediate problem was to get somewhere to live. In *Women and Children Last* Hilda Marchant describes the typical reaction of women:

> In one of the lesser damaged streets they had found a row of houses without roofs or windows, but with the first floors still waterproof. About a hundred of them, including the tenants of the houses, got together and patched up windows, moved scraps of furniture in and, every afternoon, they would sit around the fireplace gossiping, knitting and scribbling letters for the kids. They all had Anderson shelters and several lived in them.

As their children played on the rubble, women still referred to the different areas of the street as the 'Dairy' or 'number 64'. Many preferred a semi-blitzed room in their own neighbourhood to a billet in a West End mansion where all links with home were lost. Those who had jobs still picked their way over the debris every morning. 'They needed the feel of something fixed and persistent. In their normal daily work they found it and gripped it hard.'

Although thousands of builders were recalled from the forces in 1941, over two and a half million people were still living in semi-repaired, bomb-damaged houses by the end of 1942, and more than a million in condemned and unsafe housing. Yet with the arrival in Britain of thousands of American GIs after Pearl Harbor in December 1941, urgent camp-building for the troops became first priority and once again civilians were left to wait their turn.

For the victims of air raids, the need for hot water and food came even before housing. The Ministry of Food advised women to make street stoves out of mud and bricks, but they needed no telling. Hilda Marchant describes the first reactions of a group of homeless women. After the first awful numbness as they stood before the wreckage of their homes, they began 'to pick it over forlornly in search of belongings'. Then they 'made field kitchens out of the broken brick walls of their homes. With wood from their own doors and furniture, they made fires and cooked something hot for the old man's dinner. They had miles to walk to find shops, for their own butcher and grocer had been blown out.' The fact was that

there were no cups of tea or mobile canteens, no facilities to wash soot-soaked clothes and bodies, no advice centres or enquiry posts and no future for the blitzed, until the women's voluntary groups organised them. These voluntary groups advised and pressured ministries for better mobile canteens, hostels, clothing exchanges and citizens' advice centres. But only after the most concentrated bombing was over in 1941 did these official policies begin to take effect. Until then women managed as best they could. Anger and frustration was voiced loud and clear, not just at the new nightmarish conditions of life but at a system which put factory workers into billets but made no proper provision for families. Or, as a loud cockney voice announced to reporters at the scene of a particularly sensational disaster, 'We're sick and tired of being bleedin' heroes.'

Water was often a major problem after a raid. When water pipes were bombed, queues stretched for miles. Until water carts were introduced, mothers and children would take buckets, basins or whatever they had to collect their ration from leaky taps or burst water mains. One woman remembers how she used water: 'We had to work it out carefully, face first etc. By the time it got to hankies and stockings there was no water left to rinse with, nor to wash the blackened basin.' Another voluntary worker remembers using the contents of her father's hot-water-bottle regularly, 'tea first, socks last!'

The food supply was just as critical. At first women packed cars and vans with sandwiches and tea urns to tour the public shelters and, after the raid, the streets. Each night, as more were made homeless, the problems increased. During the first months of the Blitz it was left to individuals to brave the raids with cups of tea for bombed families and rescue parties alike. Tea urns were carried on wheelbarrows or prams if necessary. Within weeks, the first crude mobile canteens were organised by dedicated voluntary workers, who made sandwiches of bread and margarine, some-

Volunteers taking food to evacuees in the village of Allington.

The East End in war time

The Hand that held the Hoover helps the Bombed!

HOUSEWIFE 1944

.V.S.

When an "incident has occurred", nobody is more welcome to 'bombed out', wardens, and demolition workers, than the W.V.S. with their mobile canteens. Now there is a bite to eat, and a cup of tea to hearten them. That's only one of the many jobs W.V.S. do, voluntarily, and without pay, and they nearly all have homes to run and families to look after as well. As a token of our very heart-felt admiration for this splendid Service we say —

Salute! FROM HOOVER

times all night.

Early in 1941, 18 Queen's Messenger Convoys financed by America were put into action. Each consisted of 12 mobile canteens and water suppliers, staffed by 50 women, and rushed to each disaster. One water tank, two food storage units, three mobile canteens, two equipment lorries with army field kitchens and four motor cycles were able to feed 10,000 people a day (as they did during the Liverpool Blitz in May 1941) with meat, vegetables and puddings. Only when the worst of the Blitz was over in June 1941 was a Canteen Code organised by the Ministry of Food, to prevent voluntary workers overlapping in certain districts while neglecting others.

Although mobile food and drink facilities were vital to the homeless, British Restaurants, started during the Blitz, were seen as more comforting. 'Shocked people went to familiar places where they knew they could get a meal, or waited in dumb misery until a meal was brought to them.' The numbers of these restaurants, however, never reached the original target of 10,000. They hovered around 2,000 for the remainder of the war. During the lull after the first Blitz, the wvs organised a Pie Scheme to feed land workers, factories without canteens, schools and other institutions between major air raids. 1,144,306 pies were produced from private ovens and village baker shops to cope with the demand. To save petrol, 'they were carried out into the fields in bicycle baskets, ordinary baskets, prams, wheelbarrows and carts, or sold at depots in the village.'

In 1941 mobile emergency feeding units were set up by the wvs in Middlesex. A collapsible shed, solid-fuel burners, furniture, crockery and stores of food, water and fuel formed the basis, and were carried as close to the scene of disaster as possible. These units were so successful that the policy was soon extended to other counties. But even these were not enough. Semi-mobile kitchens, army-style, were assembled on lorries to feed 5,000 people at a time, and produced in all eight million meals a month.

The voluntary workers worked tirelessly on, in extended rotas 'in the thundering blackness with no sleep at all'. They listed names of refugees as they arrived. They scrubbed bleak dwellings for them. Flowers, when available, were put out, 'wallpaper' daubed on with a paint brush and, on occasion, curtains 'painted' around a blacked-out window to give a more homely effect. These women invented the Home Help idea for new mothers, to relieve qualified nurses for hospital duty. They knitted and darned vests and socks for the troops and those on leave. They hand-sewed rabbits' fur for the troops in Russia: they spun everything – including sheeps' and rabbits' wool. They set up mobile libraries for bored militia awaiting instructions. They had them to tea and gave them baths and precious soap. Translators, guides and a car pool were provided for foreign troops and refugees. Millions of garments were sorted at clothing depots and a successful exchange system set up once clothes were rationed after 1941. A London woman remembers: 'Some of the garments from America looked as if they had gone over on the *Mayflower*, but I first glimpsed nylon stockings in these Bundles for Britain.' Vegetables for the Navy were grown, and delivered at depots by mothers and children. In the Red Cross, women organised an educational scheme for British prisoners-of-war, sending books and exams along with life-saving parcels of bully-beef, tea, condensed milk, chocolates and cigarettes. The young were mobilised to help too.

Under the guidance of these women's voluntary groups, the new Citizens Advice Bureaux information centres, health inspections, food supply and billeting systems slowly began to flourish. Technically 'immobile', these women were unpaid, often worked long hours, and took on many of the most repetitive and joyless jobs of war as the need arose, often without warning. During the Blitz, the elation at being alive was often followed by despair at losing everything else. Goering's aim – to 'demoralise into capitulation' by the bombing – might well have been achieved but for the women who voluntarily helped to solve the enormous social and emotional problems that flooded to the surface during this harrowing time of the war.

One of five sisters running a 380-acre farm in Yorkshire feeding the chickens before taking the tractor out. The women rise at 4.30 in the morning to start in the dairy at 5 to millk the herd in time for the milk collection at 7 o'clock. They do most of the heavy work on the farm and all the work in the dairy. Even in the hard winters when, with snow drifts 20 feet deep, the flocks of sheep need digging out, they still maintain it is 'The only life for them'.

6. Lend a hand on the land

The problems of food production in the war were vast, since previously much of Britain's food had been imported. Horrifying statistics were announced by the Ministry of Food. Half an ounce of bread wasted each day would necessitate extra imports of over 200,000 tons a year. Posters warned women that 'Cargoes cost lives!' and 'Let your shopping help our shipping!'

Another problem was that British farming had declined steadily since the nineteenth century, and, with huge amounts of cheap grain arriving from the USA during the inter-war years, many farmers had concentrated on dairy produce. But now cereals and root crops were urgently needed to give the greatest yield per acre. Farming methods were often still archaic. The cart-horse, the hand-plough and the hoe were still more common than tractors. The factories that could have produced them were not only making submarines, aeroplanes and tanks, but were also luring away the badly paid farm labourer with high industrial wages. By May 1940 the nation's headaches included a shortage of 100,000 farm workers to meet the food production target. The Women's Land Army, 80,000 strong by 1944, was to be their greatest single help, along with the remaining sources of full-time labour, conscientious objectors and eventually 40,000 Italian and German prisoners-of-war.

Other helpers for the often bewildered and not always grateful farmer included an assortment of 60,000 schoolchildren, Girl Guides, Cubs and youth squads, GIs, evacuee children and their mothers, soldiers on leave and tired factory workers gasping for a breath of fresh air. Jolly posters begged those in towns to have 'Farming Holidays' – and to 'LEND A HAND ON THE LAND'. 'Why not take your children a-harvesting?' suggested one MOF (Ministry of Food) pamphlet.

Without doubt the helpers, who varied from bishops to nurses, were in need of some respite from the war-torn cities, but the farmer's wife had her own problems too. As villages bulged with people from evacuated factories, hospitals and schools, accommodation became increasingly scarce. The farmer's wife, with her quota of land girls and billeted guests was frequently obliged to rise well before dawn to cope with her extra domestic burden.

The Ministry of Food organised the huge farming programme through the 'War Ags' (the War Agricultural Committees). These were local advisers empowered to fine or even confiscate land if instructions were not followed. The illegal slaughter of an animal if not observed by a War Ag. at a certain place and time could result in prosecution and a fine. Animals, from cows to chickens, were strictly rationed according to the yield of the previous season. But the War Ags also provided help, advice on new scientific approaches and grants for the farmer. Farm machinery was in short supply in many parts of Britain and combine harvesters, tractors and ploughs were pooled so that all farmers could benefit. In March 1941 the situation improved somewhat when the American Lend-Lease Bill passed into law, and vital farm machinery was sent to Britain from the USA. (This scheme pledged financial and material help to Britain, on terms decided by President Roosevelt – including contracts with American industry and lease of bases for the US armed forces. Apart from vital supplies of money, arms and machinery,

Come on the Services!

LEND A HAND ON THE LAND

SPEND YOUR LEAVE OR SPARE TIME HELPING FARMERS

FULL DETAILS FROM YOUR CANTEEN

'Come on the Services'. This poster promised romance in the fields for men in the Services and women working in the factories. Travel and petrol restrictions made it hard to go anywhere. Only after two years of war did Ernest Bevin manage to provide a few official holiday camps for exhausted war workers.

the Lend-Lease scheme made a crucial contribution to improving the quality of the diet in Britain, which in early 1941 was at its poorest.)

Meanwhile 'Growmore' bulletins, Ministry of Food pamphlets sent to farmers with agricultural and horticultural information, advised on emergency feeding of livestock, but with a tiresomely bureaucratic tone: 'Cereal coupons may be applied for by the farmers who have grown essential crops . . . if they satisfy their Committee that they have not enough food for their livestock.' Every month more advice arrived on how to feed the animals with diminishing food stocks, along with forms and new regulations for the harrassed farmer. Farmers remember too the hazards of the blackout, helped only a little by double summer time when clocks went forward by two hours but left livestock still bright and alert at 10pm.

In April 1939, under pain of confiscation of land, the British farmer began a massive ploughing programme, encouraged by a grant of £2 per acre. As well as other problems, he had to cope with pill-boxes, anti-tank traps and barbed wire and military exercises on his land. By 1943, 70 per cent of our food was home-produced compared with 40 per cent in 1939. Twelve million acres were already arable in 1939, and a further ten million were ploughed up as well as seventeen million acres of neglected marsh and moorland, some of it untilled since Saxon times.

In order to achieve their goal, farming families were urged to plough by night as well as by day. Dangerous but blackout-proof lamps were improvised, using oil lanterns shaded by ancient hats, as farmers and their wives donned their Weatherdair macs and Attaboy trilbies and set to work. By day, especially in the South-eastern counties after the air raids had started, farm workers found it safer to work in pairs, facing opposite directions, since neither siren nor approaching aircraft could be heard above the roar of archaic tractor engines. By working with an eye on the sky, labourers could

more easily warn each other of bombs, aircraft or shrapnel if a battle was raging above. In the case of invasion, farmers were instructed to sell or give away milk to people close by and to be 'ready also to dispose of perishable fruit and vegetables by selling to those who can afford to pay and giving to those who cannot.'

This was the countryside to which 20,000 Land Girls, some of whom had volunteered eagerly from the Birmingham and Nottingham factories, were introduced by the spring of 1941. They came from all classes. With their sagging corduroy breeches, canvas leggings and felt hats they were officially portrayed as a romantic band of happy volunteers, fighting for peace by tossing bales of hay lightly on to carts. But cartoonists presented a more accurate picture. Rationed gumboots meant borrowing from the men or, with rubber in short supply, waiting for two years, unless they were working in the milk shed. Improvised clothing had to be adapted. Land Girls' tasks varied from rat-catching, tree-felling, muck spreading, land reclamation, ploughing, hedging, ditching and harvesting, to mucking out, milking cows, and caring for sheep and poultry. One girl, used to working in a warm factory, remembers the agonies of potato picking in freezing weather, tying sanitary towels around her wrists to keep a little warmer. One Land Girl on a 600-acre farm remembers pitting her strength against a huge stubborn carthorse:

> Today I took the churns of milk up the hill to the road and Bargey bolted – we did a chariot race down the three-quarters of a mile drive back to the farm – I tried to hold him back and deepened my voice hoping he'd think Jack was holding the reins. The tail board on the cart came off and the churns fell out – ahead was a closed gate. I tightened the reins and thought the gate would stop him, but he charged through the field along the deep cart ruts towards the stable. The going was rough and the ground was hard – but there was no stopping his great weight. As we got to the yard I slipped down from his back into the cart and rolled off as he came to an abrupt halt.

Feeding sheep in winter involved carrying kale and water to them twice a day. The water barrel might have to be filled from a stream, after breaking the ice from a plank stretching from bank to bank. Digging, carting and sorting vegetables, stacking pens, milking, herding and sawing could be all in a day's work. Threshing lasted for weeks. During shearing time, loads of fleeces had to be gathered and stacked in lofts. The summer months involved the sweaty job of hoeing field after field, then hours of overtime during harvesting with a further hour and a half's grooming and feeding before the day ended, after dusk if necessary.

During harvesting there was ratting:

> When the last sheaves were lifted, the men used sticks, forks and dogs to kill as many rats as possible. I tried to get out of the way but the farmer said to me: 'I'll hold the sack while you put the dead rats in.' I had to pick up the rats by the tails and count them as they were put in – forty-two of them.

Even worse was taking the remains of dead

Fences and hedges disappeared to facilitate land reclamation. A mass assault by Land Girls on a 400-acre 'field' of wheat which had hitherto been derelict and unploughed for 20 years.

Previous pages: Land Girls pause as a squadron of fighters return.

sheep and lambs to a pit. If the Land Girl missed her aim with cart or wheelbarrow she had to fork the decomposing animal into the hole.

Songs often proved a distraction:

> *When this silly war is over*
> *Oh how happy I shall be*
> *When I get my civvy clothes on*
> *No more Land Army for me*
> *No more digging up potatoes*
> *No more threshing out the corn*
> *We will make that bossy foreman*
> *Regret the day that he was born*

And as the farmers ploughed by night as well as day, the Land Army sang:

> *If you wanna go to heaven when you die*
> *You must wear a green pullover and a tie,*
> *You must wear a khaki bonnet*
> *With* WLA *on it*
> *If you wanna go to heaven when you die.*

Since about one third of Land Girls were town dwellers, there were the inevitable stories of attempts to milk the bull, of being chased by pigs while mucking out, pruning trees down to the trunk or, more seriously, having nasty accidents. Their training was often too brief for the assortment of jobs the year-round farmer needed. At one hostel alone a Land Girl recalled the belt on a threshing machine breaking and 'cutting a girl to ribbons', the end of one girl's finger being cut off while she was feeding sheaves into the machine, coats getting caught in the potato-sorting machine and going round with it, an eye poked out by a pitchfork and a girl whose ankle was sawn through while using a cross saw on a tree trunk.

Many of the town girls had been eager for a taste of country life, lured by jolly posters advertising a healthy, rustic yet patriotic life, in contrast to the prospect of working in bomb-stricken towns. They regarded the country, like most wartime town dwellers, as a land not only of milk and honey, but also of cream and eggs. They arrived bright-eyed with anticipation, only to find that except for the odd rabbit and a few more eggs, restrictions were sternly enforced. Their new life was often extremely tough and poorly paid – conditions already familiar to many agricultural workers in Britain. Land Girls' training lasted for four weeks (with only 10s a week wages). The Land Girl manual advised them to try carrying full buckets of water for half an hour and then 'attempt to pitch earth on to a barrow'. Weekly hours were officially fifty in summer, forty-eight in winter, but it was often more like fourteen hours a day. The minimum wage was 22s 6d (18s if girls were under eighteen years of age, as many were), increased to 48s a week only in 1944. A strong reaction to these conditions came from some of the voluntary women's groups in 1942, against a government that only permitted women to work during a national emergency, and then treated them inadequately:

Girls transferred away from home have to find 25s–30s a week for lodging out of wages which may be even lower . . . How can they send money home or save the fare for an occasional visit? National Service officers have been obliged in some cases to release girls from nationally important work on the grounds that the pay did not enable the girl to support herself.

Billets for Land Girls varied. Some were friendly and fairly free of discipline. Others were less so – such as the attic in an isolated, Welsh-speaking valley with no electricity, a well for water and only a roaring sermon on Sundays for entertainment; or isolated caravans and grim hostels housing between 15 and 100 girls who worked in gangs for surrounding farms.

If we were caught smoking in the bedrooms we were fined three pence and if we were to leave anything lying around during the day it was confiscated and taken to the Warden's room and to get it back we had to pay a fine from one penny to three pence according to the size.

In wartime, as at other times, town and country regarded each other as separate breeds. Some farmers' wives accordingly received Land Girls with a wariness which however often mellowed as the girls proved themselves indispensable.

A visit home was allowed after each six months of satisfactory work, with a free travel pass. There were a mere seven days' paid holiday a year, compared with twenty-eight days for those in the forces.

There were compensations – the occasional glorious discovery of a nest of quail, partridge, pheasant or pigeon eggs. And there was still much experimenting to be done with cooking other species. Swan, cormorant (soaked overnight in seawater to remove the salty taste), redshank (for cakes only) and seagull eggs were all tried by the ingenious. Or there might be other specialities. A Devon farmer's wife remembers her anger at the disgust of her two Land Girls when presented with a badger to eat for supper, a local delicacy cooked like mutton.

The girls' lunches often depended on the goodwill of the farmer's wife, who might also have to feed Italian or German prisoners-of-war. Generally the prisoner's

official ration of a twist of tea, some bacon and bread was used to make better lunchtime pies and sandwiches for everyone. After a breakfast of lumpy porridge or half a slice of bacon or a sausage of 'bread and sawdust', and with twelve to fourteen hours' work ahead of them, the Land Girls in one area complained:

> We considered we weren't getting enough and, much as we moaned, nothing ever altered so we called a meeting and the outcome of this was a 'strike'. This went on for a week and, wherever you went, you would see Land Girls sitting at the roadside. The farmers didn't take too kindly to this but could see our point of view as they said they didn't expect us to do a hard day's work on an empty stomach. Anyhow, results were achieved.

Sandwiches, following Lord Woolton's advice, were filled with

> nasturtium leaves and cheese, boiled nettles and spam, raw carrots, home made chocolate spread with lumps of cocoa in it (ugh!) grated raw beetroot and bully beef, peanut butter and spring onions, to name but a few, with a flask of stewed tea. These were supposed to last us until we got back for our evening meal of the cheapest cuts of meat and suet puddings without fruit and custard made with water.

But the Land Girls made the most of their food. 'If we were hedging and ditching then, no matter what sandwiches we had, we always sat and toasted them on the bonfire. Some would fall into the ashes or be covered in smoke but it made no difference, we still ate them.'

In the same spirit, the girls made the most of their time off.

> If it had wheels on it and it stopped we would hitch a lift on anything. One day a helicopter landed in the field and the men trooped over to see what we were doing so off we went for trips round the countryside.

The kindly warden of one hostel used to organise tea parties and dancing sessions with 'boys' stationed nearby, while they in turn organised films and dances, laying on trucks for the girls to get there and back by 11 pm, sometimes two or three times a week. If cigarettes were offered at dances, 'we would light up and, as we danced by, give the tab end to one of the other girls to light up. We NEVER threw a cigarette away. We saved them to reroll. We even smoked dry tea-leaves.'

In 1941, at a discussion group in St Pancras, a woman described two jobs as a Land Girl where she had been badly exploited:

> In a large farm in Lincolnshire we worked for twelve hours a day at very hard and monotonous work and received no training. Wages were 28s a week, out of which we had to pay £1 for billets. At a smaller firm in Huntingdon where we expected to be trained in tractor driving we were made to do odd jobs, including kitchen work for the farmer's wife. The farmer gave us no training and refused to pay us any wages.

Mostly, however, it was heroic stories that filtered through. 'The Land Girls are hard at work in Hertfordshire operating excavators on the heavy wasteland in the district. They can cut ditches at the rate of twenty yards an hour.' There were thousands of stories like this – stories of courage and prodigious energy. Farmers everywhere found it extraordinary that such an apparently unqualified band of recruits, press-ganged to the land in time of national emergency, could adapt to the rigours and demands of farm life with quite such ease. Land Girls set to with a will, and with increasing expertise to do every task required of them. By the end of the war the country's debt to them was enormous. In spite of conditions – exhaustion, very low wages, shared cigarettes and baths, and frequent homesickness, the food supply had almost doubled by 1944, thanks in the main to the WLA.

> *Back to the land, we must all lend a hand*
> *To the farms and the fields we must go.*
> *There's a job to be done,*
> *Though we can't fire a gun*
> *We can still do our bit with the hoe.*
> *When your muscles are strong*
> *You will soon get along*
> *And you'll think that the country life's grand;*
> *We're all needed now,*
> *We must speed with the plough,*
> *So come with us – back to the Land.*

Mrs Whitham, mother of sixteen, works out her ration quota for the family.

7. Food is a munition of war

FOOD AND RATIONING

In 1939, a survey by Sir John Boyd Orr estimated that at least a quarter of the population of Britain were undernourished. Sixty-
two of every thousand babies died before
they were a year old, and in Glasgow it was
over a hundred. Given existing medical
knowledge, the number should have been
no higher than ten. Unemployment and
poverty, ignorance and overcrowding as
well as inadequate health provision all con-
tributed. The rich could have private treatment, but the poor crowded in their hundreds to the out-patients' department of
charitable hospitals, sometimes to queue
for days before they were finally seen. At
least half of all working-class women were
in a state of very poor health, and only a
quarter were completely well. An appallingly
large number persisted in working when ill:
with no adequate form of family allowance
they could not afford not to work.

Compulsory directions to war work
brought some relief to the working class,
for they were coupled with official realisa-
tion that the civilians' war of ten-hour factory shifts and broken nights could not be
sustained if the populace was not 'fighting
fit'. Rationing, introduced in January 1940,
was the first food democracy, although the
situation was still unfair in that the urban
poor had usually only window boxes in
which to Dig for Victory, while the rich
could cultivate their gardens, and eat in restaurants (even though they were rationed
to protein in one course only).

Lord Woolton, the Minister of Food,
announced that it was impossible to ensure
that everyone received the same supplies.
His job, he said, was 'to see to it that everyone received the minimum amount of pro-
teins and vitamins necessary to ensure

good health under hard working conditions'.

In order to eke out dwindling amounts
of home-grown food and to cut down on
imports, ration books were issued, to be
renewed each summer. These were in different colours according to category – general adult, children, travellers, seamen,
pregnant women.

For all rationed items, coupons were
required in addition to money, and the
number required for each item varied according to availability. The famous green
ration book led pregnant and nursing
mothers and children under five to the
front of their queue, with first choice of any
oranges and bananas that filtered through,
a daily pint of milk and a double supply of
eggs. These last varied from between one
every two weeks in the winter to three or
four a week during the spring and summer.
Children under five were allowed half the
meat ration. Children between five and sixteen were allowed fruit, the full meat ration
and half a pint of milk a day with their blue
ration books. The remaining goods on
ration were distributed equally among the
rest of the civilians. The buff-coloured
ration book was issued to all other adults
except for travellers and seamen who could
not register with particular shops and
dairies.

For the next six years, many learnt to
drink watery beer, to sigh at the sight of a
banana skin, to mourn real sausages and
strong sweet tea. Modifications could be
made for those with religious, vegetarian or
invalid diets; heavy manual and agricultural
workers were allowed an extra cheese ration
for their packed lunches. If a ration book
was mislaid, or buried in the debris of a home,

an emergency one-week card could be obtained from the Food Offices who, under the Board of Trade, issued ration books and advised them on coupons used.

> The ideal consumer of rations never moved, or took a holiday, or had a baby; was not a vegetarian, or a Moslem, or an estuarial seaman, or a hop-picker; did not keep bees or poultry, or spend nights in police cells; above all, was not under 2, or under 5, or under 6 or under 18.

Families retreating to country billets or friends' houses had to show great tact about how coupons should be spent if meals were shared. The royal family rationed themselves, slightly to the embarrassment of the government who were concerned at the thought of 'spam on a gold plate'. Churchill was exempted, however. When he asked to see what his people were eating, he was brought a week's ration. He looked approving and said, 'H'mm, not bad for a meal . . .'

In November 1939 people were ordered to register with the shops of their choice – butcher, grocer and dairy – and the housewife was thus introduced to what became a way of life for the next fifteen years (rationing did not end completely until 1954 and some of the most severe rationing was brought in after the war). Ration books had to be handed in at hotels or billets, but were not needed in restaurants (including British Restaurants) or cafes. If the shop where people were registered was bombed, they had to register with another one.

From 8 January 1940 the shopper was limited to 4oz a week of ham or bacon, 12oz a week of sugar and 4oz a week of butter – amounts that were to fluctuate according to supply throughout the war. By 11 March 1940 meat was rationed to just over 1lb per person, or 1s 10d-worth (later reduced to 1s 1d-worth). Offal was not included in the meat ration. Liver became a rare treat, and Stuffed Ear, Pig's Feet in Jelly, Calves' Feet Pie, Mock Goose (pig's fry), Sausages Gratinées, Hash of Calf's Head and Melt & Skirt Pudding were some of the enthralling

new recipes found in the spate of austerity cookery books published.

By July 1940 the tea ration was reduced to a meagre 2oz a week, and Lord Woolton advised 'None for the pot'. This was a blow to morale but tea remained the national form of hospitality whether from a shelter thermos or a weak brew at home. One old woman, on being helped home after a bad raid, found her house gutted, and said rather shyly to her helper, 'I'd ask you in for a cuppa, love, only it seems I've got even less than usual.'

Margarine, butter, cooking fats and suet were limited to about 2oz each a week in July 1940. By March 1941 jam, syrup and marmalade, followed by honey and lemon curd, were put on coupons at between 8oz and 2lb a month. In July of the same year, cheese was rationed to a pitiful 1oz although, like eggs, milk and fruit, the amount varied somewhat with the season.

Basic food rationing varied during the war according to supply and production: the range was 1s to 2s 2d-worth of meat, 4–8oz of bacon, 1–8oz of cheese, 1–8oz of fat, ½–2 eggs a week, ½–2 pints of milk, 2–4oz of tea, and 8–16oz of sugar (increased during the jam-making season). Sweets and chocolates fluctuated at 3–4oz while soap eventually became a serious problem at 4oz a month. One tin of dried National Milk (four pints) was permitted every four weeks and every eight weeks the bonus of an extra twelve eggs was allowed in the form of the famous dried egg packet. Gas, petrol, electricity, coal, light and water supplies were also severely curtailed.

In mid-1940, nutrition experts for the War Cabinet presented Churchill with the 'Basal Diet'. It was estimated that *in extremis* each citizen could survive on 'twelve ounces of bread, a pound of potatoes, two ounces of oatmeal, an ounce of fat, six ounces of vegetables and three-fifths of a pint of milk a day, supplemented by either more of the same foods or small amounts of cheese, pulses, meat, fish, sugar, eggs and dried fruit'. Luckily both Churchill and Lord

Your NEW RATION BOOKS

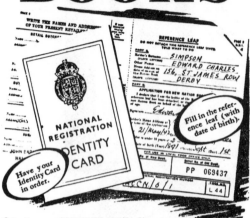

WRITE THE NAMES AND ADDRESS OF YOUR PRESENT RETAILER

NATIONAL REGISTRATION IDENTITY CARD

Have your Identity Card in order.

REFERENCE LEAF

SIMPSON
EDWARD CHARLES
156, ST JAMES ROW
DERBY

Fill in the reference leaf (with date of birth).

PP 069437

L 44

1 Look at your IDENTITY CARD. If you have made any alteration to it, or if it does not give your present address, the first thing you should do is to take it to the nearest National Registration Officer. (Usually his office is in the Council Offices.)

2 As soon as you have made sure about your Identity Card, turn to page 3 of your main FOOD RATION BOOK. This is the reference leaf. *Do NOT take it out of the book.* See that your name is clearly written in Part A (the top portion).

3 In Part B, the lower part of the reference leaf, you must fill in the details asked for — and one that isn't. The form says "If the holder is under 18 state date of birth." But this time *everyone* must give this information. It will be kept confidential.

4 Take your main FOOD RATION BOOK and your IDENTITY CARD (slipped in between page 2 and page 3) to any one of the special offices in your area at once. *Most of them will be closing at the end of this week.* Addresses are advertised locally in Post Offices, Cinemas, and elsewhere. Don't post the Books and Identity Cards—take them or send them by a neighbour or a member of the family.

5 You may take the Books of your family and friends — but see that all the reference leaves have been properly filled in and that you have the right Identity Cards in the right Books.

6 The office will hand over the counter the new Clothing Book (valid from June 1st), with a supplement for children, and also the Personal Food Ration Book. They will take out the reference leaf, and will send on the general Food Ration Book later.

APPLY AS SOON AS YOU CAN

THE MINISTRY OF FOOD, LONDON, W.1

RECIPE of the WEEK No.8

WHIT-SALAD

Time : Preparation 30 minutes. Cooking 15 minutes.

Salad. *Ingredients :* ¼ lb. cooked diced potato, 1 small shredded cabbage or ¾ lb. spinach, ¼ lb. shredded root vegetables, 1 bunch watercress.

Potato Eggs. *Ingredients:* ½ lb. cooked mashed potatoes, 2 ozs. grated cheese, ¼ lb. shredded carrot, ¼ teaspoonful salt, pinch of pepper.

Dressing. *Ingredients:* 1 teacupful milk, 1 tablespoonful vinegar, ½ teaspoonful mustard, 1 teaspoonful sugar, 1 teaspoonful parsley and 1 teaspoonful mint, chopped together.

Quantity : 4 helpings.
Method : To make Potato Eggs, mix the carrots and grated cheese together and form into balls with a little potato if necessary. Cover the balls with a thick layer of potato and cut in halves. Arrange round the dish to look like hard-boiled eggs. Place the cooked diced potato in the centre of the dish. Add the chopped cabbage or spinach and shredded root vegetables. Decorate with watercress. Make the dressing by mixing all its ingredients together. Serve with the salad.

Woolton were horrified at any plan to introduce this and it was soon forgotten.

The National Milk Scheme was launched while the 'Basal Diet' was being discussed. Poor families before the war seldom had more than about a sixteenth of a pint of liquid milk a day, but economised with the sweetened condensed variety for their tea; the average Briton consumed half a pint a day compared with one pint in the USA and Switzerland. The new scheme guaranteed a pint a day to all pregnant or nursing mothers and children under five. If the joint income of parents was below 40s a week milk was free, otherwise it cost 2d a pint. Children from five to sixteen were allowed half a pint. By 1944, 75 per cent of school children were getting a third of a pint subsidised by their school and of the poorest children 90 per cent were getting free milk. The remaining milk was shared out according to supply at about two pints a week, although the League of Nations Diet suggested a minimum of eight pints a week for both children and adults, with twelve pints a week for expectant and nursing mothers.

The milk shortage was due partly to the slaughter of dairy herds in 1940 to allow more land for vital food crops. As milkmen were directed away to fight, it was more often a milkwoman who would drive the horse and cart on its rounds to fill the householder's jug (once milk bottles were no longer made). Even bomb craters and blocked roads could not stop the dairies' deliveries.

Dried household milk, another wartime novelty, was to become as familiar as the dried egg packet. 'How to make dried milk delicious,' advised the Ministry of Food. The answer was a chocolate disguised drink, but wartime chocolate left a lingering dry taste in the mouth. Dried milk nevertheless was a great standby. Each family was allowed one tin a month (about four pints' worth) and to find the enriched version for children under two was a particular triumph. Chemists sold it to non-parents if the tins were past the recommended consumption date.

The Vitamin Welfare Scheme was launched on 8 December 1941, with cheap or free fruit juices and cod liver oil for children under the age of two. A year later the policy was extended to include pregnant women and children up to the age of five. Much of the fruit was collected by children in youth squads organised by women volunteers and helped by Brownies and Girl Guides. When the American Lend-Lease supplies of tractors, machinery, ammunition, nursery equipment, cloth and food first appeared after Pearl Harbor, concentrated orange juice was also added to the fruit juices at welfare clinics. But through ignorance of their importance, only a quarter of the cod liver oil or halibut liver oil was being claimed in 1944. Far more popular were the chocolate-covered vitamin tablets at 10d a packet. Largely as a result of improved diet, infant mortality declined from 62 per thousand live births in 1939 to 45 per thousand in 1944.

Until December 1941, those with ready cash could snap up unrationed goods like tinned foods – at a price. Average wholesale prices had risen by nearly 50 per cent between 1939 and 1941. Clothing costs were 175 per cent higher and the sale of uncontrolled foods was a goldmine for Black Market profiteers. Price freezes eventually managed to stabilise food inflation at around 136 per cent between 1943 and 1944, although luxuries like melons, grapes or good fish were naturally a source of profiteering (melons were offered at £2 each, a week's wage for some). On 1 December 1941 the points system was introduced. On top of ration coupons, sixteen points a month were granted to each shopper and increasing numbers of goods – tinned fish, tinned beans, macaroni, soup, tapioca, and eventually other foods like oatmeal, cereal and canned fruits – were each given a certain number of points, according to availability. These points were included in the back of ration books. As well as controlling food supplies, this was the second attempt at food democracy, and supplemented the first, rationing. Bargain hunters' noses were closely pressed to shop window panes, and no item low in points value, however unpopular, remained on the shelves for long.

Tedious queuing and frustrated hopes were as much a part of the shoppers' life in wartime as the elation of finding a pound of cooking apples or offal. Jokes on this flourished. The committed food hunter refused nothing. Commodities were added to the points system as they became scarce, while others became completely unavailable with shipping lines cut off (for instance, meat from Argentina, onions and tomatoes from the Channel Islands). Favourite brands disappeared – 'in short supply' was the term – and what there was often appeared in bland official packaging, wanly labelled 'Biscuits X.Y. 124', or left unwrapped. Queues lengthened, paper bags disappeared and those at the Kitchen Front kept a military eye on the changes in points value while planning their next strategy. Shopping became a battle of nerves. Fiddly coupons, the bane of shopkeeper and shopper, had to be counted as their points value changed. Shelves were at times so bare that shop windows were sometimes filled with empty crates, plaster effigies of long-forgotten bananas, or even crumpled newspaper – anything to fill the space and distract the forlorn shopper from the emptiness.

For women war workers, shopping was usually a nightmare. They could only buy where they were registered and this often involved long waits after work or during a lunch break at bus stops with few buses, followed by a long queue, often in the black-out. Often they would find that bargain goods on points had already been sold.

Queuing became an obsession for some people. If one stopped in a shopping or market district, to speak to a friend, one often found a queue forming. 'What are we queuing for?' was a common question.

A Huddersfield woman recorded the hazards of shopping without lights in a nor-

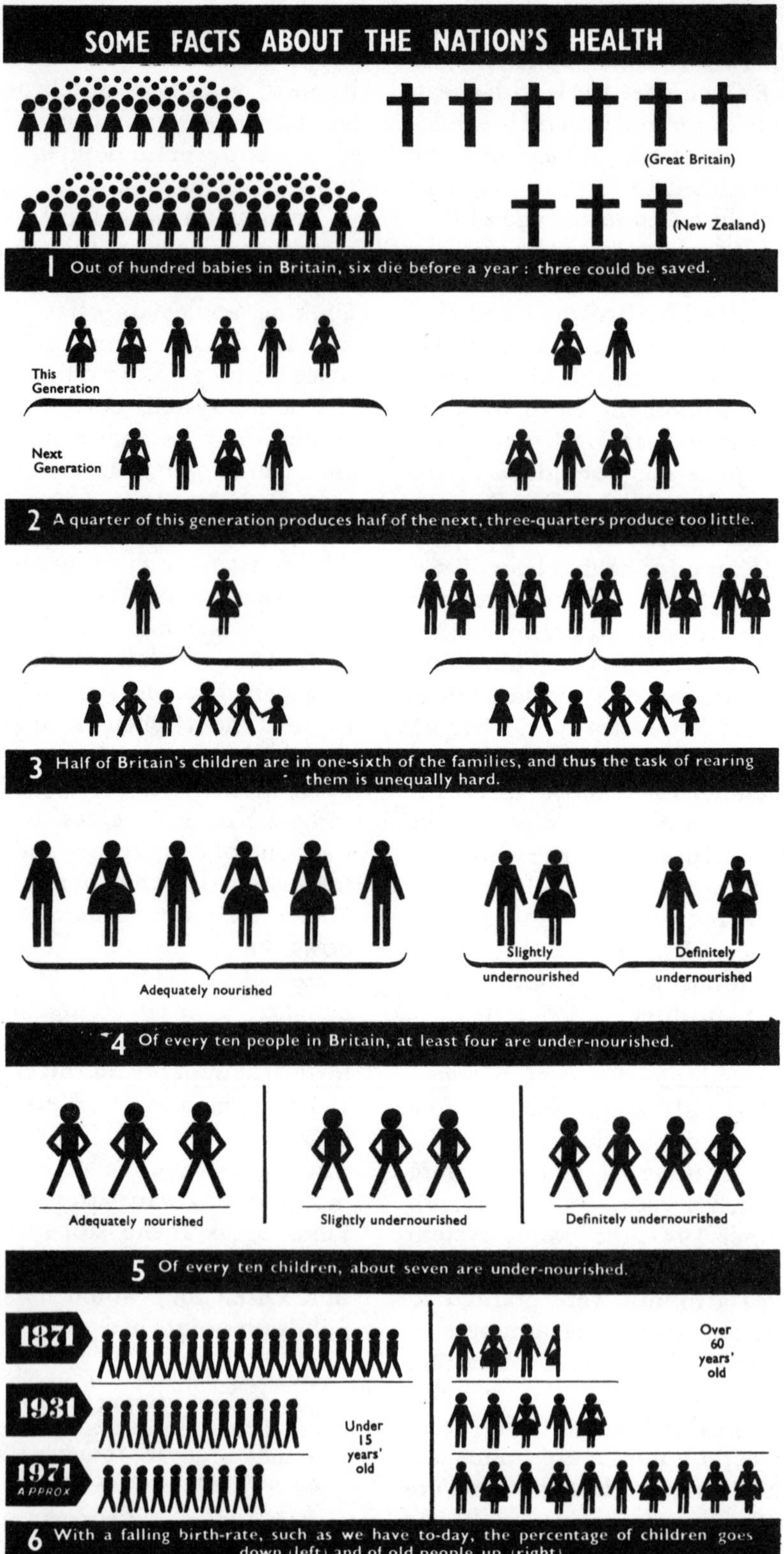

This table was published in 1941.

SOME FACTS ABOUT THE NATION'S HEALTH

(Great Britain)

(New Zealand)

1   Out of hundred babies in Britain, six die before a year : three could be saved.

This Generation

Next Generation

2   A quarter of this generation produces half of the next, three-quarters produce too little.

3   Half of Britain's children are in one-sixth of the families, and thus the task of rearing them is unequally hard.

Adequately nourished

Slightly undernourished

Definitely undernourished

4   Of every ten people in Britain, at least four are under-nourished.

Adequately nourished   Slightly undernourished   Definitely undernourished

5   Of every ten children, about seven are under-nourished.

1871

1931

1971 APPROX.

Under 15 years' old

Over 60 years' old

6   With a falling birth-rate, such as we have to-day, the percentage of children goes down (left) and of old people up (right).

90

mally bright and busy part of the town.

The business is done outside the shop and usually people are five or six deep waiting to be served. Only a few odd people were being served to-night and assistants groping around the till for change. Across the way, a door kept on opening and letting out a flood of light when all the assistants would chorus 'Shut that door!' and seemed to be getting a lot of fun out of it.

Fish was unrationed, but often scarce. Women took what rare and awful looking slabs they were given. Even the air-raid siren could not move one Paddington fish queue – women simply stayed and ducked the shrapnel if it meant a good buy. One woman queued for an hour for a piece of fish, only to weep with frustration on finding that she was left with the head after the woman in front had bought twenty-four portions for her billitees. Everyone celebrated the purchase of a few kippers, even if they had to be carried home by their tails, unwrapped for lack of paper. And as women adapted themselves to the absence of familiar delicacies, so their shopping skills increased. A London woman was astonished to meet her friend 'all dolled up on a Monday morning with stockings and the lot'. On asking her where she was going she answered, 'To the butcher's, of course.'

In order to encourage the cook coping with these dreary and limited supplies, 'Food Facts for the Kitchen Front' bombarded women's ears four times a week. The programme included recipes together with remedies for constipation from the Radio Doctor, Charles Hill. Deadly statistics were published in women's magazines of how many merchant seamen would perish if each person wasted a crust of bread each day. The Ministry of Food announced in 1941:

Nearly half of our food comes across the sea. The U-boats attack our ships . . . Now, here is *your* part in the fight for Victory. When a particular food is not available, cheerfully accept something else – home-produced if possible. Keep loyally to the rationing regulations. Above all – whether you are shopping, cooking or eating – remember, 'FOOD IS A MUNITION OF WAR, DON'T WASTE IT'.

The Ministry of Information announced, 'The housewife has the warm satisfaction of knowing how directly her sacrifice of energy and triumphs of ingenious makeshift contribute to the war'. To gain this 'warm satisfaction' women were obliged to go to positively ridiculous lengths to produce a humble meal. When the fat ration was down to one ounce a week, for example, and dry vegetable puddings were recommended by 'Dame Austerity', women took to boiling animal skins for any fatty shreds that might remain. Others used bacon rinds over and over again until the crispy results were chopped ceremoniously over such patriotic dishes as Victory Flan or Dunkirk Delight. Any dripping from meat was saved to supplement the Patriotic Pudding or spread thinly on toast as a 'nourishing snack'.

Food Education Memos, issued by the government, encouraged the use of foodstuffs as they became available. Oatmeal with everything was often the answer. And titles of dishes became important. The ingredients of Hasty Pudding, for instance, (to be served with gravy) were six tablespoons of oatmeal, three tablespoons of suet, a pint of cold water and one onion *or* parsnip. The more spartan the recipe, the more heroic its title became. Mock Haggis incorporated bacon rinds, oatmeal, bicarbonate of soda, *one* leek and milk or vegetable water. Half the battle was in the presentation. One writer advised the cook never to mention the ingredients until after the meal, never to talk about gloomy aspects of the war or dwell on the cost of the gas bill, but to deflect conversation away to some more cheerful subject.

Women workers often sacrificed their own rations of protein so that the man of the house, 'the breadwinner', should continue to have as good a meal as possible. While Constance Spry stressed the benefits of spinning out an egg in a cake or soufflé for the whole household, cartoonists

91

Clothes coupons join the food coupons in ration books. These women are making their first negotiations in Woolworths, 1941.

reflected its more usual fate, as women called up the stairs, 'How would you like your egg done this month, dear?'

From 1940, nutrition and patriotism were increasingly linked:

> To our delight we housewives of today find ourselves in a somewhat exalted position. Each time we serve a meal we stand in the limelight, facing an audience of men and children – with large appetites. We know their health and happiness depend on us ... and never before have we received such whole-hearted appreciation. We like it.

Such was the language that helped to win the domestic war. If women were not encouraged by such propaganda to accept the appalling difficulties of broken homes and lack of food, it was thought that the morale of the nation would hardly be sustained. The British government knew that it was vital that a nation of war workers should be adequately fed.

It was indeed the duty of the British to

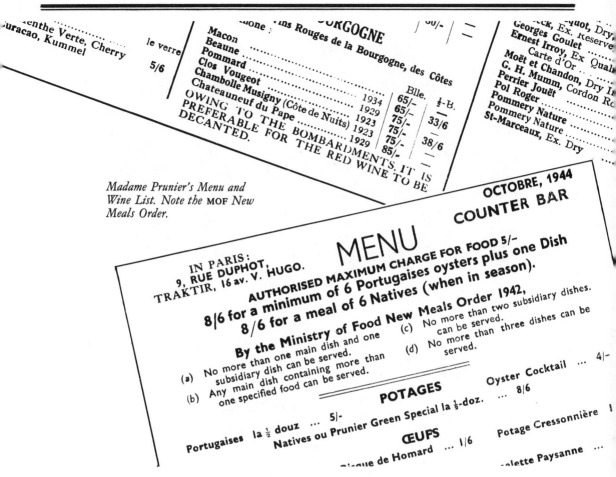

Madame Prunier's Menu and Wine List. Note the MOF New Meals Order.

feed themselves properly, even with ersatz ingredients. Coffee could be 'easily' made from ground dried acorns and cakes could rise with a little household soda. Salad dressing was improvised with soya flour or condensed milk and vinegar, and mock raspberry jam was made from marrow and quinces. The index pages of austerity cook books were full of ideas like fatless pastry, sugarless puddings, eggless cakes, meatless meals, mock cream, mock whitebait and fuelless cookery.

Women at home, the 'inessential' workers, who were caring for children under fourteen, had to cope with incessant shortages and drab surroundings. They did not have the advantage of wartime industrial wages. In reception areas they probably catered for evacuees and war workers as well, for which they received a scant 8s 6d

or 21s 0d. These were the women who were encouraged to share a neighbour's fire or dimmed light bulb to economise, and usually to do some form of outwork in the home as well. After the war, Susan Cooper described their lot in her essay 'Snoek Piquante', published in *The Age of Austerity*. Their wartime lives were never free from 'small dull makeshift meals, from darkness and drabness and making do; from the depressing, nerve-aching, never-ending need to be careful'. By September 1943 the Minister of Health was applauding them:

> In many cases they are doing this after having had the care of those children for two, three or four years: and in all cases on top of their other duties. Perhaps it is not very difficult to make sacrifices for a short period. But to give years of uneventful toil in the service of others demands the very highest qualities of human nature.

A change of air and a rest from air raids was a welcome change for city workers and their families. Although Dame Austerity did not encourage indulgences like travel and rest, the stamp of official approval was put on these farming holidays, which combined pleasure with working for Victory.

8. Sow, grow and add Oxo

Digging for Victory was the best-launched and most famous campaign of the Home Front. The merry grins of Potato Pete and Dr Carrot, personified in cartoons, became an increasingly familiar sight. Although vegetables were unrationed, they were scarce. Fruit when available was distributed to everyone, except for oranges and bananas for which expectant mothers and children had priority. Peaches, lemons and strawberries became mere memories as land was turned over to vegetables that yielded the maximum per acre, in the form of root crops. For the individual householder, the only answer was to grow your own, since the official market gardeners could be fined for growing gooseberries, say, instead of cabbages.

From the first day of war leaflets, news bulletins and magazines bombarded the ears and eyes of civilians. Ten million instructional leaflets on growing food were issued in 1942. By 1943, 1,400,000 allotments flourished and a survey showed that over half of all manual workers kept either an allotment or a productive garden. They were badgered by Ministry of Food notices: 'We need all the food we can get', or, 'Turn over a new leaf – eat vegetables daily to enjoy good health'.

Famous gardens like those of Kensington Palace, public parks, golf clubs, tennis courts and even the moat of the Tower of London were accordingly turned over to cabbages. Grass verges in towns, flower tubs in Piccadilly, window boxes, roofs, rubbish dumps and even bomb craters all served the patriotic call to 'Dig harder to beat the U-Boat'. RAF pilots grew radishes at aerodromes. Women tended allotments in railway sidings and on Hampstead Heath, where sheep mingled with anti-aircraft guns, barrage balloons and mock villages camouflaged to decoy enemy aircraft looking for landmarks.

Schoolchildren forfeited their sports time to dig around the football pitch and spent their holidays at farming camps. Brownies and Cubs were grouped into youth squads, not only to organise salvage drives and help with evacuated children, but also to gather the hedgerow harvest of nuts and berries, rosehips, blackcurrants, crab apples and selected fungi, as well as more unusual vegetation. A character called Gypsy Petulengro advised them in the Girl Guides magazine, *The Guider*: 'Gather the buds of the king-cup: Wash them well and put them in jars and cover them with vinegar in which a few spices have been boiled and you will have one of the nicest pickles imaginable.' Or butterbur (gypsy asparagus) spikes could be gently baked in dripping. Burdock could be gathered as a substitute for cabbage, dandelion leaves or wild watercress for lettuce and stinging nettles for spinach.

> To gather them without being stung you can wear an old glove between February and June. Put them into a pail under your tap and twirl them around well using a piece of wood and, when the nettles are thoroughly wet, they lose the power of stinging you. There is no fear of them stinging the throat once boiling water has touched them.

The youth squads and their mothers picked rosehips (500 tons in 1943) to supply the entire juvenile population with rosehip syrup throughout the war.

In spite of the availability of these unusual delicacies, the more common tomato and onion were sorely missed at the Kitchen

GROW FOOD FOR THE NATION

FEEDING STUFFS FOR YOUR FARMS

KEEP OUR SHIPS AND MONEY FREE

FOR BUYING VITAL ARMS

★THE
PRIME MINISTER
TO FARMERS AND
WORKERS—

The Tower of London's moat was dug up into allotments.

Front. Norman Longmate reported that onions were so highly prized that a single one made £4 3s at a raffle and one woman managed to cook with the flavour of her onion for a whole month before actually eating it. Woeful odes were written in magazines

Marmalade, butter, eggs and cheese,
I bore it when they rationed these;
But who could guess that they would seize
The sweet and lovely onion?

My cupboard might as well be bare
Bereft I wander everywhere
And try, nose in the empty air,
To sniff a whiff of onion.

Mrs Arthur Webb of *Farmer's Weekly* announced in 1939:

It may come as a shock to busy folk to be told that they should *grow* at least some of the food they consume . . . Let's hope the ground is in better heart, presenting less back-breaking labour than those allotments of twenty years ago . . . I'm desperately afraid that each housewife coming fresh to the work will think all soils are heavy soils. The busy woman with only an hour or two a day will be able to do only odd jobs of clearing and piling up the rubbish and coarser weeds ready for burning when time and weather permit, should the ground be too wet or hard to dig. It all helps.

By 1942 many urban families were producing between 3lb and 6lb of potatoes a week and between 2lb and 5lb of other vegetables and fruit. The official vegetable-eating figures show that consumption rose by 5.27oz a week between 1942 and 1945, or the equivalent of two small apples, though of course amounts varied enormously throughout the country. Lack of space was never allowed to become a problem. As Mrs Arthur Webb declared:

> The housewife who wants to grow fruit, and is determined to, can, because even if her garden is only a few pots on a sunny window sill, some sort of fruit will flourish. I have grown grapes on a flat London roof and redcurrants in a small tub on a tiny balcony, tomatoes in a window box and herbs which the sun merely glimpsed for an hour or two during the day. And so here's wishing the gift of the green thumb to all those who set out to grow the nation's food.

Anti-Nazi curses were hurled skywards when shrapnel or bombs or splinters of glass wrecked the marrow or tomato plots. Seeds and cuttings were carefully swapped or given as special birthday presents and gardening know-how exchanged at the bus-stop. Bartering a bit of land in exchange for some honey, or exchanging bottled fruit for eggs or milk were not officially encouraged, but occurred nevertheless.

Necessity became the mother of invention. Vegetables cropped up in unlikely places as recipes for jam began to advise ingredients like swede, beetroot, parsnip and carrots which could be 'nicely set in a packet of orange or strawberry jelly, but should be eaten within two weeks'. Mothers squeezed grated swede and carrot through muslin to produce a 'health-giving' drink called 'carrolade' before making sandwiches for the night-shift with grated raw turnip. Carrot marmalade, carrot flan, pastry cakes and pancakes made with mashed potatoes were hailed, rightly, as nutritious. Grated raw beetroot and carrots were used as sweeteners to replace dried fruit in cakes and to add colour. Children chewed 'nice and crunchy' carrots instead of sweets – 'And you're lucky to get them!' A new thrill arrived when toffee apples were replaced by toffee carrots, now endowed with the magical properties of help-

ing tired eyes in the blackout. This story proved so popular that the Germans, not knowing of the British discovery of radar, and thinking the British had developed exceptional eyesight, made Luftwaffe pilots eat raw carrots until the war ended. Or so the story goes.

Fruit, like vegetables, was distributed according to supply, but was so scarce that an hour's queuing for a pound of cooking apples was thought to be worthwhile. For many people fresh fruit became a luxurious memory. Once again it was a matter of growing your own or making the most of what you could get. One Hampstead woman with four small children and not enough money to make ends meet remembers: 'Our blackcurrant bush was a treasure. We used to have a few – about five each – for lunch sometimes, and collect blackberries on the Heath for fruit pies, and with the glut of plums we could make puddings that even our billetted refugees liked.' A

Manchester housewife remembers one of the rare arrivals of oranges: 'Somehow, some oranges arrived and I carefully cut the rinds and sugared them and made strips of sweets, quite a delicacy, and later a friend with whom we had shared them, asked us to tea and produced jellies in little cups from a packet she had kept by as a treat. We made a bit of jam by going out of the city to pick blackberries and we had gooseberries in the garden, and also a few apple trees.'

One lady remembers to her astonishment watching a monkey toying with a banana at the zoo. She hovered, filled with moral righteousness, outraged complaints on the tip of her tongue, only to realise the animal had been given a potato wrapped in a more seductive skin. Another family who managed to get hold of a banana, after

showing it to everyone and meticulously sharing it out, could not bear to part with the skin. They arranged it on the pavement and watched, from behind their curtains, the reactions of passers-by.

Jam-making was the answer to the official headache of how to preserve the summer crops of fruit from England's wealth of small gardens. Women, in their own kitchens and official jam-making centres, were supplied with 600 tons of precious sugar in 1940. By December, 150 tons of canned fruit, 160 tons of pulped fruit and chutney and 3,000,000lb of jam had been made by the WI (Women's Institute) and WVS, after growing, gathering and picking over the fruit and separating the good from the bad. One woman in Northern Ireland typified the patriotic fervour of millions of others when she made 4,897lb of jam in three months on two primus stoves in the bedroom of her bungalow.

As in the First World War, drugs and bandages were in short supply. Women on country herb committees set off through woods and lanes with their children to collect the raw material for chemists. Foxgloves, deadly nightshade, coltsfoot and nettles had to be gathered and dried before manufacture. Elderly women made drying trays from net curtains tacked on to grocery boxes and herbs were dried in any available space, including disused chapels. Villagers heard with triumph in 1943 that they had reduced the medicinal imports by half.

As fresh eggs and proper milk supplies faded into fond memories, the keeping of small livestock like hens, ducks, geese, rabbits, bees, goats and pigs was attempted by women dreaming of real cakes and milk puddings for the family. Hens could even be hired. Rooftops and balconies, garden sheds and wooden crates became chicken runs and communal efforts even had them squawking and laying in East End shelters. However, balancer meal for poultry was only issued on the surrender of egg coupons. This could mean months of experimenting with chick-rearing before the results, if there were any, turned into eggs. But with luck each hen might lay between two and six eggs each week. While other women wondered whether to use the tough leaves of sprouts, dandelion leaves, carrot tops and mouldy crusts for soup or pigswill, those with poultry needed no advice, and roasted crusts or boiled potato peel before mincing the mixture with enthusiasm.

Although bartering was officially frowned upon, the women with 'these shelly treasures' had a currency 'worth its weight in gold', especially in the spring when they might be rewarded with a rare glut. Eggs were swapped for anything 'in short supply' from pieces of coal to fruit, honey or meat. Even the eggshells were hoarded to be pounded back into the feeding mixture. Those with more than twenty hens, how-

Food for the picking

Blackberrying is a traditional custom that most of us have enjoyed at one time or another. There are other Hedgerow Harvests too, that provide good things for the larder. So why not take the children and go a-harvesting? Be sure, however, that in their excitement they do not damage bushes or hedges, or walk through growing crops, or gather mushrooms, for instance, in fields without getting the farmer's permission.

Elderberries are delicious stewed with half-and-half apple; or made into jam with an equal quantity of blackberries. Wash and strip them from the stems before using.

Sloes look like tiny damsons. They are too sour to use as stewed fruit, but make a delightful preserve with marrow.

Crab Apples. For a drink or flavouring Crab Apple juice is a good substitute for lemon juice. Put the apples to sweat, choose only the sound ones, take off stalks, beat the fruit to a mash and press the juice through a thick cloth. Leave for a day or two until bubbles appear. Put into clean dry bottles and cork well, securing the cork with wire. Store in a cool place. The juice will be ready in about a month's time

Rowan-berries (Mountain Ash) make a preserve with a pleasant tang, admirable to serve with cold meats. You can make the preserve of the berries alone, or with a couple of apples to each pound of berries.

Hips and Haws should not be picked until perfectly ripe. Hips—the berries of the wild rose, make a vitamin-rich jam. Haws—the berries of the may-tree, make a brown jelly that is very like guava jelly.

Nuts. Cobnuts, walnuts, chestnuts and filberts are good keepers. Choose very sound,

well-coloured nuts. Remove them from their husks, spread them out and leave to dry overnight. Pack cobnuts and filberts tightly into jars or crocks and cover with an inch layer of crushed block salt. Pack walnuts and chestnuts in a similar manner but cover with an inch layer of sand instead of salt. If the containers have lids, put them on top as an extra precaution against shrivelling. Packed in this way, your nuts should keep till Christmas. Beechnuts make good eating, too. Store them as you would cobnuts. Use as almonds.

Mushrooms are very easy to dry and make an excellent flavouring for winter soups and dishes. Small button mushrooms are best for drying. Gather them in the early morning; before the mushroom fly has had time to attack them. Simply spread them out to dry in the air.

Blackberry and Apple Jam. Here is a favourite recipe:—4 lbs. firm blackberries, 1½ lbs. sour apples, 4½ lbs. sugar, 1 breakfastcupful water. Core and slice the apples. Put in the preserving pan with the water and cook till quite soft. Add the blackberries and bring to the simmer. Simmer for 5 minutes, then add the sugar (warmed) and boil rapidly until setting point is reached. (Make first test after 10 minutes.) Put into hot jars and seal.

Hedgerow Harvest Leaflet containing many useful recipes for using wild produce will be sent to all who ask. Please send postcards only, addressed to The Ministry of Food, Room 625L, London, W.1.

ISSUED BY THE   M·F   MINISTRY OF FOOD
(S46)

ever, entered the realms of bureaucracy, with forms, regulations and inspections, and collections were made regularly.

Rations for rabbits, as for chickens, were never large enough and were only issued if half the resulting brood was handed over to the butcher. Many women grew adept at the art of midnight slaughtering. Rabbits and ducks were the easiest to feed, though like goats (kept for milk and cheese) they ravaged the garden if allowed to escape. Lawn clippings, thistles and dandelions, pot scrapings and peapods were their more usual diet, collected painstakingly. Rabbit skins too were highly prized as the foundation of many a pretty and warm collar, hat or mitten. With comparative ease they could be sewn into coats and slippers for children or, with such things no longer manufactured, into powder puffs for a rare gift at Christmas. At Make-do-and-Mend classes women sewed thousands of furry linings into military coats and were further encouraged to save the resulting fluff for spinning into wool or for stuffing into pillows.

Pigeon, goose and hen feathers were likewise used up to repair old eiderdowns after the manufacture of bedcovers was virtually banned in 1942. The homing pigeon was of vital use when communication lines were blitzed and its eggs, smaller and richer than hen's eggs, were also enjoyed. Although pigeons were bad layers, nobody sniffed at the chance to make a cake that might actually rise. Eggs galore, those of sparrows, ducks, pigeons, seagulls or hens could be preserved in isinglass, so that the shells became soft and rubbery. Many a jar was found at the back of the larder years after the end of egg rationing, still perfectly preserved.

The Dig for Victory campaign also encouraged pig clubs so that several families (or, in the case of Hyde Park in London, a group of air-raid wardens) could pool their resources and scraps so long as they obeyed strict regulations. Pigs could only be slaughtered at the exact weight of 100lb in the presence of an inspector at a precise time and place. Heavy fines and prosecution resulted for farmers and householders whose pigs suffered any untimely 'mishaps'. Pigs entered suburbia and were received with enthusiasm, as women collected swill from neighbours in exchange for a few precious rashers of bacon. Feeding and mucking out was a labour of patriotic love, as the pigs made themselves at home in the garage and the swill boiled for hours, pervading the Kitchen Front with its awful smell.

When feeding stuffs became really short, Growmore leaflets announced that although raw tulip bulbs were all right for cows, they really ought to be steamed for pigs, especially young ones. Both laymen and farmers were allowed small amounts of bran, but were advised by the Ministry of Food to augment the pig's diet with chopped reeds, beech nut kernels and young bracken fronds, all well steamed. Gorging on acorns, beech nuts and sprouting potatoes should be avoided. One woman remembers their pigs, housed at the local fire station: 'How we watched these pigs and gladly paid our money when it came round to Christmas and we were given permission to kill them. There were ten of us round the table for Christmas dinner. I don't think pork has ever tasted the same since.'

In order to supplement the sugar ration, some householders started bee-keeping for honey, not always successfully. The bees sometimes behaved with an oddness befitting the wartime spirit. One London visitor sunbathing at a friend's cottage and pondering on the unusual peace was deafened by the sound of a bomb landing close by. Darting naked to inspect the damage, he realised that all the roof tiles had been blasted off, and the hive roofs too. Following the first moving object they could vent their anger on, the swarm chased him, still naked, on to the lane and half a mile through the village to the nearest lake where he remained underwater until the bees disappeared.

"STEP LIVELY WITH ME"

says Potato Pete

You get the *extra energy* you need in wartime from potatoes. They guard you against illness too. Don't just serve potatoes once a day, cook them often and buy less bread. Give the family such tasty dishes as Floddies for supper or Potato Pancake for dinner. There are so many easy dishes to make — and they're all energy-givers.

POTATO PANCAKE

Cooking time : 20 minutes. *Ingredients :* 1 lb. mashed potatoes, ¼ lb. cooked carrot, milk, salt and pepper. *Method:* Whip the mashed potato to a loose creamy consistency with a little milk. Season well with salt and pepper, add diced cooked carrot. Pan-fry slowly in very little fat until crisp and brown.

FREE—ask at any of the Food Advice Centres or, Bureaux for a free copy of the Potato Pete Recipe Booklet, or write direct to the Ministry of Food, London, W.1.

Potatoes keep you FIGHTING fit

While weeds flourished on the tarmac of roads, women tended cauliflowers and beans on the local rubbish dump or bomb craters according to the instructions of the latest Growmore bulletin. The Dig for Victory campaign encouraged people to grow food in the most likely and the most unlikely places. A sense of wellbeing could be achieved after a good meal, it was felt by the government, and responsible citizens should eat sensibly to serve Britain in her hour of need. The dangers and difficulties of wartime life could be lessened on a well-nourished stomach, and the fatigue of shift workers greatly reduced. So went the message – and it gradually sank in, with the help of a bombardment of nutritional propaganda from Lord Woolton and Co:

> *Dig! Dig! Dig! And your muscles will grow big,*
> *Keep on pushing in the spade!*
> *Never mind the worms*
> *Just ignore their squirms*
> *And when your back aches, laugh with glee*
> *And keep on diggin'*
> *Till we give our foes a wiggin'*
> *Dig! Dig! Dig! to Victory.*

Dr. Carrot

BETTER POT-LUCK

with
Churchill
today

THAN HUMBLE PIE

under
Hitler
tomorrow

DON'T WASTE FOOD!

9. Women, save your bacon!

If an air-raid signal takes you away from your kitchen for an indefinite time, the first thing to do is *stop the heat*; if you do this your food cannot get burnt, and we will tell you how to continue the cooking when you come back to the kitchen... an accident, a sudden call for help may call the housewife away from the stove.

In case of disaster, the advice was: 'On no account throw any food away if there is any way of using it. After a few experiments, and perhaps one or two failures, you will find ways to rescue food that has had to look after itself for a time.'

This advice could hardly have been news for most women – though an air raid at meal times must have been the last straw after long hours of compulsory work, queuing for rations, waiting for buses and trains and the inconveniences of the blackout. There was also the problem of saving fuel.

After the great domestic headache of rationing, the fuel crisis produced the second battle of the domestic front. Paraffin, coal, electricity and gas were desperately short, after thousands of young miners were called up because of a surplus of unexported coal in Britain. By 1941 factories and power stations as well as homes were so bereft of power that 33,000 men were released from the Army to return to the pits. Accordingly the Ministry of Food produced a pamphlet called *Food without Fuel*. The most ingenious and simple alternative to using a stove was the hay box – after porridge or stew, for example, had been heated on the gas ring it could be transferred to a sturdy wooden box stuffed with straw or newspapers and left all day or night to continue cooking in conserved heat. The MOF also issued copious hints on how to save other forms of fuel.

Cooking methods

Cooking without Fire

Instructions

This is a slow method of cookery you can follow either with the help of dry sweet hay, or newspaper balls. Before starting to make a fireless cooker, decide on the size you want. Unless living alone, make one that will take 2 pans of the same size, but if living alone, a cooker to hold one cooking vessel may be large enough.

To make a hay box

1. Choose an oblong box large enough to take the number of pans or deep casseroles you mean to use, and ample hay padding round them. An old packing-case will do if you can't rake up a box with a hinged lid.

2. Line the box smoothly with 3 or 4 newspapers, that is, with anything from 15 to 20 layers of newspapers, and fasten papers in place with drawing-pins. Then pack it tightly over the bottom with a 5-inch layer of dry sweet hay. Now make a mattress the size of the interior of the cooker and fill it with dry sweet hay.

3. Choose cooking pans with short handles made of aluminium or enamel, or you can use casseroles of fireproof china or glass so long as you have asbestos mats to put under them when heating on the stove preparatory to placing them in the hay box.

4. To prepare food successfully in hay box, the pans containing food must be as full as possible, and the food should be really boiling when the pans are covered and slipped into the box. Pack dry sweet hay about 4 inches closely and tightly round the sides of the pan.

5. Lay hay mattress on top, and press it firmly down on pans, then cover with lid of the box. If it doesn't fasten down, weight it down.

Hints on fireless cookery

1. Bring all the food to a full rolling boil before covering and putting in hay box.

2. Quickly transfer the pan from stove to hay box.

3. Don't open box till time is up.

4. Always re-heat food in pan on stove before serving.

5. If you want to cook only a small quantity of

food in box, place it in a covered basin in the inner pan, which should be half-full of boiling water.

6. If using one pan only, fill the other with boiling water. It helps to conserve the heat, and can be used for washing up.

Three-tier Steamer

Steamed meals are easy to prepare if you have a three-tiered steamer. Here is a menu for a complete dinner for 4 persons in a tiered steamer:

Chicken with Parsley Sauce
Steamed Potatoes   Steamed Cauliflower
Canary Pudding with Apricot Sauce

Half-fill the bottom of the steamer with boiling water and keep a kettle of boiling water on the side so that the steamer can be replenished with boiling water through the spout.

Grease each compartment. Place peeled potatoes in the first, prepared cauliflower in the second, and chicken in the third. Season the chicken to taste. Dab with bacon fat or margarine. Cover and steam according to age. Prepare the pudding and put into greased basin, covering with greased paper. Cook in bottom of steamer for 1 hour.

To Use a Pressure Cooker

A high-pressure cooker is the greatest of fuel-savers. A single-course or a three-course meal of soup, roast meat, vegetable purée, etc., can be prepared in these cookers in a minimum of time.

To Save Gas

Remember that a gas oven usually retains its heat from 8 to 10 minutes after the gas has been turned off, so it's possible to finish cooking milk puddings and many other baked foods without any gas at all.

Buy a sheet of metal which will enable you to boil 2 saucepans or kettles on one gas-ring.

To Save Electricity

Use pans which cover the whole surface of an electric boiling plate. If they don't, a certain amount of heat is wasted.

Use utensils with ground flat bottoms, especially made for using on hot plates, of thick aluminium, cast-iron, copper, seamless nickel or steel.

When counting time required for cooking or baking, remember that the enclosed boiling plate will continue boiling operations for about 10 minutes after switching off, and that you can continue to bake in oven from 20 to 30 minutes after switching off.

To Save Coal

Place all old papers, newspapers, bags and wrappings as well as pasteboard boxes in water. When pulpy, squeeze into tight balls the size of your fist and roll in coal dust. Use them for stoking after you've got a good fire going.

Soups

No matter what rations you're allowed, you need never go without soup because your meat is rationed. You can always prepare meatless soups, or broth or soup from stock made from odds and ends of gristle, trimmings of chops, cutlets, etc., as well as from used bones or carcasses of cooked birds.

All the wartime recipe books and ministerial pamphlets emphasised the importance of soups for nourishment and economy. The less good ones propounded the use of the soup tureen as a sort of spare dustbin to get rid of all scraps and leftovers unless they were needed for chicken or pig swill. Better advice came from writers like Ambrose Heath, one of the most popular wartime recipe experts and a regular broadcaster, and Constance Spry, who also examined the best continental recipes.

They advised their readers and listeners not to mix strong-tasting meat or game remains together, but suggested instead clear fresh soups like watercress, carrot or peapod to substantiate the meagre main course 'now that rationing controls our figures', or soups that were a meal in themselves, like cabbage soup made with pork. With only one fillet of fish or half a pound of meat to hand, excellent soups for the family could eke out the ration, with the extra advantage of being the easiest meal to warm up for those working awkward shifts.

Country people were officially encouraged to kill rabbits, pigeons or crows for the sake of protecting vital crops, and like game, these were unrationed, though hardly plentiful in the shops. Those with their wits about them also managed to shoot a grouse or duck while aiming for the pestilential pigeon. A wealth of game soups was the result. Recipes from the countryside, like those sent to *Farmhouse Fare* (compiled by Mrs Arthur Webb) from women all over Britain, had more plentiful quantities than were available to those in the town ration queue.

Oatmeal came into its own as a thickener. A listener wrote to Ambrose Heath and Freddy Grisewood at the Kitchen Front department of the BBC: 'Sometimes I think you all fail to stress the importance of oatmeal as a means of thickening soups. Tomato soup with a good handful of oatmeal is delicious and saves imported tapioca.'

Soups were also produced by women's voluntary groups in emergency field kitchens where a mixture of petrol and sand might be used as fuel among the black dust and rubble. Here a good nourishing soup would be provided for air raid victims.

Cabbage Soup (which also provides a meat dish for the next day)

1 lb pickled pork
1 carrot
1 turnip
1 large savoy
1 clove of garlic
pepper
thyme, parsley, bay leaf
3 pints water

Put the pork into a saucepan of cold water with parsley, thyme and the bay leaf. Bring very slowly to the boil and simmer for 1 hour. Take out the pork and put in the carrot and turnip, cut small, and the savoy, shredded finely. Add a little pepper. Bring to the boil and simmer for 1½ hours. Then add 1 dessertspoonful of chopped parsley, the clove of garlic, chopped fine, and 1 slice of the pork, cut in dice. Cook for ½ hour more. Keep the pork for breakfast or luncheon, on the next day.

Fish Soup

a handful of spinach or sorrel
1 or 2 small onions
1 carrot
1 potato
2oz butter
parsley, mint, chives
2 small whiting, plaice or whatever you can catch at the fishmonger

Chop together the spinach or sorrel, 1 or 2 small onions, a carrot, a potato, parsley, mint and chives. Brown these in butter and add boiling water, salt and pepper. Add the whiting or other fish whole, and cook for about 20 minutes. Take out the fish and remove the skins and bones. Strain soup and serve with pieces of fish and vegetables in it.

Rich Hare Soup

a large hare
¾lb ham or bacon
2 onions
2 blade mace
1 large wineglassful port wine
3 quarts beef stock
a little salt and cayenne
½lb breadcrumbs
a bunch of thyme, parsley and sweet marjoram

Cut the hare into pieces, and the ham or bacon into slices. Put into a stewpan with beef stock, onions, bunch of herbs and mace. Stew all together for about 2½ hours. Take out the bacon and pound all the inferior parts of the hare with it in a mortar. Strain the soup back into the stewpan, add the pounded meat and the breadcrumbs and the port wine. Simmer for nearly ½ hour. Rub through a sieve, season with a little salt and cayenne. Make it very hot, but do not let it boil, and serve it up quickly.

The carcass and stock from a jugged hare provide quite enough meat for this soup.

Sheep's Head Broth

1 sheep's head	
1 cup of dried peas	
1 cup of barley	SUET BALLS
1 small turnip	2oz suet
2 carrots	3oz flour
2 onions	salt
1 cabbage heart	nutmeg

Soak a sheep's head overnight in cold salted water. Pour off the next morning, wash well and place the head in a good-sized pan. Cover the head with water and put on to boil. Simmer for 30 minutes, skimming all the time, then add the peas and barley, both having previously been soaked. Add 2 carrots, 1 small turnip, 2 onions all sliced and one firm white heart of cabbage cut up. Simmer for 1 hour, then throw in a suet ball for each person. Simmer for another hour, taking the scum off as it appears. Remove from the fire and take the sheep's head out on to a plate. Serve the soup with squares of bread.

For the suet balls, mix 2oz suet, 3oz flour, a little salt and water. Roll into balls in a little flour. See that the soup is boiling when the balls are put in.

After the sheep's head has cooled, remove all the meat from the bone and put it through the mincing machine. Add salt, pepper and a good scrape of nutmeg, and stir it together with 3 tablespoonfuls of the clear liquor it has been boiled in. Press into small jars and run melted butter over the top.

Cold Cream of Pea Soup with Fresh Mint

Take young fresh pea shells and cut off the stringy parts at top and bottom. Cut or break them roughly, just so that the juice from them will run easily. Have ready a pan of boiling liquid, for choice the water in which the peas themselves have been cooked, or potato water, or plain water, or a mixture. Plunge the pods into this, add an onion and a few pieces of mint. When cooked put through a hair sieve. Return to the pan and reheat, season with salt and pepper and a touch of sugar and add as much milk as you like and can spare. If you have it, put a spoonful of cream in each cup, sprinkle very finely chopped mint on the surface, and chill well.

Chestnut Soup

1lb chestnuts
1 small, scraped carrot
pinch grated nutmeg
1 peeled, medium-sized onion
1 quart water or chicken or veal stock
salt and pepper

For 4 or 5 persons. Make a sharp slit in each chestnut. Place in a saucepan. Cover with cold water. Boil till the outer and inner skins are soft enough to be peeled off together. Drain off water. Remove nuts from pan. Peel and return nuts to pan. Add the water or stock. Slice in the carrot and onion. Cover and bring to a simmer. Simmer till the nuts and vegetables are soft. Rub through a sieve. Turn puree into pan. Season with salt and pepper to taste. Add nutmeg. Reheat and serve.

Potato and Watercress or Sorrel Soup (Emergency Meal No.5 for 100 persons)

75lb potatoes	water or stock
6lb watercress (or sorrel)	seasoning
1lb oatmeal or wheatmeal flour	1lb cooking fat
30 pints milk	

25lb wheatmeal bread
1½lb margarine
3lb carrot (grated) } sandwiches
3lb cabbage (shredded)
1lb onion (grated)

Serve sandwiches with oil and vinegar or mayonnaise if available.

Standard Ham Bone Purée

¾ pint haricot beans, butter beans, lentils, split peas or
dried green peas
1 small peeled turnip
1 peeled potato
½oz dripping
pinch of baking soda
1 ham bone
1 peeled onion
1 stalk celery
¼ pint hot milk
1 sprig parsley
1 quart cold water
salt and pepper

Rinse the beans, lentils or peas in a colander
under the cold water tap, and drain well. Place in
a basin. Cover with 2 quarts boiling water. Add a
pinch baking soda and soak overnight. Strain
and rinse again under the cold water tap, then
drain well. Cut the vegetables into small pieces
(add sliced carrot when making a ham bone soup
of any pulse except haricot bean). Melt dripping in the soup pan, and add the sliced vegetables. Cook over slow heat until all the fat is absorbed. Add the ham bone, water, the pulses,
parsley and salt. Bring to the boil, then cover
and simmer for 2–3 hours. Stir occasionally
during that time. Now rub the contents of the
pan, except for the bone, through a wire sieve,
then rinse the pan, and pour in the purée.
Reheat the purée, stirring occasionally, then
add the milk, and salt and pepper to taste. Pour
into a hot soup tureen and serve with croutons.

Fish

England's coastline, beaches and inland
waters were covered with barbed wire,
wrecks, mines and booby traps. Most battle-
worthy fishing boats, notably the modern
trawling fleet at Hull, had been command-
eered by the Navy. Fishermen, in the rusty
relics left to them, caught their spoils with a
machine gun in one hand and nets in the
other. The enemy 'hit and run' raids on the
south and east coast of England often aimed
at any boats in sight, while in the North Sea
itself fishing boats were sitting ducks. Fishing was one of the jobs that conscientious
objectors could do. It was often one of the
most dangerous and unpleasant tasks.
Eventually much of the fishing fleet moved
to the slightly safer waters of the west coast.
Once the V1 flying bombs were aimed at
London all spare guns were moved to the
coast in order to shoot them down over the
sea. Many London lives were saved but it
was yet another danger for fishermen.

Although fish was unrationed it was a
scarce luxury, until by 1941 fish prices were
seventeen times higher than before the war.
A Lancashire trawler might make a profit of
£600 with a single catch. The skippers hardly knew what to do with their new wealth.
One is reported to have bought forty new
pairs of shoes, and deckhands often got
double their peacetime pay. In Scotland
some fishermen were reported to be stunned by their prosperity and generally saved
their new fortunes.

Fish had previously sold at 4s for fifty
baskets. Strange new species were grate-
fully accepted by both fishmonger and
housewife, while an apologetic though opti-
misitic note crept into many fish recipes. A
new range of fish names like saith or ling,
slabs of salted cod 'like boiled flannelette',
and eventually whalemeat and the mysteri-
ous snoek were gingerly introduced to the
housewife along with a lot of clever, though
lemonless sauces. In their food leaflets the
MOF advised canteens to provide fat fish,
which was very nutritious, at least once a

week if it was available.

Meanwhile the Ministry of Food tried to rally the public:

When fisherfolk are brave enough
To face the mines and foe for you
You surely can be brave enough
To face a fish that's new.

But even Ambrose Heath was daunted by the new fish: 'Cheese is usually cooked with fish to give added nutrient as well as flavour to the often rather tasteless sorts of fish to which wartime has accustomed us, and for making savoury and attractive dishes out of tinned fish or the remains of boiled fish.' Similarly Mrs Arthur Webb of the *Farmers Weekly* put fish meals in second place, and with the shortage of fuel in mind, suggested: 'It is well to remember that the coolish oven or stove top is capable of cooking herrings which will serve as a good stand-by on washing day, or when spring cleaning demands labour and devotion. Or they may be cooked on Saturday to serve with a salad on Sunday.'

At the other end of the scale fish restaurants like Prunier's and Wheeler's were strictly rationed to 480lb of fish a month,

and faced regular checks by inspectors. Lobsters and scallops were controlled, although oysters were unrationed. Sometimes no fish were supplied. At one restaurant, the chef, with a wonderful sauce prepared, made a well-cooked, fish-shaped, dried-egg omelette and poured the sauce over it. None of the guests guessed.

Sardine Pancakes

Make some thin pancakes with a slightly salted batter. Roll each round some mashed and boned sardines, and serve them in a long row, with a sauceboat of thinnish tomato sauce.

Stuffed Herrings (if an egg can be spared)

Split open some large herrings with soft roes, which you will remove and chop up with parsley and soft breadcrumbs. Mix well together and season with a little pepper. Now melt some butter – not too much – in a saucepan, break into it an egg, stir it, add the mixture of chopped roes, stir again so that it does not set before it is all well mixed. Remove the backbones of the herrings as best you can, stuff the fish with the egg and roe, and bake them in a fireproof dish with a little butter for nearly half an hour. They should be served with a sauce of the liquor in which they have baked, stirred over the fire for a few minutes with a little milk.

Fish and Leek Pudding

'Men like this dish as well as women,' says the prime minister's wife, Mrs Neville Chamberlain in *Kitchen Goes to War* – a selection of recipes by 'Big Names'.

¾lb self-raising flour or plain flour and 1 good teaspoon
baking powder
6oz chopped suet
a little salt
2 thick slices of cod or other white fish
4 or 5 leeks

Line a 7-inch pudding basin with a light suet paste. For this mix the flour, the chopped suet and a little salt into a stiffish paste with water. Wash, trim and cut into cubes the 2 thick slices of fish. Cut the leeks into 2-inch pieces. Place fish and vegetables, well seasoned with salt and pepper, into the lined basin. Fill up with cold water. Cover with suet paste. Tie up securely with a pudding cloth and steam or boil 2½ to 3 hours.

Fish Puffs

½lb cooked fish
liquor in which fish was boiled
2oz self-raising flour
salt and cayenne to taste
½oz finely chopped parsley
2 eggs
milk

Flake the fish with a little of the liquor it was boiled in, add the flour, seasoning and eggs, and add sufficient milk to make the mixture of a soft consistency like sponge sandwich dough. Have ready some very hot fat, and drop in tablespoonfuls of the mixture. Fry until golden brown. Add chopped parsley. Serve very hot, with mashed potatoes.

MEDALS FOR HOUSE-WIVES

THE BRITISH HOUSEWIFE is helping to make a second front — the Kitchen Front — against Hitler. That is why we say "Medals for you, Madam." *Is there anything else you can do?* Read the list of awards below and see how many your household deserves. *More* medals for you, Madam!

A Medal for this . . .
Making delicious dishes from home-grown vegetables, with just a *flavouring* of meat or fish.

A Medal for this . . .
Trying new things — fresh-salted cod for instance — acting on recipes and hints from Kitchen Front Wireless Talks, Food Advice Centres and Ministry of Food Magazine Announcements.

A Medal for this . . .
Saving all bread crusts and crumbs, even the crumbs off plates, drying them in the oven and making crisp rusks or crumbs to use in cooking.

A Medal for this . . .
Never accepting more than the rations; and going without rather than pay unfairly high prices for foods that may be scarce.

A Medal for this . . .
Serving larger portions of vegetables than usual; because more are needed to get the same amount of nourishment that used to be had from the scarcer, concentrated kind of foods. Serving three or four different kinds of vegetables at the same meal, and dressing them up with different sauces to get variety.

Salmon in Custard

1 small tin of salmon
2 eggs or substitute
½ pint milk
seasoning

Flake the salmon with a fork and season well. Place in a greased fireproof dish. Pour over a custard made with 2 eggs beaten in the milk, and bake in the oven for about 30 minutes till set. To prevent custard boiling, stand the dish in a shallow tin with a little water in it. Serve hot or cold. A dish that is quick to prepare.

Scrambled Eggs with Smoked Flaked Haddock

Lupino Lane, who swaggered to greater fame in the 'Lambeth Walk', gives us this recipe also from *Kitchen Goes to War*:

2 eggs
2 tablespoons cooked smoked flaked haddock
salt and pepper
1oz margarine
2 tablespoons milk
2 slices hot buttered (margarined) toast

Beat the eggs, add seasonings, milk and flaked haddock. Melt the margarine, add beaten eggs, etc., and cook gently, stirring all the time over a low gas flame until the mixture is thickened. Serve piled on hot buttered (margarined) toast.

Mock Oysters

6 sardines boned and skinned
6 large artichokes boiled and rubbed through a sieve
2 tablespoons cream
pepper and salt
breadcrumbs

Mix all the ingredients together thoroughly, put lightly into oyster or scallop shells. Sprinkle breadcrumbs on top. Brown in oven and serve very hot.

Tasty Emergency Snack

Take a slice of Scotch bap (no other bread gives equally good results) not more than ½ inch thick, and toast it crisp under a hot grill. Remove it and butter or margarine it liberally all round the edges. Then pile on to it broken-up pilchards in tomato, using about a third of the contents of a small tin. Sprinkle with pepper and salt and replace the bap under the hot grill for 2 or 3 minutes. It is then ready to serve – hot, crisp tasty and nourishing.
NB Sardines and herring roes may be substituted for pilchards.

Meat

The lack of meat became both a headache and something of a national joke, as cartoons testified. Women invariably 'went without' in order to feed the men well. The ration per person varied from 13oz to 1lb 2oz a week and the families that fared best were those with young children, who from the age of five were allowed a full adult ration. This left a traditionally meat-eating nation with about 2oz of meat per day per person. Offal and game were not rationed. Liver was a thrilling treat, crow and redshank less so to the ordinary English cook. The rush of new austerity books was suddenly full of enthralling dishes—Stuffed Ear, Pig's Feet in Jelly, Mock Goose, Hash of Calves Head, Melt and Skirt Pudding, Sausages Gratinées—all fairly presentable meals as it turned out but far more acceptable to the cook with an element of French disguise. For *Mou en civet* (lights) for example, Ambrose Heath wrote bravely, 'The French are rightly called more frugal than we are, and I do not think that Pussy will approve of this savoury treatment of her usual prerequisite even if her master does.'

One Yorkshire butcher managed to fill his more or less empty window with illegal supplies of venison, while others sold horsemeat under the counter to many a grateful customer and at least one famous hostess entertained with mysteriously huge steak and kidney pies. Chicken was an almost forgotten luxury at a time when many families were happy to have a larger than usual shepherd's pie at Christmas time. Hens were kept in gardens for their precious eggs—they were even to be heard on the rooftops of Harley Street. The inevitable end of a good hen's laying days was often a sad moment for the family.

Statistics showed that in some areas health improved with the enforced reduction of cholesterol. The drop in heart disease and liver complaints as well as in infant mortality was attributed to an improved diet. The lack of cooking fat was another contri-

The Butcher says..

"That's right, Mrs. Smith. We're getting a seventh of our meat now in corned beef—twopence in the 1/2 as you might say. Lord Woolton's watching his stocks — he likes to be sure he's got a bit in hand. I don't mind telling you I was rather afraid the whole ration would be cut down. It's lucky for everyone there is this corned beef to help out with. Cold or hot, you can dish it up in a dozen different ways—and very tasty, too. No, Mrs. Smith, I don't want any points coupons, it's all part of the meat ration."

And here are some new recipes :—

HARICOT BEEF

Soak ½ lb. small haricot beans for 24 hours, then cook for 1 hour. Slice 1 lb. corned beef and shred one small cabbage. Put the beans, meat, cabbage and a chopped leek, if possible, in layers in a fire-proof dish, with a few peppercorns and a little salt sprinkled between. Mix one dessertspoon mustard and 1 tablespoon gravy thickening with ½ pint vegetable stock and add to the dish. Cover closely and cook in a slow oven for about 45 minutes.

CORNED BEEF WITH CABBAGE

Wash and slice a leek and fry lightly in a little cooking fat, in a stout saucepan. Add 1 lb. corned beef cut into small pieces. Cut 1 lb. cooked potatoes into small pieces, add to the pan, sprinkle with 1 dessertspoon flour and pour in ½ small cup vegetable water. Add a little made mustard, if liked. Stir all together until very hot.

Wash and shred a cabbage and cook in a very little salted water with the lid on the pan for about 10 minutes. Drain and serve on a hot dish with the meat mixture on top.

AMERICAN CORNED BEEF HASH

Mix together 1 breakfastcupful of chopped corned beef with the same quantity of diced raw potato, and season with pepper. Put into a frying-pan ½ a teacupful of vegetable water and a teaspoonful or two of dripping or cooking fat. When the pan is hot, put in the meat and potatoes, spreading them evenly. Dot another teaspoonful or two of fat over the top. Place a plate over the pan and cook *quite slowly* for about 45 minutes. A thick delicious crust will form on the bottom. Fold across and serve on a hot dish with cooked green vegetables.

Food Facts

NUMBER 76

THE MINISTRY OF FOOD, LONDON W.1

How to make *four small chops* provide a man-sized meal

4 SMALL CHOPS don't look much in the hand. But cook them this way and they'll provide a man-sized meal for the whole family.

To make the dish, it's best to use a " Pyrex " brand casserole. Then the food cooks in its own juices — none of the goodness is lost. It cooks evenly all through — doesn't frizzle up or burn or boil away. And, of course, there's no waste from dishing-up. You cook and serve in the same lovely glass dish. Washing-up is quicker and easier, too.

Another point — because glass retains heat, you won't have to leave the oven on for so long. That means a saving in fuel.

The recipe given here is approved by the Ministry of Food. To make it, you need 4 small chops (about 1-lb.); ¾ to 1 lb. onions or leeks; a heaped breakfastcup of grated stale bread; 1 dessertspoon dried parsley; 1 teaspoon dried thyme; 1 teaspoon dried egg (dry); salt and pepper.

First, cook the onions or leeks in boiling, salted water. Keep the water. Mix the breadcrumbs and seasoning with the dried egg. Add the onions or leeks cut up, and enough of the cooking water to make the stuffing nice and moist. Put chops in the " Pyrex " brand casserole with rolls of stuffing between the chops and on the top. Cover with the lid and bake in a hot oven for half an hour.

bution to better health. The fact was too that some families managed to earn more money during the war than before and the diets suggested by the government were often better balanced than those they had been used to.

America sent unfamiliar tins of meat in the most economic form possible of Supply Pressed American Meat (Spam), Prem, corned beef, Tang and Mor on the Lend-Lease Scheme, while Oxo, Bisto and Marmite (although the last two contained no meat) took on new importance in the kitchen as the chief substance of many a sauce for mock goose, mock chops or bread steaks, the new batch of ersatz meals that invaded each household.

On the subject of sausage, a 'higher authority' was overheard to explain that, 'I have held the view for a long time that the wartime sausage is one of the most serious blots on the achievement of the Ministry of Food.' Shoppers jokingly asked each other whether they were joining the meat or bread queue for their sausages, until 1942 when it became illegal to make sausages with less than 30 per cent meat. But not until June 1944 was the use of udders, melts and paunches prohibited in sausage making.

Generally, the best economies suggested with meat were ingenious, cheap and nutritious. Oatmeal, providing essential vitamin, was added to minced meat, stews and stock, to further the ration. 4oz of meat with fresh or tinned tomatoes could make a very good filling for pancakes. Small amounts of chopped meat with potatoes and carrots made traditional pasties. Stews were augmented with spiced dumplings. Roly-polys, meat puddings and pies, all using the minimum of meat, fed war workers at home and in canteens. Small pieces of veal or chicken were frittered in batter to spin the ration twice as far, and as the national flour was compulsorily 80 per cent wholemeal the result was always nutritious. Leftovers went straight into little bowls of potted meats for the more traditional tea table so that barely a scrap of goodness was ever wasted. At a time when butchers often had only a single type of meat to sell like pickled pork or mutton according to the season a larder full of little pots of fish and meat paste was a godsend.

One listener sent this answer to Ambrose Heath after his appeal from the 'Kitchen Front' programme for suggestions about eking out the meat ration:

> I am sending particulars of 3 days' meat courses I have myself used this week, having only received 1lb steak from the butcher during this temporary shortage.
> WED – Pasty, using one-third of steak supply, with turnip and sliced potato.
> THURS – Beef olive (stuffing of brown crumbs, parsley, herbs, etc.) with carrots and suet dumplings
> FRI – Steak and leek pudding. Remainder of steak with alternate layer of leeks and sliced potatoes.
> Sprouts also served on those 3 days. Family: 4 adults.
> Pasty made with uncooked meat and vegetables. It really irks one of West Country extraction to hear of pasties made of previously cooked meat and vegetables!

Sausages en Surprise

Grill some sausages, skin them, and let them get cold. Beat an egg into some mashed potato. Wrap each sausage, or half of each, in some of the potato purée and when cold and set, egg-and-breadcrumb them and fry them, or gild with beaten egg and bake in oven.

Sausage Pancakes

1lb small sausages
BATTER
4oz flour
½ pint milk
½oz custard powder
salt and pepper

Combine the flour and custard powder and mix to a smooth batter with the milk. Beat well for about 5 minutes, stir in the rest of the milk, season, and set aside. Fry the sausages until golden brown, remove from the pan, and keep hot. Pour off the fat, leaving just enough in the pan to fry a pancake. When browned on both sides, roll up with a sausage inside and lay on a hot dish. Add a little sausage fat to the pan, fry a second pancake, and fill again with a sausage. Repeat until all the batter is used, serve very hot with an accompaniment of fried tomatoes.

Corned Beef Hash

One can mix corned beef, cooked potatoes, purée of tomatoes (made from bottled tomatoes), cover the mixture with browned crumbs and bits of margarine, and bake in the oven. Fresh hot chutney is good with this.

Trench Meat Pudding

½lb steak
2oz shredded suet
salt and pepper to taste
2 cups oatmeal
2 small peeled onions (if available)
cold water as required

For 2 persons. Chop steak and onions finely. Mix with suet and oatmeal. Season with salt and pepper to taste. Mix to a thick dough with cold water. Three-quarters fill a greased pudding basin. Cover with greased paper. Tie down securely. Steam for 3½ hours. Serve with mashed potatoes and brown gravy. To make gravy, melt 1oz beef dripping or margarine. Stir in ½oz flour, then ½ pint stock. Stir till smooth and boiling. Season.

Economical Beefsteak Pudding

6oz flour
2oz breadcrumbs
½ teaspoonful salt
1 teaspoonful baking powder
3oz suet
4–6oz minced steak and kidney
1 large onion, minced
pepper
milk to mix
1 egg if liked

Mix together all dry ingredients and add the minced steak, kidney and onion. Mix to a soft dropping consistency with milk, adding a beaten egg if liked. Put into a greased basin, cover with greased paper, and steam 2–3 hours. Turn out and serve with gravy or sauce.

Rabbit Pudding with Mushrooms

2 young rabbits cut up in joints
a few slices of fat bacon
4 large sage leaves chopped fine
tablespoonful chopped onions
pepper and salt to taste
¼lb suet
½lb flour
mushrooms

Line a good-sized pudding basin with a suet crust, put in a layer of rabbit, chopped sage and onion, then a layer of peeled mushrooms and continue until the basin is full. Sprinkle plenty of flour between each layer, as that makes good thick gravy. The slices of bacon should be cut up in thin strips and put in each layer. Nearly fill the basin with water, cover with suet crust, and steam for about 3 hours.

Toad Special (Veal)

First make a batter with 2 eggs, 5oz flour, a pinch of salt, tablespoonful of water and sufficient milk to make a thick, creamy consistency. Allow this to stand 1 hour or longer. In a well-greased flat fire-proof dish, lay small rolls of thinly cut veal stuffed with breadcrumbs, parsley, milk and seasoning and a quarter slice of a rasher of bacon. Pour the batter over the neatly arranged rolls, and cook for ½ to ¾ hour in a moderate to hot oven. Ornament the top when nearly cooked, with cooked mushrooms or uncooked slices of tomato. This is a good way of using up the remains of a joint.

Two Dishes from One Fowl

1 small onion
a sliced carrot
1 stick of celery
pepper and salt
sausage meat, ham or tongue
chicken or boiling fowl

Prepare chicken or boiling fowl, removing both legs. Boil the giblets, onion, 2 or 3 slices of carrot and a little celery in water to cover for 1 hour, adding a few peppercorns and salt to taste. Strain and replace in the pan. Put in the trussed chicken; add enough water or stock just to cover the chicken. Simmer gently till tender, when cool, cut into pieces, removing any protruding bones.

Meanwhile, boil the stock with any trimmings for 1 hour or till reduced to 1 pint. Pour in a dish to make a layer of 1 inch. Melt 2oz butter; blend in some flour, stir in 1 pint milk; cook, stirring over gentle heat till thick. Coat each piece of chicken separately; place the pieces on the layer of jelly. Decorate with cooked pieces of turnip and carrot, cut in pretty shapes, add slices of tomato and cucumber. Serve cold.

Stuffed Legs of Fowls

Remove the bone without breaking the skin. For each leg allow ¼lb of sausage meat or veal passed through a mincer. Season to taste, add any flavouring liked; with sausage meat, a little chopped ham or tongue, or add to the veal a few breadcrumbs. Press the forcemeat inside the legs, form them into plump rolls, tie in muslin, simmer gently with the fowl for 1 hour or till tender. Serve cut in thick slices with a good brown gravy.

Liver Mould

Cut a calf's liver in pieces, put them into a stewpan with a little seasoned stock or gravy, and stew gently for an hour or so. Strain off the gravy, , and add enough gelatine or meat jelly to set it. Arrange the pieces of liver in a mould with a sprinkling of herbs and some sliced hard-boiled egg between, packing fairly loosely. Pour in the gravy and let it set. Turn out when cold.

Chicken Liver Paste

Dip in seasoned flour. Fry till tender with a slice of finely minced onion, then smooth it to a paste. Season the paste to taste with margarine, cayenne and anchovy essence. Serve spread on fingers of hot toast or fried bread at high tea or supper.

..*Shoot straight, Lady*

You've got a fighting job on hand, too. These are significant days and anyone — man, woman, or child — who is less than fighting fit is a pull back on the total war effort.

FOOD is your munition of war. The Government sees that you get the right stuff and it's vital that you should know how to use it to full advantage . . .

There's cheese : it makes muscle and bone.

There are potatoes : they give energy and warmth.

Carrots, that give vitality and help you to see in the dark.

Green vegetables, with their valuable salts and vitamins, which are so very important for clear complexions and sound teeth.

Did you know that 5 quarts of summer milk—milk at its richest and when it is most plentiful — go to the making of 1 lb. cheese?

Or that swedes, the juice of which you used to give to babies because of its valuable Vitamin C, are now to be had at most greengrocers cheap enough and in big enough quantities for you to serve as a second or third vegetable to the entire family?

All good live stuff. And you need them all : *every day.* Serve everything appetisingly as you so well can do. Then you can be proud of your vital, active part in the drive to Victory.

The Right Stuff . . .

You want to get through your work and difficulties with the same spirit you expect of the Forces in action . . . Well, thanks to Government planning, the foods that will feed you and your family to the pitch of fighting fitness are right at your hand. They have been deliberately chosen to that purpose.

To release ships and seamen on the fighting fronts, you, on the "Kitchen" front, have the job of using these foods to the greatest advantage. Here is how to do it:

*FIRST : **Your rations and allowances.*** These are the *foundation* of your fighting diet. Take your full share of them always.

*NEXT : **Vegetables.*** These provide much of the precious vitamins and other health factors that keep you bright and vital.

*THIRD: **Unrefined or whole-grain Foods*** — flour, oats, etc. These also supply valuable health factors, and, of course, add bulk to build up satisfying meals.

Spread your rations and allowances so that you get part of each of them *every day*, making sure that each member of your family gets his proper share. On those days when you've no meat, make up for it with cheese, fish, or dried peas or beans cooked with dried eggs or milk. *Every day* serve a lb. of potatoes per head, plenty of lightly and quickly cooked green vegetable, or root vegetable (don't forget swedes, especially when greens are scarce)and a salad."Something green and raw every day" as the Radio Doctor says. Round out each meal with porridge, bread, biscuits; or a milk or boiled pudding, according to the occasion.

Keep to the above principles *every day ;* but, of course, vary the ingredients and extras as much as you please.

SPICED BEEF. 3 to 4 lb. boneless brisket, or rolled thin flank. Mix together 1 teaspoonful each sugar, made mustard, salt, 2 tablespoonfuls vinegar, and rub well into the meat. all over with back of a wooden spoon. Leave meat in dish. with 2 bayleaves, 4 cloves, ½ teaspoonful peppercorns, for about 12 hours. Turn occasionally. Put the meat, with all its juices and spices into a pan, add 2 small onions (home-pickled ones do nicely) sliced, and ½ lb. sliced carrots and small bunch parsley. Just cover with water, put on lid and simmer slowly for 3 hours. The meat may be served hot. with the liquid thickened as gravy, or placed between two plates with a weight on top and left to get cold, the thickened liquid served as a cold sauce. If the oven is on, the meat can be cooked in a casserole ; 4 hours at very low heat.

ISSUED BY THE MINISTRY OF FOOD (S 53)

Kidneys with Horseradish

Grill the kidneys, fill them with grated horse-radish, and serve them with fried potatoes.

Wood-Pigeons

2 wood pigeons
seasoned flour
2 slices of fat raw bacon
2 large Spanish onions (or their equivalent bulk in home-grown ones)
about 6 large leaves of sage
good beef dripping
hot water
seasoning   } for gravy
1 meat cube
cornflour

Pick and clean the wood-pigeons, cut them through lengthwise and cover with seasoned flour. Cut the bacon in dice and fry to extract the fat. Place the bacon in a stewpan, leaving the fat in the frying pan, into which put the onions and sage leaves. Fry together till onions are tender; then add them to the bacon already in the stewpan, still leaving the liquor in the frying pan and adding to it the dripping or lard in which to fry the birds till browned all over. Lay the pigeons on the onions.

Pig's Cheek Baked

Wash the pickled cheek in several waters, put it into a saucepan covered with cold water, and bring it gradually to the boil. Then simmer for 2½ hours. Now drain it and skin it, cover it with lightly browned breadcrumbs, and bake it in a moderate oven for half an hour.

Meat Stew with Mixed Vegetables

(Emergency Meal No. 2 for 100 people)
for cooking in large air raid shelters, field kitchens, British Restaurants

10lb meat (bully beef, etc.)
5lb haricot beans
10lb onions or leeks
20lb carrots
     (or 30lb of any mixed vegetables)
65lb potatoes
1lb oatmeal or wheatmeal flour
1lb parsley (chopped)
water or stock
1lb cooking fat
25lb wheatmeal bread
1½lb margarine

This stew can be cooked in a clean dustbin after an air raid emergency.

Vegetables and vegetarian meals

The first dishes in this chapter are intended for those of my readers who live outside the danger zone, and who will almost certainly have extra people in the house. I have heard many stories about evacuated children (some of them sad, most of them funny), and many of the women who write to me for advice about their cookery difficulties have asked how they are to feed town children. 'They don't like vegetables and they won't eat soup,' these women say. 'In fact, they don't seem to like anything but fish and chips and bread and jam.' Well, there is no reason why they shouldn't eat bread and jam, and if you spread their bread with Stork before you put on the jam your town guests will get plenty of nourishment, in the form of food they like. I have found that all children like a good hot dish with plenty of gravy in it and a good thick slice of bread to eat with the gravy. Here are three dishes of this kind, and although one of them is made with vegetables, it is savoury and nice to eat. Try it on your evacuees and if at first they don't like it, try, try, try again. Give them a slice of bread and Stork to eat with it, too.

As the virtues of vitamins in vegetables were widely expounded in the humblest of cookery books, few remained ignorant of their culinary potential. As *Food Facts for the Kitchen Front* published by the Ministry of Food explained:

We have never eaten enough protective foods. Even in peacetime doctors have urged us to eat more of them. They guard against infection; they help us to fight tiredness and depression, they keep our complexions clear. Their vitamins and essential mineral salts are indispensable to our daily diet ... In these days when we are all beginning to concern ourselves with essentials and to discard things which do not matter, it is necessary to remember these two facts:
1. What we *can* get is good for us.
2. A great deal of what we *cannot* get is quite unimportant.

Methods of serving raw vegetables (for their nutritional value) concealed in various dishes were explained to canteen cooks and housewives, as in spotted mash, a potato purée with *any* raw vegetable grated into it. Outer leaves were always to be kept for soups, chutneys or chickens. Great efforts were made to persuade people not to prolong the boiling of vegetables, which would have destroyed most of their food value. 'Let them remind us of gardens and fields and fresh air', wrote one government adviser.

British Restaurants and canteens were advised to popularise thick vegetable soups, hotpots, curries, vegetable pies and puddings, to add grated carrot, cabbage and parsley to all meat pies and pasties and to increase the portions of vegetables if the supplies of milk, cheese, eggs, liver and fat fish were limited. Raw cabbage was to be used instead of lettuce in salads (an unusual idea then, new from America) and watercress, parsley and carrot were to be chopped into soups before serving. Mashed vegetables were described as an excellent sandwich filling and potatoes were considered an essential, not just an accompaniment. Potato consumption rose by 15 per cent and ministerial advice to caterers concerning nutritional values in wartime diets was clearly set out in MOF pamphlets:

1. Potatoes:
a. An essential energy food full of vitamin C and essential vitamins throughout the year.
b. Serve large helpings if meat amounts are small.
c. Use in pastry, scones and cakes.
d. Use mashed potato flan cases and pie coverings.
e. Use potatoes as the basis of all dishes.
f. Mix with meat rissoles, fish, sandwich spread, etc.
g. Serve baked potatoes stuffed with vegetables as snacks.
h. Use grated raw potato in place of half your suet in steamed puddings and suet pastry.
i. Serve potato pancakes and scones for tea, not buns and cakes.
2. Increase the portions of green vegetables and carrots if the supply of protein is small. Serve two vegetables as well as potatoes, the greener the better.
3. Raw carrots added to steamed puddings and cakes will help to sweeten them.

4. Serve well-flavoured mashed potatoes as sandwich fillings.

In *Food Facts for the Kitchen Front* all cooks were told that ½lb carrots and 4oz cabbage would almost satisfy daily requirements of Vitamin A, that 4oz oatmeal and 4oz wheatmeal would provide enough Vitamin B, that ½lb potatoes and ¼lb of cabbage satisfy the total daily requirements of Vitamin C – and that a perfectly balanced meal would be a fat fish, like herring, eaten with potatoes and a green vegetable.

Woolton Pie

The ingredients for this pie can be varied according to the vegetables in season. Potato, swede, cauliflower and carrot make a good mixture.

Take 1lb of them, diced, 3 or 4 spring onions, if possible, 1 teaspoon vegetable extract and 1 tablespoon of oatmeal. Cook altogether for 10 minutes with just enough water to cover. Stir occasionally to prevent the mixture from sticking. Allow to cool, put into a pie-dish, sprinkle with chopped parsley and cover with a crust of potato or wheatmeal pastry. Bake in a moderate oven until the pastry is nicely browned and serve hot with a brown gravy. Enough for 4 or 5. If you are short of fat, use this pie-crust which is made without fat: mix together 8oz wheatmeal flour, 1 level teaspoon baking powder, a pinch of salt, and a pinch of powdered sage if liked.

Stir in nearly ¼ pint of cold milk, or milk and water. Roll out the mixture and use it as you would an ordinary crust, but serve the pie hot.

The public were also reminded that: 'Those who have "dug for victory" will surely be interested in new ways of cooking and serving their young carrots, their early peas and new potatoes, not to speak of all the wealth of green stuff that will be coming along with the late spring and summer.'

Mushrooming too, announced the MOF food pamphlets, should now include what most British people had formerly regarded as deadly, nasty-looking fungi – Parasol Mushrooms, Blewits, Morels and Puffballs. 'With the recent influx of refugees and armed forces of all the Allied nations our country folk have seen the despised "toadstools" being collected eagerly for food, and this, coupled with the desire for variety in

for vitality
eat greens

Start gradually with your vegetarianism. Cut down the amount of meat you are accustomed to, even before rationing starts; adults don't need it unless they are doing heavy physical work. Give your share to hard workers and children. Take some fish at first, with vegetables, salads and cereal dishes. Then replace the fish with cheese, eggs or milk.

The Oslo Meal

4oz any raw mixed vegetable (i.e. shredded cabbage, lettuce, chopped parsley)
Grated carrot (if available)
sliced tomato
grated beetroot, cooked or raw
salad dressing
2tbs dried milk powder
2tbs vinegar
water
salt, pepper and mustard

Mix well together. Accompany with wholemeal bread and butter, 2oz cheese, apple and as much milk as rations allow.

The Oslo Meal in particular was found to be so nutritious that the health of schoolchildren who were given it daily was much improved; they grew taller, learnt faster and were better tempered.

the restricted wartime diet, has led to a greatly increased demand for information'.

Many people were obliged to be vegetarian at times through circumstances. Those who were vegetarian from conviction or for medical or religious reasons were able to exchange their meat coupons for a larger ration of cheese, about 8oz a week. They were also allowed extra eggs and so could on occasion indulge in a soufflé which could feed a household. Reluctant vegetarians were offered encouragement by Leonora Eyles in *Eat Well in Wartime*.

A good many people in wartime will be forced to adopt a largely vegetarian diet, and it may reassure them to know that it can be both pleasant and healthy. Hitler and Mussolini – and our George Bernard Shaw – are vegetarians and whatever else one may think of them they are all men of strength and energy.

This summer I had to do the work of this ten-roomed house (and it has fifty-four stairs), all the cooking, my journalistic work and reviewing and I was no worse for it. So you can see that a diet without meat need not be weakening.

Tops

Allow 1½lb for 4 portions. Broccoli tips, turnip tops, and beetroot tops have good food value, so have the broad bean tops which gardeners always pick off. Shred with a sharp knife after removing any coarse bits for soups and stews. Cook quickly in a little water. All sorts of additions may be made: a few bacon rinds chopped small; a few teaspoons of vinegar and a sprinkling of nutmeg or a shake of caraway seeds, and you have something quite new and intriguing.

Braised Kale

Cut into quarters, removing coarse stems, throw into salted boiling water and blanch for a few minutes. Strain. Line a stewpan with scraps of bacon, ham fat or lard, an onion stuffed with 1 clove, a carrot, and a bouquet of herbs.

Put the leaves on top with, if liked, a little ham in the centre, add stock till half full, season, cover with greaseproof paper and the lid and put in the oven for at least an hour. The kale is nicest when all the moisture has been absorbed.

FOOD FACTS

HARVEST HOME

Apple pudding on wintry days? Runner beans for dinner in December? This is the time to make sure you will have these dishes later on. Preserve every ounce of home-grown food you can spare for the winter. You are on a *fighting food standard* now. Nothing must be wasted. Gather in the garden harvest now, so you can enjoy your 'Harvest Home' in the winter.

ELDERBERRY AND APPLE JAM

Ingredients : 3 lb. elderberries, 3 lb. apples, 5 lb. sugar. *Method :* Remove berries from stalks and wash. Warm them to draw juice. Simmer for ½ hour to soften skins. Core apples and simmer until quite soft in another pan with very little water, pass through sieve or pulp well with wooden spoon, add apples to elder-berries, reheat and add sugar. Stir until dissolved and boil rapidly until jam sets. Make first test for setting after 10 minutes.

RECIPE of the WEEK No. 20

Marrow Surprise

Cooking time : 20 minutes.
Ingredients : 1 medium sized marrow, 4 oz. grated cheese, ½ pint household milk and vegetable stock, 2 tablespoonfuls flour, 1 oz. margarine, ½ lb. carrots, 1 cup sliced beans, salt, pepper. **Quantity :** Four helpings. **Method :** Peel marrow, unless garden fresh, remove seeds, slice beans and carrots, cut marrow into large pieces. Put carrots and beans in one saucepan with a little boiling salted water. Cover and cook till almost tender. Add marrow, cook for five minutes. **Cheese Sauce :** Melt margarine in a saucepan, blend in flour, cook for a few min-utes, add milk and vege-table stock to make thick sauce, stir until smooth, add grated cheese. Pour sauce over marrow, carrots, beans. Brown under grill. Serve with potatoes.

How are you? **FIGHTING** *fit, thanks!*

Salting Beans

Salting is the best way of preserving runner or French beans. Use young fresh beans. Take a lb. of cooking salt to 3 lb. of beans.

Wash the beans, dry, string them and, if large, break into pieces. *Crush* the salt with a rolling pin. *Put a layer* of salt about 1 inch deep into the bottom of a crock or jar (any large jar will do). *Press* in a layer of beans, then another layer of salt ½ inch deep, and so on. The secret of success is to pack the salt well down on the beans. *Finish* with a layer of salt 1 inch deep. *Cover* with a cloth or paper and tie with string. *Leave* for a few days for beans to shrink.

Don't worry if contents become moist. *Just add* more beans and more salt until jar is full again. If beans are well covered with salt it doesn't matter how moist they are. *Re-cover.* Store in a dry cool place.

Before use, wash beans thoroughly in *hot* water, then soak for 2 hours in warm water. Cook in the usual way, but with-out salt.

Apple Rings

Here's a way of keeping apples that can be used for windfalls or blemished fruit. Wipe the apples, remove the cores and peel thinly. Cut out any blemishes. Slice into rings about ¼ inch thick. Steep the rings for 10 minutes in water containing 1½ oz. of salt to the gallon. Thread the rings on sticks or canes to fit across the oven or spread on trays. Dry very slowly until they feel like chamois leather. The tem-perature should not exceed 150° F. Turn once or twice during cooking.

Pears can be treated in the same way, but they must be cut in halves or quarters and spread on the trays.

DRYING HERBS

Parsley, mint, sage, thyme, marjoram and bay leaves can be dried and stored for the winter. Gather the leaves on a dry day. Wash small leaved herbs such as thyme, tie in muslin bags and hang from the fire to dry. Large leaved herbs such as bay leaves should be tied in muslin, dipped in boiling water. Then dried in a cool oven, this takes about 1 hour.

FREE — Ask at any of the Food Advice Centres or Bureaux for a free copy of the *Hedgerow Harvest* leaflet, or send a post-card to the Ministry of Food, London, W.1. The leaflet contains many useful recipes for preserving wild fruits and berries.

THIS IS THE 2nd WEEK
OF RATION PERIOD No. 2.

Beet the Cold

1 large or 2 small beetroot
½ pint milk
¾ oz flour
¾ oz margarine
2 teaspoonfuls vinegar
salt and pepper
little grated horse-radish (if liked)

Cook the beetroot very carefully, without peel-ing, to preserve its red colour. Skin and cut into dice. Melt the margarine in a pan and mix in the flour. Add the milk by degrees and bring to the boil, stirring continuously. Boil for 2–3 minutes and then add the seasoning and vinegar. Add the cubes of beetroot to the sauce and heat until the beet is hot through and the sauce coloured pink. Dish and serve at once, sprinkled with a little grated horse-radish.

Mushroom Puffs (to be served with soup)

Stew some mushrooms with margarine and sour cream, salt and pepper. Have some puff pastry ready. Cut into rounds and place a few mush-rooms on each. Cover with another round closing the edges well. Bake in a quick oven.

Sweet Corn Pudding

Take the contents of one tin of American sweet corn and drain it free of all liquid. Mix with 1 egg, which has been beaten to a froth. Add two tablespoons of mock cream, a lump of margarine the size of a walnut, season with salt and black pepper, and bake in a moderate oven for 40 minutes. The pudding, when done, should be moist on the inside and slightly browned on the surface. Serve with small pats of butter and chopped chives, if procurable. Good with ham, bacon and fowl.

Bean and Tomato Pie

½ lb butter or haricot beans
2 oz margarine
½ lb tomatoes
1 oz rice
1 large onion
pepper and salt to taste
pastry

Soak the beans, and then boil them with the onion until they are soft. Put them in a pie-dish with seasoning, tomatoes and rice in alternate layers, putting small pieces of margarine on each layer, until the dish is full. Cover with pastry, and bake in a brisk oven. Serve a little of bean liquor as sauce, or use it to make a parsley sauce to hand with it.

Oatmeal and Herb Sausages

¾ pint water (salted)
1 cupful flaked oatmeal
1 medium-size onion, chopped finely
1 teaspoon mixed herbs
salt and pepper to taste
a little tomato sauce, if liked
1 egg or dried equivalent
breadcrumbs
chopped parsley

Bring the water to the boil, stir in the oatmeal and cook for ½ hour, stirring frequently. Pour the oatmeal mixture over the onion, herbs, parsley, salt and pepper and tomato sauce. Then add a well-beaten egg and enough fine breadcrumbs to make a stiff dough, flour the hands and roll the mixture into sausage shapes. Dip the 'sausages' into flour, egg and breadcrumbs, and fry a golden brown. Serve with hot sauce.

Lentil Chick

1 pint lentils
½lb dry mashed potato
2 tablespoons dried egg
2 level tablespoons household milk powder
2oz flour
1 teaspoon thyme
½ teaspoon lemon substitute
salt and pepper
2 or 3oz dripping

Cook the lentils in a little salted water, taking care they do not burn. When they are tender, drain off any superfluous liquor – saving it for soup. Add the milk powder, dried egg, mashed potato, thyme and lemon flavouring. Season with salt and pepper. Beat all together until the paste is smooth. Form into an oblong shape and coat thickly with flour. Put into a baking tin in which the dripping has been melted. Baste well and bake in a hot oven for 35 minutes. Baste once or twice during the cooking to make the flour into a crisp crust. Serve with bread sauce, and sausages, if liked. (Reg. mark 7)

Cheese Pudding

Mix together 6oz grated cheese and 4oz breadcrumbs, and add to these a breakfastcup of milk into which you have beaten one, or if possible, two eggs or their equivalent in dried egg powder. Leave this for half an hour, and then add more milk, enough to make the pudding the same consistency as pancake batter. Season with salt, pepper and either nutmeg or a little mustard. Pour into a greased pie dish, and bake in a moderate oven until the pudding is set and the top a lovely brown, round about three quarters of an hour.

Baked Vegetable Roll

½lb potato pastry
1½ breakfastcups boiled vegetables, diced small (as large variety as possible)
1 pint thick gravy
salt and pepper, and if liked a pinch of mixed herbs
4 tablespoons chopped parsley

Potato pastry is made with half the usual amount of flour being replaced by mashed potato – more nutritious and surprisingly good. Roll out the pastry thinly on a well-floured board. Toss the vegetables in enough gravy to moisten them. Spread them on the pastry, leaving a margin of about 1 inch all round. Season. Roll up and seal the ends and down the side securely to prevent the gravy oozing out. Put the roll on a well-greased baking tin, sealed side down. Brush all over with melted dripping or milk and bake in a moderately hot oven for 35–40 minutes. Garnish with parsley. Serve with the rest of the gravy made very hot.

Marrow and Walnut Cutlets

1½ cups finely chopped walnuts
1 beaten egg or 2 tablespoons of dried egg
1 teaspoon salt
2oz nut butter
½ cup fine breadcrumbs
1 cup mashed potatoes
1 tablespoon hot milk
1 cup chopped cooked marrow

Mix in a basin the nuts, marrow, potatoes, crumbs, milk, nut butter, egg and salt. Stand half an hour. Shape into cutlets. Crumb, then dip in slightly beaten egg diluted with a quarter cup of milk. Crumb again and fry in deep smoking hot fat till crisp and golden. Serve with white sauce flavoured with onion.

Cheese and Potato Custard

6–8 cooked potatoes
3oz dry cheese
pepper and salt
a little made mustard
½ pint milk
1 egg
parsley

Slice the potatoes and grate the cheese. Arrange in layers in a small pie dish or casserole. Beat the egg and add the milk, pepper, salt and mustard. Pour the custard on top of the potato and cheese and stand in a meat tin containing a little cold water. Cook in a moderate oven until the custard is set, about 30–40 minutes. Garnish with a little parsley.

Patriotic puddings and cakes

The British flair for pudding- and cake-making was displayed with even more resourcefulness during the war years. With tapioca, sago, rice, eggs, dried fruit, sugar, milk and custard powder all scarce or on points it is surprising to find cooks at their most confident in this area of the Kitchen Front.

Cakes and puddings were the most acceptable way of presenting the reconstituted egg, which more often resembled a sort of scrambled custard. Custard powder was often used instead of eggs in tarts, potatoes instead of flour, carrots or beetroot instead of fruit, honey, saccharine or treacle instead of sugar and water instead of milk. One Dorset woman's Christmas allocation of dried fruit was three prunes, four dates, twelve raisins and one ounce of sultanas, but even so she made a Christmas cake augmented with grated vegetables.

Icing sugar was made illegal. There was a ban on all candied peels, crystallised cherries and sugar ornaments. 'No person shall put or cause to be put any sugar on the exterior of a cake after the same has been baked,' instructed the MOF. Stocks of sugar ornaments were legally sold until 31 December 1941, but in 1942 Woolworths had left 412,666 non-edible sugar candle holders in store. Brides had to make do with cardboard-covered cakes, ornamented with plaster of Paris. GIs sent home to their mothers for icing sugar as well as nylons, soap and cosmetics as the most valuable presents they could give.

In March 1941 anything containing sugar was rationed to a 'minimum share' of 8oz a month. All preserves, marmalade, syrups, mincemeat, lemon curd and honey went on coupons (even the bees were government-rationed to small amounts of sugar for their honey-making efforts). In July the minimum share changed to a straight ration of about 1lb a month for the jam-making season only and everyone looked forward to the extra sugar rations at Christmas.

Although some parents made mammoth efforts to produce surprises for their sweet-deprived children, there was seldom more than a stocking with one orange, one sweet and perhaps some tiny treasure on Christmas morning. One uncle managed to find a banana for each of his nieces and nephews and was stunned into amused speechlessness while they ate them – skins and all. One niece remembers 'It wasn't at all bad, if you didn't know what you were meant to be eating.'

Party food consisted of stewed fruit juice to drink, pilchard sandwiches, cheese potato puffs, prune jellies, snowballs (baked apples covered in rice), potato or parsnip spread flavoured with strawberry or banana essence, perhaps saccharine-sweetened cakes decorated with improvised icings of gelatine and sugar dyed with coloured sweets and sometimes a sort of scrambled egg ice-cream made from dried eggs, syrup and milk. One family with children who had birthdays close together drew a line down the centre of the cake with the right number of candles on each side. Even candles could be home-made.

After six years of a virtually sugarless war that had also ensured a milk supply to everyone, the beneficial effects on height, mental health, weight, teeth and bones were dramatic. In 1937 80 per cent of the deciduous teeth of British children were imperfectly developed and rickets were common. A report in 1937 stated: 'In a recent enquiry in London schools it was revealed that, among children of five years old, there were 67%–80% of abnormality of the bones, 67%–82% of cases of adenoids, enlarged and septic tonsils and 88%–93% having badly formed or decayed teeth.' The 'iron ration' of war years did much to change this. As one teacher remembers: 'Those who had lived on bread and cakes with jam, cheese and chips, as many of the poor did, no longer had them and were much healthier for it. There was enough and it was simple.'

The prohibitions on milk and cream in April and October 1940 seriously affected the manufacture of cakes, biscuits and sweets when it became illegal to use milk in ice-cream, chocolates and all confectionery and bakery goods, except at home, of course. However cookery books advised women to save fuel and fats by buying cakes from shops that used cheap commercial shortening. Home baking, it was estimated,

not only used nine times more gas than factory baking but also wasted residues that could be used for the soap or oil industries or even for ice-cream.

Ironically the desire for something sweet was exacerbated by war conditions that left people drained of stamina. Nothing was so welcome during or after air raids as the buns and homely cakes of the Salvation Army food van, baked with saccharine if necessary to comfort the worker and the destitute.

While children's craving for sweetness was often fobbed off with a scraped carrot, homemade sweets were occasionally made (although most recipe books omitted them altogether), with golden syrup, saccharine and honey eking out the sugar ration. Honey toffee and honey twists were popular; sweets were made from condensed milk; marzipan was made with soya flour and almond essence. Jellies, jams and sometimes the scum from jam-making sessions went into improvised sweets as well as oatmeal, cereals, grated carrots and grated raw beetroot for colour. Very good and wholesome they were too, closely related to health food recipes today. Chocolates and sweets became so scarce from 1940 onwards that deliveries to Lyons Corner House produced an instant crowd and supplies were exhausted within half an hour.

This Week's FOOD FACTS

SHIP-SAVERS

Ships and more ships are wanted for war materials. *Less cargo space can be spared for food.* That's why we must all think of food in terms of ship-savers. Dried eggs and cheese are splendid ship-savers. They take up far less room than shell eggs or meat, and they are first-class food. Other ship-savers are home-grown foods such as vegetables and oatmeal. Give your family cheese often for their main meal. Bottle or preserve home-grown fruit and vegetables. Don't waste a scrap of food. *Pin this up on the larder door* and let it remind you that thoughtful shopping saves shipping.

Trench Cake (An excellent cake for the troops. It needs no eggs and makes a good-sized cake)

6oz margarine
6oz brown sugar, or granulated can be used
2oz chopped peel (optional)
¾lb mixed fruit
¾lb flour
1½ teaspoonsful bi-carbonate of soda
Nearly ½ pint of milk

Cream the margarine and sugar. Warm the milk and pour on to the soda. Add the prepared fruit, the milk and the flour. Mix well. Bake in a moderate oven for about 2 hours in a 7-inch cake-tin, or in slabs, for about 1 hour.

A slab of this cake was sent to the Front in France, travelled round France, chasing the owner, missed him and came back. Other things in the parcel were spoilt, but this cake was good after 10 weeks. It finally was sent out again and was much appreciated.

Sultana Pudding

This recipe can be varied by using other flavouring ingredients, such as figs, dates, prunes, etc., in place of the sultanas, and by the addition of spices.

3oz medium oatmeal	*3oz suet*
1½oz breadcrumbs	*3–4oz sultanas*
1½oz flour	*little grated nutmeg*
½ teaspoonful baking powder	*about 1½ gills milk*
1½oz sugar or syrup	

Mix all dry ingredients together and add enough milk to make a soft dropping consistency. Pour into a greased basin, cover with greased paper, and steam about 2 hours. Turn out and serve with a custard sauce.

Ice Cream for Wartime (without sugar)

¼ pint cream (a threepenny carton of 'Economy' cream can be used)
2 tablespoons sweetened condensed milk
2 whites of eggs
vanilla or other flavouring

Whip the cream until it begins to thicken. Add the condensed milk and vanilla essence. Whip the egg whites stiffly and fold them in. Spread the mixture into one of the freezing trays of the refrigerator and freeze for 2 hours. It is advisable to turn the gas to maximum before making the ice-cream. If the tray is lined with greaseproof paper this will facilitate removal of the ice-cream.

Sour Milk Pancakes

½lb flour
1 level teaspoon salt
1 small teaspoon bicarbonate of soda
sour milk to mix

Mix together the flour, salt and bicarbonate of soda and sieve them. Add enough sour milk to make a batter that will drop from the spoon, mixing the milk in gradually. The batter must be smooth and free from lumps. Well grease a girdle or stout frying pan. Drop a large tablespoon of batter onto it, and when the edges are cooked, turn and brown the other side. Serve with jam or marmalade.

Honey Nut Tartlets

6oz flour
½ cup sour cream
salt
½lb butter (slightly salted or fresh)
1 yolk of egg
honey
walnuts
castor sugar (or demerara)

Sift the flour with a pinch of salt, rub in the butter, and blend with the beaten egg yolk and cream. Leave in a cool place for an hour, then roll out and line small tartlet tins with the paste. Mix together 1 teaspoon of honey with 1 teaspoon of demerara sugar and 1 teaspoon of minced walnuts, fill up the tartlet tin, and bake in a moderate oven till crisp.

Wartime Trifle (Trifle – what memories!

But where are the sponge cakes, jellies, etc., necessary for the real thing? Never mind, this will be very good too.)

1 small ordinary teabun (stale will do)
*   per person*
fruit juice (bottled) or cooked fruit, or very thin
*   apple sauce.*
Thin custard made with custard powder or potato flour
*   and flavouring*

Cut the buns across and put either on individual plates or a large dish. Soak with the fruit juice, pour a little thin custard over them and top with a little fruit, if you have it.

Do it the other way round. Soak the buns with thin custard, pour the fruit juice over it, again use fruit, if any, for decoration.

Always pour the juice or custard *hot* on the buns.

Quick Bread Pudding (without lighting the oven)

Soak the stale bread overnight in milk or water with chopped dates or figs if available. Next day mash with a fork. For every cupful add a dessertspoon of custard powder, 2 saccharine tablets and a pinch of salt. Heat a little fat in a saucepan and add mixture, stirring until thick.

You can (a) fill small dishes and serve with a little cold milk and nutmeg or (b) leave to cool in a wetted basin and when cold turn it out and serve with fruit or fruit juice.

Beehive Cake

½lb self-raising flour
3 tablespoons honey
2oz candied peel
3oz Stork margarine
1 large egg, beaten in ¼ pint milk
pinch of salt

Brush a cake tin with melted Stork and dust with flour. Sieve the flour and salt into a basin, rub in the Stork. Add the chopped peel, stir in the egg and milk, add the honey and beat well. Put into the prepared tin and bake for 1 hour in a moderate oven. (Regulo mark 4)

CALLING ALL MOTHERS

Date and Nut Loaf

6oz dates, weighed after stoning
2oz Stork margarine
7oz self-raising flour
½ teaspoon bicarbonate of soda
¼ gill boiling water
1 tablespoon golden syrup or 2oz sugar
1 egg
pinch of salt
2oz shelled walnuts

Brush a cake or bread tin with melted Stork and dust with flour. Stone and chop the dates and mix them with the golden syrup or sugar, melted Stork and boiling water. Leave to cool, then add the beaten egg. Sift the flour, salt and bicarbonate of soda together. Stir in the date mixture, add the walnuts, roughly chopped, and mix well. Put into prepared tin and bake for 50 minutes in a moderate oven (Regulo mark 4).

Siege Cake

4oz dripping or lard
4oz moist sugar
4oz golden syrup
1½ teacupsful buttermilk
lemon flavouring
1 level teaspoon bicarbonate of soda
12oz flour

NB To save sugar 6oz of syrup and 2oz of sugar can be used. If buttermilk is not available use ordinary milk, 1 level teaspoon of cream of tartar, and ½ teaspoon bicarbonate of soda.

Grease a cake-tin measuring about 7 inches in diameter. Beat fat, sugar and golden syrup until the consistency of whipped cream, gradually work in the buttermilk. Sift the flour with bicarbonate of soda and work it lightly into the mixture. Add the lemon flavouring. Bake in a moderate oven for about 1¼ hours.

Eggless, Fatless Walnut Cake

4 cups flour
1 cup chopped walnuts
1 good cup milk
1 cup sugar
4 teaspoons baking powder
1 good pinch salt

Mix flour, sugar and chopped walnuts together. Add salt and baking powder, then the milk. It should be slightly wetter than an ordinary cake mixture. Leave to rise for 10 minutes. Bake in a greased cake tin in a slow oven till risen and brown.

Cheese Muffins

1½ cupfuls flour
½ cupful grated cheese
¼ teaspoon salt
4 teaspoons baking powder
1 egg
¾ cupful milk

Beat the egg lightly, add the salt and milk. Sift the flour and baking powder together, and then put in the grated cheese. Make into a dough with the liquid, beat well and roll out. Cut into rounds, brush with beaten egg, and bake for 10 minutes in a sharp oven. Spread with butter and eat hot.

Baking Powder Rolls

½lb self raising flour
1oz Stork margarine
½ teaspoon salt
milk and water to mix

Rub the Stork into the sifted flour and salt. Mix to a dough with the milk and water. Turn on to a floured board and knead lightly. Divide into six portions and shape into rounds. Cut across the top, place on a baking sheet and bake for 20 minutes in a hot oven (Regulo mark 8).

Health Bread

1½lb self-raising flour
1 teacup granulated sugar
1 breakfastcup syrup
1 egg
1 breakfastcup large raisins (stoned)
1 breakfastcup milk
Pinch of salt

Mix flour, sugar and a pinch of salt together and add raisins. Well beat egg and add together with milk and syrup. Thoroughly mix all ingredients (sufficient for two loaves) and bake in well-greased bread tins in a moderate oven for 1½ hours. After a couple of days the loaf can be buttered and cut into slices, wafer-thin, or as required for the menfolk. If kept in a tin cake-bin, these loaves will retain their flavour and moisture for at least a month.

Christmas Pudding (with dried eggs)

1½lb fruit (6oz raisins, 8oz sultanas, 8oz currants, and 2oz candied peel if available, though grated carrots & mashed potatoes make very good substitutes for the fruit.)
5oz self-raising flour
5oz fresh breadcrumbs
4–6oz margarine
grated rind and juice of 1 orange or 1 heaped tablespoon marmalade
3 level tablespoons dried egg
¼ pint milk
2 tablespoons cider, beer, brandy or milk
4oz Demerara or granulated sugar
1 heaped teaspoon mixed spice
1 level teaspoon cinnamon
½ level teaspoon nutmeg
pinch of salt

Clean the fruit, stone the raisins and chop the peel. Sieve together the flour, salt, spices and dried egg. Melt the margarine, adding the marmalade if used. Mix all the ingredients together in a large basin, and stir thoroughly. Place a round of greaseproof paper at the bottom of two medium-sized basins, brushed with melted margarine, and add the mixture. Cover with greaseproof paper and a pudding cloth, and steam for 4 hours. When the puddings have cooled, remove pudding cloth and top paper and cover with clean, dry greaseproof paper and a dry pudding cloth, and store in a dry place. Steam again for 2 hours before serving. (Makes 2 puddings each serving 6 portions, or 1 large and 1 small pudding serving respectively 8 and 4 portions. This pudding keeps well, and can be made at least a month before Christmas.)

Let's talk about XMAS FOOD

There won't be turkey on many tables this year; but the Christmas atmosphere will be there and the children's eyes will sparkle at simple treats, served gaily. From what we know of you, you'll make your Christmas catering a grand success in spite of difficulties, and we're out to help you all we can. Here are a few suggestions of general interest from letters we have sent to correspondents. A Happy Christmas to you!

Wartime Christmas Cake without Eggs

½lb plain flour
½lb ground rice
½lb granulated sugar
½lb currants
½lb sultanas
¼lb mixed peel
¾lb butter or good margarine
1 teaspoon bicarbonate of soda
12 drops essence of almonds
½ pint boiling milk

Mix the flour, rice, sugar, fruit and peel altogether. Cream the butter and stir well. Put the soda into a tablespoon of cold milk, add the essence to the boiling milk, then gradually blend the milk into the mixture while boiling hot. Beat well all together, put into a fairly large tin, and bake in a good oven for 4 hours. The cake will keep for months and improve.

STAND-UP MEAL
for a
wartime journey

EGG AND CRESS SANDWICH
CHEESE SANDWICH, APPLE

and best of all

Fry's SANDWICH
CHOCOLATE 2½d.
and 6d.

Mock Marzipan

½lb haricot beans
4 tablespoons sugar
2 tablespoons ground rice
1 teaspoon almond essence
1 tablespoon margarine

Soak the beans for 24 hours, then cook until tender in fresh, unsalted water. Put them on a tin in a warm oven to get dry and floury. Rub them through a sieve. Beat the sugar into the bean purée, add the ground rice, warmed margarine and finally the flavouring. Beat until quite smooth and well mixed. Use for cake covering or sweet making. Any kind of flavouring and a few drops of colouring matter may be added.

Apple Bombes (no sugar)

Mix grated raw cooking apples with condensed milk and whip. Add a little orange juice. Arrange in large spoonfuls and top with ground nuts or grated chocolate.

Potato Pastry

4oz mashed and sieved potato
½ teaspoon salt
8oz plain flour
3oz fat
2 tablespoons baking powder

Method: Sieve dry ingredients. Rub fat into flour and lightly mix in potato. Mix with a little water into a dry dough. Knead well and roll out.

Teatime: jam and preserves

During wartime it is especially important that there should be no wastage of home-grown fruit and that any surplus should be preserved for winter use. The Ministry has, therefore, thought it advisable to publish information on the subject giving particular attention to methods requiring less sugar than usual.

Supplies of sugar have been made available for soft and stone fruits, but in many households it is now found possible to save a little of the weekly sugar ration. *Growmore Bulletin No. 3*

The jam-maker had two alternatives – either to use the full amounts of sugar (the 'supplies' made available were a mere 2lb) and have jam that lasted well, or to economise and eat the results, which were more susceptible to fermentation and mould, within two or three months.

Instead of sugar, the fruit-preserver could try using 20 per cent glucose, if available, or experiment with honey and syrup. Saccharine with added gelatine was another method, but much of the jam bulk would disappear without sugar.

The long-lost lemon was replaced by citric acid to provide enough pectin, or artificial lemon flavouring. Failing even this a little vinegar might be used. Vegetables flourished in jam-pots, lending colour and bulk to rather wan jams. Beetroot, cooked and chopped, in crab apple jelly was considered 'scarcely recognisable', while carrots were grated to look like orange peel, or chopped to resemble apricots. Rhubarb was added to strawberry and black-currant preserves, marrow was added to damsons or used alone with ginger, and windfall apples featured in all jellies – bramble, elderberry, quince, sloe and bilberry. Fruit pulp from jelly-making could be used twice after re-heating with half the former amount of water, while jelly 'scum' was hoarded for puddings and syrups.

Jam-making centres, run by women volunteers, were sent instructions, as strict as those for any vineyard, about honest labelling of their products. Labels had to state the kind of jam, including the extras, the registered number of the jam-making centre, the day of work, the boiling of jam: 'Example: If the Centre number is 365, the marking on the label for jam made on the third day of work and at the fourth boil would be,

365.3.D

Ministry of Agriculture and Fisheries,
Jam-Making at Preservation Centres.'
During the summers of 1941 and 1942, 1,500 tons of jam were made by Women's Institutes.

The expression 'money for jam' took on a new and poignant meaning. It was a fineable offence to sell jam made with both real fruit *and* sugar outside the rationing system, although it was considered 'all right' to give a genuine present of jam to friends. Jam, like bananas, oranges, lemons and onions, became one of the most sought-after prizes at raffles and tombolas.

While many shops grew more adept at selling some marvellous vegetable jams – marrow and green tomato were popular, parsnips and beetroot less so – schools and institutions became familiar with an odd sort of concentrated marmalade. It was still severely rationed and had to be spread very thinly on bread and margarine.

Scum from Jam

When making jam or jelly, there is sometimes a good deal of scum to be removed. This of course contains sugar and fruit flavour, and can be used again. I add water (not very much), boil up the scum in it until it becomes a syrup, and then strain it. The syrup thus obtained can be used for stewing fruit, when of course no extra sugar is needed, or for making a jam pudding without having to boil it with water first.

Alternatively place a small piece of butter in the pan to prevent the scum from rising

Preserves when Sugar is Short

To make with glucose To each pound of fruit, allow ½lb sugar and ¼lb glucose. Prepare fruit. Place in pan with amount of water necessary, if water is required. Bring to the boil. Simmer gently till fruit is soft. Add sugar and glucose. Stir till sugar is melted. Bring to boil. Boil till a little sets when tested on a cold dish. Skim. Pot and seal.

To make with honey or syrup Allow ¾lb clear honey or golden syrup to each prepared pound of fruit. When fruit is soft, add the honey or syrup. Stir till boiling. Boil quickly, skimming frequently, till jam sets when tested as usual.

To make with salt Allow ½ teaspoon salt and ¼lb sugar to each pound of fruit. Boil fruit till soft. Add salt and sugar. Boil rapidly till jam becomes thick. Pot and seal.

NB If preserves made with honey, syrup or salt don't thicken to your satisfaction, add for every pound of fruit used ½oz small tapioca, soaked overnight in cold water to cover, after adding salt and sugar.

Parsley Honey

5oz parsley, including the stalk
1lb sugar
1½ pints water
½ teaspoonful vinegar if you have it

First pick your parsley, wash it well and let it dry. Chop the stalks roughly. Then put it into a pan with 1½ pints of boiling water and boil until it reduces to a pint. Now strain it, add the pound of sugar and boil until it goes all syrupy. This takes about 20 minutes. Then you add the ½ teaspoonful of vinegar.

The honey ought to jell perfectly well next day. It tastes very good – like heather honey. Do not make too much at a time; it is best used up in a couple of weeks or so.

Orange Skin Marmalade

6oz sweet orange skins
1 teaspoonful citric or tartaric acid
3½ pints water
1lb sugar

Cut the orange skins in quarters, and soak them in the water for at least 24 hours. Then put them in a pan with the water they were soaked in, and add the citric or tartaric acid. Tie the orange pips (if any) in a muslin bag, and add them to the pan. Simmer gently for 1½–2 hours, until the skins are perfectly tender, and the liquid reduced by about one third. Leave overnight, then shred the skins finely and put them back in the pan with the liquid. Add the sugar, stir till dissolved, and boil briskly for about three-quarters of an hour or until the marmalade will set when tested. Put into pots and tie down immediately. The above quantity makes about 1¾lb of delicious well-set marmalade.

As the peel contains 5 to 6 times as much vitamin C as the orange itself, this jam is preferable to ordinary marmalade.

Green Tomato Jam

4lb tomatoes
flavouring
3lb preserving sugar

Break up the tomatoes, put them into the preserving pan, and let them come to the boil. Add the sugar, a few cloves, or a small piece of whole ginger, or the grated rind of a lemon for flavouring. Boil fast for 20 minutes. It will set when placed on a plate in a cool place. This is an excellent way of preserving outdoor tomatoes that do not ripen well, and tastes like fresh figs.

Vegetable Marrow and Pineapple Jam

6lb marrows
6lb sugar
1 large tin pineapple
3 lemons
3 inches cinnamon stick
½oz white ginger

Peel and cut marrow into cubes, put it into a pan with the sugar, grated lemon rind and juice, and finely chopped pineapple. Next day put it into the preserving pan with ginger and cinnamon tied in muslin. Boil all slowly for 2 hours. When thick and syrupy put into hot jars and tie down.

Cheap Mincemeat

8oz grated carrots
1lb apples
2oz currants
2oz raisins
grated rind and juice of 1 lemon
2oz sugar
2oz mixed peel
½ teaspoon mixed spice

Peel apples, core them and chop them up finely. Stone the raisins and chop them. Finely chop peel. Wash currants, dry them and pick them over carefully. Mix all the ingredients well together, put into jars and tie down.

This mincemeat will keep one month if stored in a dry place.

Dried Apricot Jam

2lb dried apricots
2oz bitter almonds
6lb sugar, or equal quantity glucose and sugar
3 quarts water
1oz sweet almonds

Wash the apricots and pour water over. Stand 24 hours, or longer. Boil till tender. Add sugar, and when dissolved bring to the boil. Boil 20 to 30 minutes. Blanch and split the almonds and add them to the jam just before potting. Cover as usual.

Family Jam without Sugar (An adviser sends this with the caution 'to be eaten within a few weeks'.)

2lb stoned dates
1 packet lemon jelly
1½ pints water

Boil all together for ½ hour with any flavouring, eg ginger, crabapples, elderberries, sloes, etc.

Treasure the FRUITS *of* SUMMER

Carrot Jam

carrots
sugar
cooking brandy
lemon
sweet almonds

To 1 pint of purée allow 1lb sugar, 1 lemon, ½oz sweet almonds, and 1 tablespoonful cooking brandy.

Wash and clean carrots, and cut into small pieces. Cook until tender in as little water as possible, and rub through a sieve. Measure the purée, put it into a preserving pan with the sugar, grated lemon rind and strained juice of the lemon. Stir until the sugar is melted, then boil until the jam will set. Add the almonds (blanched and shredded) and the brandy. This jam will not keep without the brandy.

Potted Cheese (stale cheese will do)

Mix together ½lb grated cheese, 2oz margarine, salt, pepper and cayenne pepper and 2oz of ground nuts of some kind. Beat well together, press into small pots and cover thinly with melted margarine. This will keep for several weeks in a cool place.

Cottage Cheese

Place a jugful of sour milk in a warm place until the milk is quite thick, then salt should be added in the proportion of ½ small teaspoonful to 1 pint. Stir well, and place in a muslin bag (well washed flour bags do excellently for the purpose). Hang it up to drain overnight, press between two plates for an hour, then work up with fresh cream and make into a pat.

Hard Roe Butter

Boil a hard herring roe or two for a few minutes in salted water. Drain, then mash or pound it. Add pepper and salt, a few drops of vinegar or lemon and a very little softened (not oiled) margarine. Beat together and press into little jars.

'All Clear' Sandwiches

Spread fish or meat paste on to bread and margarine. Wash young dandelion leaves and spread on top to make sandwiches.

One Pound of Butter into Two

Warm 1lb of butter to a consistency that will permit of its being beaten up with a fork to a cream, care being taken that it does not oil. On no account must the butter be whisked with an egg whisk. Boil ½ pint milk, with a pinch of salt, and allow it to cool to blood heat. Then stir the milk gradually into the creamed butter. Put in a cool place to set and you will find that you now have 2lb of butter.

Flavouring Margarine (How to eke out the butter ration)

ONE
4 sprigs parsley, finely chopped
4 spring onions or a bunch of chives
garlic, crushed
1 dessertspoonful vinegar
¼lb margarine
Mix all well together.

TWO
2 gherkins
chopped parsley ⎫
chopped chives ⎬ *any or all mixed*
chopped chervil ⎭
chopped tarragon
1 pickled onion
capers
1 tablespoonful cream
¼lb margarine
seasoning

Cook cream and margarine for a minute or two, stirring, season and add remaining chopped ingredients. Allow to cool or serve on hot toast.

THREE
1 tablespoonful chutney
1 teaspoonful mustard
3 teaspoonfuls vinegar
4oz margarine
½ teaspoonful curry powder
salt, pepper and cayenne
½ teaspoonful Worcester sauce

Pound the chutney and the curry powder in a mortar, add the mustard and the margarine, moisten with vinegar, and work well together. Season with salt, pepper and a pinch of cayenne, and add a few drops of Worcester sauce. Very good on hot toast.

Beat the squanderbug with your store cupboard

As the war progressed and favourite brands of foods and goods disappeared completely, women had to rely on their own devices and their grandmothers' secrets for such essential standbys as soap, polishes, flavourings, baby lotions, medicines, ointments, dried fruits and vegetables and alcohol. Here are some of the more ingenious economic recipes that beat Dame Austerity's cartoon character . . . the Squanderbug.

Three-in-one Cleaner

Shred into a pan ¼lb white Castile soap, and pour on 2 quarts boiling water. Simmer until soap dissolves. Add ½oz saltpetre, stir well, strain. Now add (carefully) ½ pint ammonia. Bottle and cork tightly.

Damp your carpets, brush in some of the cleanser, and clean off with a sponge, and clean water. Add enough whitening to make a thin cream, and you have a wonderful cleanser for white paint. Make the cream a bit thicker and it cleans silver.

'Reviver' for Blue Fabrics

This preparation is for the cleaning and reviving of navy or dark blue woollen materials, suits, greatcoats, uniforms, blazers, gym tunics, felt hats etc.

Take a saucepan, an old one for preference – iron or enamel, not brass or copper – and fill it full of ordinary green ivy leaves. When as many as possible have been pressed into the pan, cover with cold water and bring to the boil. After boiling for 20 minutes, stand the pan by the side of the stove and simmer for 3 hours. Strain off the leaves and to every pint of liquid add one tablespoon of liquid ammonia. Put into a bottle and cork, and for safety label 'Poison'. It keeps indefinitely. Spread the garment to be cleaned on a table, and, with a cloth (preferably a piece of old blue serge), sponge, giving extra attention to the most soiled patches. Press with an iron afterwards.

Furniture Cream

Take equal parts of turpentine, linseed oil and vinegar. Add 1 teaspoon of granulated sugar to each ½ pint of polish and shake well. This is a cleanser as well as a polish.

Farmhouse Herb Salve

1 lb home rendered lard
1 good handful of each of the following: Elderflowers, Wormwood, Groundsel.

Cut the herbs into 1-inch lengths. Put into an earthenware pot with the lard, and bring to the boil in the oven. Simmer for ½ hour. Then strain into pots and tie down when cool. This salve can be made from dried herbs, but it is better to use them fresh.

This is good for a baby in case of a rash, also for heat bumps, insect bites and chapped hands and lips. This salve is excellent for all sores and bruises, and is particularly good also as a veterinary aid for softening the udders of newly-calved cows, or for sore teats. Its healing properties are remarkable.

A Good Liniment

1 cupful vinegar
1 cupful turpentine
A piece of camphor
1 egg

A good old-fashioned liniment for sprains and chilblains can be made from the above ingredients. Mix all together well in a bottle until the resulting liquid is white and creamy. It is then ready for use.

Medicinal Jam

1 lb prunes
1 lb seedless raisins
1 lb demerara sugar
¼ lb whole almonds

Remove the stones from the prunes. Chop prunes and raisins very finely, together with the blanched almonds and kernels from the prune stones. Soak all overnight in 1 pint of water. Next day add the demerara sugar, bring to the boil and cook for ½ hour, boiling not too fast. Pour into hot jars and seal down immediately. If you can spare the sugar to make this jam you will find that it is delicious (especially on brown bread), and is a mild natural laxative for children.

Honey Cough Mixture

Put into a bottle 4 oz pure cod liver oil, 1 oz of glycerine, 4 oz honey (pure), and the strained juice of 3 lemons. Shake well. This mixture should be taken 3 times a day after meals and shaken well before pouring.

Rosehip Syrup

Take 5 lb undamaged hips. Top and tail and wash them. Tip into 3 pints of water, bring to the boil and simmer for 15 minutes. Rub the hips through a sieve and mix with half the fruit's weight in castor sugar. Cook and stir for about 20 minutes or 10 minutes after it begins to simmer. If glass jars are used they must be kept in the dark. Allow to cool and seal with waxed paper. This will keep for 3 or 4 months. One teaspoon should be given to children daily as a Vitamin A and C tonic. The thick syrup can be thinned down for drinks.

To Dry Vegetables and Herbs

Pick mature peas and beans, pod and spread them out on plates or pans or sheets of paper in a sunny room. Stir frequently to prevent them moulding. But even if you haven't a room to spare and when there is no sun, you can dry vegetables and fruit without expensive apparatus. Nail together cross-strips of wood and cover with wire gauze or cheesecloth. These trays can be stood on the rack above the kitchen range, or in a warm oven. To dry herbs such as parsley, mint, sage, thyme, etc., as well as onion and celery tops – wash well, then drain and toss lightly in cloths to remove water. Place on racks and dry very slowly in a cool oven. Remove occasionally and stir.

TIME-TABLE FOR DRYING VEGETABLES

VEGETABLE	TIME TO BLANCH	TIME TO DRY	TEMPERATURE FAHRENHEIT
Beans (string)	3 to 10 mins.	3 to 4 hrs.	110–145°
Carrots	6 mins.	2½ to 3 hrs.	110–150°
Celery	3 mins.	2 to 4 hrs.	110–140°
Parsnips	6 mins.	2½ to 3 hrs.	110–150°
Peas	1 to 6 mins.	3 to 4 hrs.	110–140°
Pea Pods	3 to 4 mins.	3 to 4 hrs.	110–140°

A Simple Way to Dry Fruit

Apples: (1) Wash, dry, quarter, remove the cores, then pare. Save parings and cores for jelly. Dry the apples in the sun or in a very slow oven until dry like leather. Put into muslin bags or tins and store. (2) Prepare the apples by washing, drying and coring, then pare. Cut into slices ½-inch thick. String on to thick thread or cotton, using a coarse needle for the operation. Tie ends and hang these strings, each about 1 yard long, in the sun to dry. Put into muslin bags and hang in a dry place.

Pears: Wash, dry and core the pears, which must not be too ripe. Dry in the sun, or in a very cool oven until they are dry like a piece of leather. Tie up in muslin bags and hang in a dry place.

Plums: Gather the plums when ripe but not too soft. Do not peel. Wash and dry carefully. Cut into halves. Remove stones. Dry in the sun or cool oven until quite hard. Put in muslin bags, then in paper bags. Fasten securely and hang up in a dry place.

TIME-TABLE FOR DRYING FRUITS

FRUIT	HOW TO PREPARE	HOURS TO DRY	TEMPERATURE FAHRENHEIT
Apples	Peel, core, slice. Dip in salt water.	4 to 6	110–150°
Apricots	Halve. Remove stones.	4 to 6	110–150°
Pears	Peel, core, slice. Dip in salt water.	4 to 6	110–150°
Plums	Halve. Remove stones.	4 to 6	110–150°

Parsnip Wine

To each gallon of water take 3lb parsnips cut into pieces ½ inch thick, two lemons and one orange cut small. Boil until the parsnips are soft, strain and pour over 3lb white sugar. Stir till dissolved and bottle while warm, adding to each bottle a small piece of German yeast (about the size of a marble). Keep the bottle full while fermenting; after fermentation has ceased, cork and wire. This is an excellent imitation of champagne.

Plum Port

1 gallon water
4lb sugar
4lb damsons

Boil water and pour over damsons. Leave until the next day. Squeeze and stir daily for 5 days, then strain through a jelly bag. Stir in the sugar, adding 1 breakfastcupful of boiling water, and leave to ferment for 8 days. Then skim and bottle.

Gorse Wine

½ gallon flowers
1 gallon water
2oz root ginger
1oz compressed yeast

3lb demerara sugar
1 orange
1 lemon

Simmer flowers, water and ginger together for 15 minutes, stir in sugar until dissolved. Slice orange and lemon and add to cooling liquid, and when just warm float yeast on a piece of toast on top. Cover with a folded blanket, leave undisturbed for a week, then skim off the head. Strain into a jar, allow to work for another week before corking tightly. A few raisins and a lump of sugar candy keep it lively. Bottle off in November.

Ginger Beer (Without the bitter taste which is apparent if all the white pith of the lemons is not removed.)

5 quarts boiling water
1¼lb sugar
1oz whole ginger, bruised
2 lemons
¼oz cream of tartar
good tablespoon of yeast (about 1oz)

Remove rinds of lemon as thinly as possible. Strip off every particle of white pith. This needs a very sharp knife. Cut lemons into thin slices, removing pips. Put the sliced lemon into an earthenware bowl with sugar, ginger and cream of tartar, and pour on the boiling water. Stir in the yeast, and leave, covered with a cloth, in a moderately warm place, for 24 hours. Skim yeast from the top, strain ginger beer carefully from the sediment. For bottling, screw stoppers are best; if corked, tie corks securely. In 2 days, beer will be ready for use.

Ad nauseam – some heroic recipes

'Grate swede and mix with seedless jam for the children's tea'

Good Substitutes

For eggs read reconstituted egg powder
For milk read national dried milk
For butter read margarine or dripping
For cream read whipped margarine with vanilla
For flour read mashed potato or oatmeal
For fruit read grated vegetables
For mayonnaise read condensed milk with vinegar
For meat read offal
For cheese read sour milk
For pepper read grated turnip
For lemon juice read rhubarb juice
For coffee read barley or acorns

For Christmas read substitute

Advice to the austere wartime kitchen or canteen was unceasingly patriotic. 'Waste the food and help the Hun,' 'Don't take the Squanderbug when you go shopping!' For many women the war became a dreary and endless battle with rations, leftovers and planning – rarely any treats.

> Then there was the lugubrious chef 'Curly Kale' to whom the so-called pleasures of the table were but a source of deepest gloom. 'What's cooking?' asked Tom. 'Don't ask *me*, Sir,' whined Curly, 'It makes me ill to think of it.'
> (Excerpt from Tommy Handley's radio programme ITMA)

The national loaf was a dusty, grey, unpopular though healthy 85 per cent wholemeal bread that turned mouldy very quickly. White bread became an impossible luxury with cheap supplies of grain from the USA cut off. A report on the letters of complaint to the Ministry of Food announced:

> For a few weeks people indignantly ascribed every minor ailment or malaise from which they suffered to this 'nasty, dirty, dark, coarse, indigestible bread'. The more ingenious found out how to sieve it – through old silk stockings

– and one old lady wrote triumphantly, 'I got
all your vitamins out and gave them to the
pigs.'

Extravagance was severely judged:

> BREAD WASTED
> Miss Mary Bridget O'Sullivan, Normandy
> Avenue, Barnet, Herts., was fined a total of
> ten pounds, with two guineas costs, at Barnet
> today for permitting bread to be wasted ... It
> was stated that the servant was twice seen
> throwing bread to birds in the garden, and
> when Miss O'Sullivan was interviewed she ad-
> mitted that bread was put out every day.

Eggs, 'those shelly treasures', were the
most sorely missed food of all. But the dull
wartime package of dried egg powder became a necessity in the larder, and was
viewed with stoicism. From 1942 with the
USA's Lend-lease Scheme, the equivalent in
dried egg powder of a dozen eggs was available per person every four weeks, still on
rations, but at least nearly always available.
The Ministry of Food tried to popularise
this novelty: 'Shell eggs are five-sixths
water. Why import water?' Cookery books
introduced the egg powder. 'Do not hesi-
tate to use this. It is perfectly harmless. It is
actually nothing but a raising agent coloured
for the sake of illusion.' It is remembered as
rubbery, leathery, biscuity and dull, endow-
ing Yorkshire puddings, cakes and pancakes with a solid dryness – but it was better
than nothing!

When one of the first groups of Americans came to survey Britain's shortages for
the Lend-lease Scheme, they landed in a
remote part of Scotland. Their first meal
was breakfast, and a very generous one by

wartime standards. They ate dried scrambled eggs, a slice of toasted national loaf with a cup of the earliest attempts at dried coffee, and bothered to travel no further, but reported our needs as dire.

Humour as always during the war rescued the cook from despair. A comic postcard sang out:

Sing a song of blitzkrieg
Deutschland full of troops
Roots and sticks and acorns
Made into soups

When der lid was lifted
Der soup was strong and thick
Der Führer tried a spoonful
And, Mein Gott, was he sick!

It was the lack of variety that made meal planning so tedious, although recipe books advocated crow, rook and seagull pies for a change. The Ministry of Food advised on the lack of familiar ingredients:

HOW TO OVERCOME CONSERVATIVE FOOD HABITS:
1. Avoid sudden changes in size of portion.
2. Introduce unfamiliar foods like oatmeals and vegetables into meat pies.
3. Accompany new dishes with a popular gravy or custard.
4. Serve a popular pudding with a novel first course or vice versa.
5. Attend to flavour and appearance.
6. Serve raw vegetables first as an accompaniment and later as a salad.
7. Talk about nourishment.

With their backs to the kitchen wall, women dreamt up the most heroic ways of sustaining morale and it was by such tortuous efforts as these that the domestic war was won;

HOW TO BEGIN EVERY DAY WITH THE SMELL AND
FLAVOUR OF A BACON BREAKFAST
One of the most difficult tasks repeated every day, is the getting out of bed. Involuntarily we turn towards a consolation. For some people it is the first cup of tea and the newspaper, for others the early morning cigarette, a hot bath or even a cold shower. But for the majority it has been decidedly the smell of sizzling bacon. If we come to think of it, it is the smell and later the flavour of the bacon more than the actual rasher which meant so much.

Well, we can have this pleasure every day.

FOOD FACTS

In winter even the most patriotic cows give less milk — war or no war. Yet the demand for milk is greater than ever before. The National Milk Scheme is chiefly responsible for this increase. Those who need milk most — expectant mothers, children and invalids — are allowed the *same* amount of milk winter and summer. In winter, in order to secure enough milk for these priorities the rest of us must do with less.

If we economise with our rations one rasher of bacon, used with skill and imagination, can make a whole family happy.

Josephine Terry in *Food for the Future* invented a wonderful recipe, 'Eggs, None for Breakfast'. Her answer was to cook tinned apricots in bacon fat and served, as egg-like as possible, on toast.

Other advice tells the cook how to sustain the morale of the family.

At Mealtimes:
Don't tell the family what the dish is made from until they have tasted – and liked – it.
Don't moan about the food you couldn't get before you serve it.
Do praise your cooking in advance to encourage their appetites.
Do use favourite flavourings ruthlessly to cover less popular meals and serve them with grace.
Do talk pleasant small talk at each meal.
Don't mention the gas bill until everyone has finished.
Don't panic if large numbers arrive; you can dump almost anything into your original dish to spin it out, just like the miracle of the loaves and fishes. Oatmeal, tapioca, rice, vegetable tops, chutneys or soups can all substantiate almost any meal.

Snoek Piquante

4 spring onions, chopped
liquid from snoek
4 tablespoons vinegar
1 can snoek, mashed
2 teaspoons syrup
salt to taste
½ teaspoon pepper

Cook the onions in the fish liquor and vinegar for five minutes. Add the snoek, syrup and seasoning and mix well; serve cold with salad.

Somerset Rook Pie with Figgy Paste

6 rooks
weak stock
pieces of fat bacon cut in chunks
pepper and salt to taste
FOR THE PASTE
1lb flour
½lb fat
4oz currants
4oz raisins, stoned
pepper and salt to taste

Bake the rooks, which must have been skinned, using only the legs and breast, as all other parts are bitter. They should be left soaking in salt and water overnight. In the morning drain away the brine and put the legs and breast in a good-sized pie-dish, adding the fat bacon. Cover with the stock and season well with pepper and salt.

For the paste, rub the fat well into the flour, adding pepper and salt, then add the currants and raisins. Mix well, and add sufficient water to make a stiff paste. Roll out to about ¾in thick, then place right over the pie, letting it come well over the sides. Cover the pie with a piece of greaseproof paper, and then put the pudding cloth on top. Tie well down and see that the water has no chance of getting in. There must be sufficient water in your boiler to cover it. Do not put the pie in until the water is boiling. The pie takes a good 3 hours to cook, and is delicious served with gooseberry jelly.

Black Pudding Toast

½lb black pudding
1 onion
seasoning
a little dripping
1 small cupful of oatmeal

Heat the dripping in a pan and add the black pudding. Mash well and add chopped onion and oatmeal. Stir for a few minutes and cook gently till onion is tender. Season. Serve on hot toast.

Crow

The crow is first cooked in a blanc.
Blanc: Mix gradually a good tablespoonful of flour with cold water, so that there are no lumps, make the water up to 2 quarts and add a level tablespoonful of rock salt and 3 tablespoonfuls of vinegar or lemon juice. Bring to the boil, stirring all the time, and put in the meat to be cooked. Now add a bouquet of parsley, thyme and bayleaf, and lastly either 3oz very finely chopped suet or 3 tablespoonfuls of the fat off the top of the white stock. Draw the pan to the side of the fire, put the lid on three-quarters, and boil gently without intermission. The purpose of adding the suet or fat is to exclude all air, and therefore to keep the meat as white as possible. This blanc besides being used for other meat is used for cooking certain white vegetables.

It can then be served in the following ways:
Fried Cut in pieces, egg-and-breadcrumbed and fried, and served with fried parsley and sauce diable handed separately.
A la Lyonnaise Fry in smoking olive oil, and arrange in a circle on the dish, garnishing the centre with fried onions. Swill the frying-pan with a few drops of vinegar, and pour over the dish.
A la Vinaigrette Serve as it is, and hand round a sauce vinaigrette.

Home-made Mayonnaise

1 level tablespoonful standard custard powder (use flour when custard powder is not obtainable)
2 level tablespoonfuls of household milk powder
1oz margarine
½ teaspoonful dry mustard
2 tablespoonfuls vinegar
salt and pepper
½ pint boiling water

Method Mix together the custard powder or flour, milk powder, mustard, pepper and salt in a basin. Warm the margarine, and blend it smoothly with the dry ingredients until soft and creamy. Gradually stir in the boiling water, then put it into a saucepan. Bring very slowly to the boil, stirring all the time. Cook until the sauce is smooth and thick. When it is cool, beat in the vinegar. Any kind of spiced vinegar may be used instead of plain malt vinegar to give variety of flavour.

To Make a Baked Custard with Dried Egg and Household Milk Powder

Regulo mark 4.

Mix together 4 level tablespoonfuls of Household milk powder and 3 level tablespoonfuls of dried egg with 1 tablespoonful of sugar. Gradually stir in a pint of water, beat thoroughly with a fork, pour into a pie-dish and stand the pie-dish in a shallow tin of water. Bake in a moderate oven for 1 hour. Once or twice stir the ingredients before the custard begins to set. If liked, sprinkle the top with grated nutmeg after the last stir.

To Cook an Old Duck

1 duck
breakfastcupful of cold water
¼lb dripping

Ducks up to the age of 5 years may be cooked in this way. Truss and stuff as for roasting. Melt ¼lb of dripping in a saucepan. When hot, put in the duck and braise for about 15 minutes, turning twice. Add a breakfastcupful of cold water, cover closely and simmer for 4 hours.

Thrushes

thrushes (1 for each person)
chopped & peeled tomatoes
clove of garlic
½ cupful of olives (optional)
fat or butter
an onion
seasoning
bacon or oiled paper

Hang the thrushes for 3 to 6 days. Prepare and gut them before cooking. Brown them in fat or butter and add chopped and peeled tomatoes, onion, a clove of garlic, seasoning, and, if available, half a cupful of olives. Wrap the birds in bacon or oiled paper and cook until tender.

Sparrow Pie (not encouraged by the Ministry)

12 sparrows & the occasional lark
bacon
mace
forcemeat
sage

Put a piece of bacon between each bird and spread a leaf of mace, sage and a little forcemeat on the top of the pie, under the crust. Make a thickened gravy and add the juice of a lemon and serve quickly.

Helping hands...

You, and you alone, can take over from the Government, the vital work of keeping your family fighting fit. The Government makes available the essential foods. In your hands lies the rest!

Helping hands must be guided by thinking heads. To-day there are new facts to absorb; new ideas and improvements on old ones. Wider knowledge of nutrition, for example, gives a new importance to vegetables.

Vegetables give us our greatest supplies of invaluable Vitamin C and many other precious vitamins and minerals without which we should soon flag. Furthermore, our vegetables, the finest in the world, are home-grown. Every lb. of vegetables you eat in place of food that would otherwise be imported — every lb. of potatoes instead of bread — releases that amount of shipping space for the transport of essential food, machines, tools, men; and lifts unnecessary strain from our seamen. Multiplied 45 million times, think what that contribution means to the winning of the war!

You have done magnificently during the past three years. Let us keep working together and this year do still better.

DO'S and DON'TS with Vegetables

DO serve swedes when greens are short, or for a change. Of all the root vegetables, swedes are richest in Vitamin C.

DO provide at least one pound of potatoes per head every day, and less bread.

DO cook potatoes in their skins; this prevents their goodness dissolving into the water.

DO serve "something green and raw every day."

DON'T soak vegetables long; their vitamins and minerals seep out into the water.

DON'T overcook vegetables; shred cabbage and greens, break cauliflower in sprigs, cut carrots and swedes in pieces before cooking; they take much less time to cook this way and it saves fuel.

DON'T throw vegetable water away; use it for soups and sauces.

ISSUED BY THE  MINISTRY OF FOOD

Imitation Eggs

Make a batter. Cut a tomato in two and put it into the batter. Lift each half out with a spoon keeping round side up and put it into hot fat. The tomato shines through looking like the yolk of an egg. If cooked in bacon fat you can almost imagine that you have the bacon as well.

Leftover Porridge

Mix with breadcrumbs and form into cakes. Fry and serve with bacon.

Mock Fish

Add 2oz ground rice to ½ pint boiling milk. Add a teaspoon of leek and a large teaspoon margarine. Also ½ cup of mashed potato. Simmer for 25 minutes. Remove from heat, add 1 teaspoon egg powder, and mix well. Spread out ¾ inch thick on a flat dish. Divide into pieces like fish fillets. Spread with milk and breadcrumbs and fry until brown. Serve with white sauce.

Victory Sponge

Regulo mark 5

2oz margarine	a little milk
2oz cooking fat	jam
3oz sugar	
2 level tablespoonfuls dried egg	
6oz flour	
½ teaspoonful baking powder	
½ teaspoonful vanilla essence	

Cream the fats and the sugar together until pale and very fluffy. Whisk the egg well with 2 tablespoonfuls of water and the vanilla essence. Beat it well into the fat and sugar. Mix together the flour and baking powder and fold it lightly into the egg, fat and sugar. Stir in enough milk to make a creamy dough. Divide the dough in two greased sandwich tins. Bake in a moderately hot oven for 20–25 minutes. Cool and sandwich together with jam.

This cake makes very good custard trifle when a special pudding is wanted.

Four 'Fruit' Jam

Wash and peel four ounces of cooked beetroot and carrot. Chop finely. In half a pint of water dissolve two cubes of strawberry jelly and ½ tablet of blackcurrant jelly. Add the vegetable chunks and three tablespoons of fruit sauce or jam. Leave to set and eat within three days.

Mock Plum Pudding

1 cup grated raw carrot
1 cup breadcrumbs
1 cup shredded suet or mashed potato
2 teaspoons salt
1 teaspoon ground ginger
1 tablespoon chopped, mixed peel
1 cup minced raisins
½ cup flour
¾ cup sugar
1 teaspoon ground cinnamon
½ teaspoon ground nutmeg
cold water as required
½ teaspoon baking powder

For 2 or 3 persons. Sift the flour with spices, salt and baking powder. Stir in carrot, crumbs, suet, raisins, sugar, peel, and cold water to make a stiff batter. Steam for 4 hours.

Bread Soup

3 slices white bread
1 medium-sized onion
1 cup hot milk
2oz dripping
3 cups boiling water
1 heaped teaspoon chopped parsley
pinch grated nutmeg
salt and pepper

For three persons. Remove crusts from bread. Break bread into small pieces. Melt the dripping in a saucepan. Add bread. Chop and add onion. Fry together for 3 minutes. Add water and salt and pepper to taste. Cover and simmer for 20 minutes. Rub through a sieve. Pour purée into a pan. Stir in milk, nutmeg, parsley, and salt and pepper to taste. Re-heat.
NB: When you've any stock to spare substitute it for all the water or part of it.

Emergency Pudding (Adapted from 1st World War recipe for soldiers in the trenches) 'How to cook in your Tin Helmet'

Smash up some old (Army) biscuits with a bayonet, or suitable instrument. Place them in a canteen. Half-fill with water, and add some orange peel. Boil to a delicious orange-flavoured paste. Serve with condensed milk.

ENEMY SHIPS TORPEDOED
with the help of Old Rags

It sounds impossible doesn't it? But the charts that guide our submarine commanders are made from old rags. In addition rags help to make maps for our bomber crews and tank crews, paper for medical supplies, wipers for cleaning machinery, battle-dress, blankets and other equipment, roofing felt for army huts, etc.

Give all the old rags you can find and spare for salvage at once. Rope, string and twine are also urgently needed. Keep rags clean and dry in a rag-bag, ready for the salvage collector or rag-and-bone man when he calls.

That's right **SAVE WASTE PAPER** *carefully*

If the collector calls less frequently in your district this may be due to labour shortage. Please keep your waste paper until he comes.

Waste paper isn't rubbish. It's precious. And it's *doubly* necessary now to save every scrap for the salvage collector. Munitions and spares to fight Japan need an average of nearly three times as much paper as for the war in Europe. Waste paper is used in the making of those munitions too. So remember—your waste paper is urgently needed—it's got a big job to do.

WASTE-PAPER
is urgently needed for **SALVAGE**

Issued by the Ministry of Supply

Austerity Picnic—To Save Paper

Now that the spring days are coming and we'll all be trying to get as much fresh air and sunshine into our lungs as possible, many people will be eating out of doors. Please remember that sandwiches wrapped in grease-proof paper and a table napkin keep just as fresh as if they were wrapped in the peacetime layers of tissue—and you'll be saving lots of valuable paper toward the war effort.

10. Start a rag bag

THE SALVAGE DRIVES

War strain has been particularly felt by mothers living in bombed districts, but this has not prevented them from attending to such matters as cleaning and drying bones for the salvage collector, ransacking the house for scraps of paper, metal and rubber, nor from making the daily journey down the road with the food scraps for the kitchen waste bin.

With the serious shortage of natural resources, Britain had to make the best use of those materials she already had. From 1939 onwards demands for salvage in newspapers and magazines plied women with statistics they could hardly resist.

Think of your waste salvage
Think of the amount of munitions we need
And remember that
one newspaper makes three 25-pounder shell cups
one magazine the interior components of two mines
six books one mortar shell carrier
one soap powder canister four aero engine caskets
five medium size cartons one shell fuse assembly
60 *large cigarette cartons* one outer shell container
20 *breakfast cereal cartons* one case for three-pounder shells
six bills one washer for a shell
four assorted food cartons one box for aero cannon shells
one envelope one cartridge wad
twelve letters one box for rifle cartridges

So you see   We must
GO TO IT!!

Collecting salvage was one of the most boring and never-ending chores of the war. The most difficult part was to persuade already overburdened working women to sort out every little scrap of rubbish. In four months, ten million household calls were made, over seven million of them organised by the WVS.

With pleas to the Kitchen Front to save fuel for the factories, with civilian petrol abolished, with appeals to save water and heat it in the oven while cooking, there was hardly any sphere of the home unaffected by the need to save. 'Five lb of coal saved in one day by each household will provide enough coal to make 13 bombers'; 'How much will you save to make bombers?'; 'Save fuel for battle'.

Women were urged to carry on with their first aid to clothes. Even Rinso soap advertisements announced: 'If everybody can prolong the life of garments by only *one third* then reduced supply will meet all needs.' The Ministry of Information expanded on the theme to clothes-hungry women obliged to spend coupons on dungarees: 'One additional clothes coupon granted would take 8,000 people from essential work and mean that 5,000 tons of raw materials would have to be imported – sufficient to equip half a million men overseas, overcoats, boots and all.'

Dustbins, accordingly, took on a new importance, with the 'tireless slogging' of sorting different forms of waste, from pigswill to rabbit fluff, to be called for by women, Brownies, Cubs and children from the children's salvage group (the Cog Scheme). Some salvage, however, was never collected, especially in the more remote villages where ugly piles of tins, old machinery and the offal of the household were to remain for years, much to the indignation of the organisers who were still under compulsion to find yet more.

The head of the WVS, Lady Reading, appealed to women in a broadcast in July 1940: 'Very few of us can be heroines on the battle-front, but we can all have the tiny thrill of thinking as we hear the news of an epic battle in the air, "Perhaps it was my saucepan that made a part of that Hurricane!" ' Households were implored to 'give' all the time. 'What you give at once is worth double'; 'If in doubt, give.' A Hampstead woman, involved in the wvs, remembers the desire to donate as 'almost manic'. One woman gave her new three-tier steamer, others valuable copper saucepans and pewter jugs. A patriotically imaginative woman, aware of the great value of her pewter donation, was so keen for it to reach its airborne destination that she drilled holes through the rarer pieces as a safeguard against theft. Another woman gave an old saucepan and then replaced it with a newer one. The greater the sacrifice the better – this was the general attitude.

But as women so willingly donated to the war effort many of the domestic oddities that make life easier, they soon found them almost impossible to replace. To cope with the shortages 'Make-do-and-Mend' classes were popularised, backed up by wireless programmes. And women's books, even after the war, were full of good advice. If you could find a packet of needles, worn-out carpets could be 'easily' mended, made into rugs or foot-muffs; if you could find good glue or cement, old linoleum could be 'easily' patched. Magazines explained how to make toys out of cotton reels, match boxes, buttons or dusters – 'and then when dusters became scarce we had to unpick them again'. Simple diagrams showed women how to mend their saucepan handle or resolder a new base to a burnt-out kettle. Any spare time was often spent knitting for the troops from unravelled jumpers, although in the cold winter of 1941 an indignant private wrote to *Picture Post* from 'somewhere in Scotland':

> I have just been visiting our battalion stores and was shocked to see the numerous bundles of comforts knitted by women's guilds for the troops being hoarded instead of distributed – a scandal when one considers the amount

of energy and time put into these articles by womenfolk, and the cold weather we've been having. Possibly they'll be issued in June in proper Army fashion.

The Ministry of Works collected metal salvage while the Ministry of Supply was responsible for everything else. It was impossible to escape their pleas: 'Paper, metal tins, bones, string and other materials go into your house every week. But how much comes out again as salvage?' Campaign after campaign was launched, appealing for different commodities. Official salvage helpers wore a round brown badge with an s for salvage on it. Children recruited from schools had salvage songs they bellowed on their hunts, 'There'll always be a dustbin...' And the Brownies alone managed to finance an aircraft and a lifeboat with their salvaged jam jars.

As the paper shortage became a famine, a suggestion was sent to *Picture Post* in 1942, under the heading, 'How to Spring-clean and Save Paper':

> The interior walls of British homes provide an untapped source of paper for the national salvage effort. We'll soon be spring-cleaning. Repapering walls is wasteful and unpatriotic but one stripped room in every house would yield an enormous amount of paper salvage, and a coat of distemper would be a pleasant and hygienic substitute.

The Control of Paper Order in 1940 declared that: 'No person shall in connection with any sale by retail wrap or pack with paper any article which does not reasonably require such wrapping or packing for its protection.' A Capstan advertisement for cigarettes suggested: 'In the national interest empty your packet at the time of purchase and leave it with your tobacconist.' It became 'good form' to write business letters on the used side of correspondence, pamphlets, memo sheets or whatever was to hand, and to re-use envelopes until the address became unintelligible. Some people made newspaper Christmas cards.

Waste fats. An American poster.

Street by street, women and children filled wheelbarrows and prams with paper, metal, tins, jam jars and rags.

The worst domestic result of the paper shortage was the lack of lavatory paper. It became such a national problem that it was finally discussed in the House of Commons in 1944. People used torn newspapers or raided office wastepaper baskets, and often kept their own supply for public lavatories where it was handed out only on request.

Magazines like *Vogue* appealed to the public to share their copy of the magazine, footnoted as it was with familiar maxims like 'Waste paper is vital to the war effort!' and 'Use as little paper as possible for fires'. The editor of *War Illustrated*, Sir John Hammerton, explained to his readers in May 1940:

> Something over 80 per cent of the paper made in British mills comes through Bergen (Norway) as pulp. Think then what it means to have this source of supply even temporarily blocked. Let me give some details: When the war started there were ample supplies of paper and it cost the publishers just over £12 a ton. The ruthless U-boat campaign directed as viciously against neutral Norway as against British shipping slowed down maritime transport, greatly increasing the cost of woodpulp. The ever-growing demand for ships to carry Britain's war materials from USA or Canada made the cost of Canadian and Newfoundland pulp supplies uneconomic if not inaccessible. I look to the approaching paper famine improving many publications by demanding a more selective taste of editors.

Paper was nevertheless the easiest item to salvage, and love letters, autograph books and library books as well as newsprint were enthusiastically given and collected by the lorry-load, usually under the supervision of women. All books and magazines were published according to the Wartime Economy Standard, on a sort of very thin blotting paper, and in 1943 the Ministry of Supply promoted a books for salvage drive throughout the country, although the forces were desperately calling for any kind of reading material. The public responded with fifty-six million books to be pulped, of which six million were considered too valuable to be destroyed and five million were sent to the troops.

Privilege was removed in the form of the iron railings of London squares and large houses, supposedly to be used for bullets. Only a few, including Osbert Sitwell, protested to *The Times* of the 'vandalistic sabotage', while another reader in July 1940 calculated that 250,000 razor blades were being thrown away each day that could yield a precious 90 tons of metal yearly. In September 1941 the government realised the antiquarian value of much metal scrap and allowed a fortnight to appeal against compulsory council collection on historic, artistic or safety grounds. By September 1944 the total weight of railings demolished at the rate of about 10,000 tons a week, was a million tons. It was not always clear how useful they were, for three-quarters of the scrap piles remained where they were for many years. Unsightly chicken wire or fences sometimes replaced the railings, as mothers worried about the safety of children, chickens or allotments in the areas left, and the effect was generally an unaesthetic and demoralising one.

By 1943 each household in the country had provided about half a ton of salvage. By 1944 the 'unflagging effort' of women was rewarded with the information that the diligence of the housewives had produced: '1,117,788 tons of waste paper, 1,334,171 tons of metal, 82,889 tons of rags, 25,298 tons of scrap rubber, 43,948 tons of bones and thousands more tons of kitchen waste.' The metal alone would suffice to build over 100 cruisers or more than 50,000 Churchill tanks, and 408 cargo ships were saved, along with many lives and months of time. The thought of the 210,000 pigs being fed on 31,000 tons of kitchen waste they had collected each month must have been of some comfort to the woman struggling to give to the war effort and at the same time keeping the home running with little more than her own ingenuity to help her.

ISSUED BY THE BOARD OF TRADE

Mrs. SEW-and-SEW on

Steps you can take to save your SHOES

Buy shoes wisely. Remember that fit is more important than appearance. It's worth a little search to find really comfortable shoes.

New shoes will last longer if worn first on a dry day.

Give your shoes a rest — don't wear the same pair two days running if you can help it.

When you take off your shoes, use shoe-trees or stuff them with paper to keep the shape. Always undo fastenings first.

Damp shoes should be dried out slowly—*never* near strong heat. Put wet "woodies" sole-side up.

Clean regularly — a little polish every time is better than a lot now and then. Use dubbin on boots and shoes for rough wear.

See to repairs promptly — heels especially. A 'run-over' heel spoils the shape of the whole shoe *and* tires the foot. Leather studs and 'rails' on Woodies must be replaced before worn down to the sole.

Rubber studs, rubber soles and iron tips help shoes to wear longer.

* * *

Children's Boots and Shoes
Always buy on the large side to allow for growing. Extra socks will make a slightly big shoe comfortable. Ask the retailer to advise you which shoes are most durable and suitable for your children

Teach your children to change their shoes on coming indoors.

148

11. Wot, no rags?

The disappearance of household goods started slowly enough. Early in 1940 it was still possible for the rich to buy a new car, Parisian clothes and good furniture polish, and for the poor to buy tin-openers and kettles. But the Limitation of Supplies Order of that year was to ban 'inessential' goods and cut down production of many more by between 33 per cent and 75 per cent, so that all labour and raw materials could be concentrated in the war industries. Almost overnight factories changed from making prams to aeroplanes. The clothing industry now produced uniforms, parachutes or dungarees, leaving an ageing force of women in insufficient numbers to maintain civilian requirements.

By the sixth month of the war clothes prices had risen by 25 per cent and food by 17 per cent. Rents at least were pegged but income tax rose from 5s 6d to 7s in the pound to help cover the government's new expenses. Millions of tons of imports were being bombarded and sunk on the merchant shipping lines with little chance of replacement. With each new military disaster more trade was cut off or became too dangerous to risk. Even before the first bombs dropped, women were urged to be good patriots by giving away saucepans, kettles, pram wheels and spanners. Within months kitchen tools were high on the list of 'inessentials' and the breakage of a mixing bowl, the rusting of a potato peeler meant hours of queuing to replace old stock at inflated prices. The plight of evacuees and refugees meant that women took every 'spare' boot or blanket to the post office, old clothes to the clothing exchanges. Women gave and gave, unprepared for the effects of controlled distribution of stock.

The Limitation of Supplies Order of 1940 curtailed the production of everyday objects, like cups, glasses, cutlery, buckets, kettles, clocks, clothes, shoes, prams, furniture, toys, jewellery and cosmetics. The result was that many 'luxuries' like paper clips, needles, pencils, gardening tools or ball-cocks for lavatories just quietly disappeared as stock ran out. What remained was distributed as fairly as possible. Spades went to farms, thermos flasks to the Fire Service, musical instruments to the BBC, clocks to shift workers and sewing machines to voluntary groups.

By 1941 shops were more or less bereft of goods. A cartoon showed a woman asking a shop girl standing before her empty shelves, 'Is this haberdashery?' Pointing to another bare counter the girl answered, 'No, that's it'. Increasing numbers of goods went 'on coupongs'. Clothes, shoes, socks and bedding were now on points. By February 1942 only 4oz of soap a week was allowed (soon reduced to three ounces) although babies got a bit extra. Shaving soap wasn't rationed, considered as important to men's morale as cosmetics were to women. Very heavy fines or imprisonment were introduced for anyone searching for or selling these 'frivolities' on the Black Market.

With devastating air raids on most cities and ports and with increasing numbers of homeless, the Board of Trade in 1941 at last permitted a special furniture allowance for those who were bombed out, setting up home or expecting a child. Their 60 unit quota, reduced to a mere 30 in 1944, could only buy a selection of the following: a chair (1 unit); a table (6); a sideboard (8); a wardrobe (12); an armchair, bookcase or dressing table (6); a double bed (5); and two

single beds (6).

The ordinary 'non-priority' householder was reduced to delving in ruins if she needed stair rods, curtain rails, extra mattresses or curtains. 'Digging for Victory' became a special kind of victory if curtain rings or coat hooks turned up in the process! The only alternative was to overbid at auctions for expensive second-hand furnishings.

British women, after two years of war, turned a blind eye to their dreary surroundings, but GIS coming from a centrally-heated, refrigerated, carpeted and painted world were warned not to be shocked at the unkempt appearance of a country at war. For the house, distemper was the only alternative to cream, green or brown paint. Some women attempted to mix it with dye, perhaps to surprise a husband on leave. Others tried stippling their walls with it and created a sort of instant rustic wallpaper. Floor coverings like carpets or linoleum were almost unobtainable.

By 1941 the Board of Trade had banned the production of the latest 'luxuries' – bedspreads and curtains. Sheets and blank-

What Norman Hartnell could do with 'Make-Do and Mend'. Here the mannequins are young, but when they were mobilised, older women replaced them.

ets joined the list of 'fripperies' and were made for 'priority' groups first, which left an unrationable penny three-farthings' worth a week for the remainder now facing the third cold winter of the war.

Curtains and wedding dresses, were made from materials available – parachute silk, butter muslin, 'a horrible hessian' and blackout materials, bleached and dyed. Even towels and tea-towels were rationed from 1942. Everything was made into something else. Old shirts would make baby clothes or knickers, though elastic was hard to find. Flour sacks and sugar bags became cushion and furniture covers, or shorts for cadets. The fabric used to fill broken windows after air raids was found to make excellent tea cloths. Architects' and engineers' offices were raided for discarded drawings on linen which could be boiled and re-used for hospital supplies or children's clothes. Laddered stockings were cut into strips and knitted into rugs for the homeless, while all remnants made useful pillow stuffing for rest centres.

Pregnant women were advised to make a cot out of an old drawer, to pad it with newspaper and line it with an old nightdress. Prams too were in very short supply, and women were lucky to find the most archaic sort until a Utility version was produced – little more than an unsprung box on wheels, cumbersome and difficult to push. The availability of rubber teats and rubber knickers fluctuated with the complicated rubber shortage until the Board of Trade suddenly informed mothers that 'Rubber knickers are not necessary, and quite apart from the fact that rubber is very scarce, they are uncomfortable for the baby.' It also announced that 'babies don't need nearly as many clothes as people used to think'.

With an estimated shortage of 100,000,000 pieces of crockery a year, people were drinking their watery and expensive beer from jam jars or toothmugs which they took to the nearly nicotine-free pubs if necessary – to the further astonish-

ment of the GI troops. In cafés and hotels the sugar spoon was attached to the bowl by string, which at least produced a certain camaraderie.

The most welcome wedding presents were now the most practical ones: a packet of soap flakes, a curtain or a fuel-saving pressure cooker. For birthdays and Christmas, a powder puff made from rabbit's fur, a packet of seeds, a banana or orange all made handsome presents and jumble sales became Aladdin's caves.

As goods disappeared completely and prices rose steadily, the only course of action was to standardise production. Hitherto points were awarded irrespective of quality. The Utility scheme, from autumn 1941, asked top designers to ensure that working-class families (the worst hit) could actually afford to buy things that they needed and at competitive prices.

By 1942 Utility carpets, housepaints, clothes, shoes, torches, alarm clocks, crockery, prams, lamps, blankets and so on, were of functional and limited design and the ration was continually reduced. But at least they were being made again, even if the cups were usually without handles.

But with the return of Sir Stafford Cripps from Russia to the War Cabinet, as leader of the House of Commons early in 1942, even stricter bans came into force. The Board of Trade's Austerity Regulations, presided over by Hugh Dalton, informed women that if they wore stockings that summer there would be none for the winter. Soup spoons, billiard tables and most toys were prohibited, and only the simplest of glassware was to be made. Biscuit packets, tin labels and pencils were plain, paper like blotting paper. Tobacco was often home grown, or an eye was cast round the allotment for acceptable alternatives in the form of dock seeds, oak and coltfoot leaves or sorrel.

Doctors were badgered for curious prescriptions. Buckets and mops were needed for women with 'back trouble'; extra cheese for husbands allergic to offal; hot water bottles for 'insomniacs'; and extra milk, cream and orange juice for 'weakling' children.

Humour in the form of Chad, a cartoon

"I suppose in about thirty years' time people will insist on describing this as the good old days."

A Birmingham shop in 1940, and still well stocked. Later in the war, empty tins might be kept for display with NOT FOR SALE *written on the shelf.*

character, came to the rescue yet again and 'Wot, no toothbrushes?' (or whatever) became a popular slogan to which the shop assistant would reply, 'Don't you know there's a war on!' Shop assistants were wooed energetically with eggs or invitations to tea as they stood before their empty shelves, their shop fronts covered in perverse advertisements for what they did not have. Advertising itself reflected the need to remind women tantalisingly of brand names. 'Won't it be nice when the war is won and we can buy . . . again?' 'In these days, you're lucky to get Meltis Newberry Fruits', or 'P & B Wools – scarce but worth looking for'. Children rushed home to announce the great news of deliveries to shops. One mother remembers her child shouting to neighbours, 'Plums! Tobacco! Sanitary towels!'

1942 was the year that clothes coupons were reduced by twelve points, to 48 a year, the Board of Trade having caught on to the ruse of 800,000 people who had 'lost' their clothing books. Austerity regulations dictated the number of pleats, seams, pockets

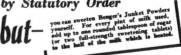

and buttonholes. Embroidery and sequins were banned. Underclothes were limited to six shapes, with the favourite garment of the middle-aged – bloomers or 'passion-killers' as they were called by the young – costing 3 coupons a pair – a twelfth of the year's ration and an unnecessary waste of material in Sir Stafford Cripps's eyes. In 1941 a Bourne and Hollingsworth woman's suit cost 11 coupons, by November 1943 a lined woollen overcoat was 18 points, a woollen dress 11 and a pair of knickers 2. But more usually knickers were home-made, and worn under dungarees, overalls, boiler suits or siren suits – the standard civilians' uniform.

On 28 June 1942, the *Observer* wrote about the new first aid classes for clothes: 'Women must expect to wear clothes now until the elbow wears out, but garments can be sent back to be refashioned as above – elbow sleeved dresses – or to have sleeves remade.' Millions of garments arrived from the Commonwealth and the USA, needing sorting and perhaps altering, and women gathered in village halls and parlours for any thrift classes and exhibitions put on by the Make-Do-and-Mend volunteers, encouraged by sickly posters of 'Mrs Sew & Sew'. In the clothing depots and exchanges, worn children's clothes could be exchanged – but only if the mother had renovated them, which she often had to be taught to do. But the quality of clothing did slowly improve by these means. It became a matter of pride to achieve good results out of unlikely materials. The Make-Do-and-Mend classes showed millions of women how to reverse collars and shorten sleeves, to make plus-fours into a child's coat, a pillow case into baby clothes or a school uniform into a maternity dress.

A military functional look was in fashion, with brass buttons, square shoulders and dyes mainly limited to dusky blues, bottle greens, burgundies or red and black. But for the last few years of war fashion petered out of most women's lives. False shirt fronts on suits, minimal hems and linings and a regulation short sock length (not more than 9½ inches) were used more and more.

Men's suits were single-breasted, often with fake pockets, narrowed trousers and no turn-ups. There were no deep pockets or extravagant shirt tails or cuffs. A careful man could only buy one pair of pants and a vest every two years, a pair of shoes every 8 months, a shirt every 20 months, one pair of socks every 4 months, a pair of trousers and one jacket every 2 years, one waistcoat and pullover every 5 years and one overcoat every 7 years. GIS were advised to 'cut out the swank' and not to be surprised by people's dull garb. They themselves brought a breath of sophistication and excitement with their beautifully pressed and cut uniforms.

Women in uniform took great pains to look as well-kept as possible and had their own inter-service snobbery as to which uniform held the most prestige. Naval uniforms were considered the smartest, although the WAAFs thought their uniforms the prettiest and looked down on the uniforms of the Army, who in turn sniffed at Land Girls and the ATS, sometimes to the extent of ignoring them in otherwise friendly queues or dances.

Meanwhile the very rich could still find haute couture, at a price. All the youthful beauties had been called up, leaving a world of ageing mannequins and private tailors whose prices had multiplied six-fold. By 1943 a pre-war 25s nightie cost about £13, a 14 guinea coat and skirt £42, and a guinea hat between £6 and £8. (This was far above the average 31 per cent rise in cost of living between 1938 and 1945, although the average weekly wage rose from £2 13s 3d to £4 16s 1d.) Good taste became officially superfluous and flashy smartness a cause for mistrust, not admiration.

Even *Vogue* was adamant that women should look as if they worried less about their faces than what they had to face. Figures should be tautened by exercise not corsets (in short supply anyway through the metal and rubber shortages).

On the production line, long hair was dan-

Clothing Exchange. Only good quality clothes were accepted. Queues of the destitute would form after each air raid.

155

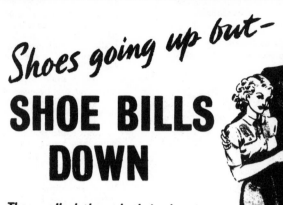

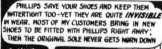

156

gerous, so women in shapeless overalls (bitterly resented if extra coupons were not supplied) tied their hair into scarves with knots above the forehead to keep the popular rolls of curls and 'bang' fringes out of the machines, though kirby-gripped curls sometimes poked out 'becomingly'. The magazines' advice was to tuck hair into nets under tin helmets, caps or berets. For the evening, hair was washed with home-made shampoo, either soapless or incorporating vinegar and detergents. Women used pungent home perms or peroxided their hair like American film stars, brushing it forward over their face. After tying a stuffed stocking around the head (or, according to a WAAF sergeant, a disguised sanitary towel for a thicker roll) the hair was flung back and tucked in to make a roll of hair around the head. This was a favourite fashion since it dispensed with the need for kirby grips. For women shift workers in industry earning a small amount for themselves but without much to spend it on, some hairdressers stayed open till midnight to cope with erratic hours.

With so many women in uniforms, caps and boiler suits, hair tucked out of sight, only their faces and legs differed from the men's. This, coupled with the clothes shortage, meant that many young girls used to 'plaster our faces with thick make-up – anything to look a bit different from the next person'. One factory manager considered that £1,000's worth of cosmetics would do more for women's morale than the same sum in cash. But with women at the Yardley factory assembling small parts for machinery at one end and only a quarter of their normal output of cosmetics at the other, chemists after 1941 had to experiment with their own home-made versions, sometimes disguised as medicaments. A WAAF girl remembers:

> Our lipstick was like dry chalk to put on though it looked like garish enamel or greasepaint. It had a bitter taste and we waited for it to dry with our mouths open! It often broke in the tube if left open. At the Anglo-American club we used to watch the American girls putting on face-packs before dances as if they were men from Mars. It was every girl's dream to have one of those leather cases of different make-ups in bottles.

From 1941 onwards women became used to darning and redarning their cotton, rayon and lisle stockings. When supplies of even these began to fail, women resorted to complicated methods of simulating stockinged legs. Shoe polish mixed with face cream was one frequent experiment. Others tried an unsatisfactory yellow dye on the market, painting the seam up the back of the leg with eyebrow pencil. Another method for an overall tan was to bath (in the five inches of water permitted) in purple potassium permanganate. These stains generally streaked the skin or marked clothes indelibly. In the summer of 1942 even *Vogue* tried hard to illustrate the charm of ankle socks with elegant summer frocks.

Stockings were the one commodity that many women guiltily felt it was acceptable to buy on the Black Market. Prices on average varied between 5s and £2 a pair. One woman remembers steeling herself to approach a likely-looking spiv and returned home only to find she had been sold a pair with odd seams. 'It serves me jolly well right,' she remembers thinking. Another queued regularly for fifteen hours to get her under-the-counter stockings at 15s a pair.

It was to this world of drab legs, of soapless, fuelless and almost bathless women, some hugging their wireless sets for company, that the GIs came early in 1942. They brought with them flimsy nylons and superior cosmetics, symbols of glamour, prosperity and hope, and found their way to many a girl's heart.

"That's Gilchrist—in charge of post-war planning."

12. The parasites are at their filthy work

UNDER THE COUNTER: THE BLACK MARKET

With rising prices and tight controls on trade there developed speculation and profiteering. Paradoxically many people were earning more money than they had during the Depression through compulsory drafting into the services or factory war-work, but with rationing and shortages they had only a limited amount of spending power. The government encouraged people to save with War Bonds, a system to invest money in the war effort and prevent speculation, to be repaid at a certain percentage after the war. But if people chose not to invest there was a certain amount of money about.

The *Encyclopaedia Britannica* explains how rationing was bound to lead to a Black Market: 'When value rationing came in all it did was to trim off the peaks without filling in the troughs. At any level of supplies above that at which practically every customer was bound to demand his full ration, a surplus was bound to arise for which there was no legitimate outlet.' Some of this surplus came into the hands of the familiar 'spivs', mainly through theft from depots. The rarer the goods, the 'blacker' the market. *The Times* wrote in January 1948, at the height of Black Market dealings: 'Between the person who lightheartedly takes advantage of an easily evaded regulation and the person who is a determined Black Market operator, there is a whole range of dishonest and anti-social practice.'

People talked of 'knowing a man' who might have spare parts for radios, alcohol, rubber tyres, petrol, or even dolls, nylons and perfumes – known to be illegally acquired. The grey market was a more individual process of being in the right place at the right time, whether shop or lorry depot.

Many tradespeople, much to their irritation, found their supplies already nibbled away on arrival. This meant a painstaking reorganisation of rationed amounts and sometimes tedious explanations to the rampant Ministry inspectors. Some people would regularly tip, or try to tip, shop assistants in the hope of getting something under the counter when stocks did arrive, and shopkeepers who knew which side their bread was margarined would keep rare consignments like salmon or peaches for their richer customers. A lorry driver, saving for Christmas, might leave the cab door open during a tea break, after a wink and a nod, and return to find a few crates missing and a fiver on the seat.

Attitudes were very mixed to these dealings. They varied from moral outrage at even a whiff of Black Market dealings to the view that if sharp dealing was the only way to provide for family and friends at a time of stress, then it was the obvious course to take.

In 1942 *War Illustrated* wrote:

> Not a day has passed but somebody has been prosecuted or imprisoned. The small fry have paid their fines or gone to gaol but the big bosses behind the scenes have not infrequently managed to escape . . . To what end are our seamen facing death night and day to bring in the food necessary to our salvation if such vermin as the Black Market dealers are allowed to wax fat upon this scandalous business?

A letter to the same paper from the Commander-in-Chief, Admiral Sir William James in Portsmouth, commanded people to fight the Battle of the Parasites to the hilt:

> We can win the battle in this part of England and win it quickly if every member of the Naval personnel in the Command, and every

Don't let the SQUANDER BUGS fool YOU!

The Squander Bugs get a good laugh to see money thrown away on needless things. They can't bear money going to help to win the war. They hate to see a bit put by for a rainy day. They like it all squandered and nothing to show for it. Don't let them laugh at *your* expense! `Join a Savings Group and put every penny you can into Savings Certificates!

Savings Certificates cost 15/- and are worth 20/6 in 10 years—increase free of income tax. They can be bought outright, or by instalments with 6d., 2/6 or 5/- Savings Stamps through your Savings Group or Centre or any Post Office or Trustee Savings Bank. Buy now!

man and woman in the Royal Dockyard will from now on consider his or her bounden duty to report to his or her commanding officer when they have evidence that the Parasites are at their filthy work.

But the grinning spivs, the 'wide boys', the barrow boys and the 'wheelers' gradually endeared themselves to the general public. The archetypal spiv wore yellow shoes, a wide-lapelled suit and wide tie, and sported a shifty little trilby pulled rakishly over the forehead. He symbolised a flashy flaunting of authority and petty regulations – especially towards the end of the war when people were long tired of self denial and the many wartime restrictions.

The inconsistent fines inflicted by magistrates only added to the feeling of irritation: a woman was fined twelve shillings for feeding her own bread to birds; workers were sent all the way home from their factories to collect forgotten gas masks; a shopkeeper was fined five pounds for selling homemade sweets out of his own sugar ration; farmers were subject to ludicrous penalties for slaughtering a pig a day late or in the wrong building – even if the kill had been witnessed by the right Inspector.

A mass of petty bureaucratic rules failed to meet the spirit of a people who by 1944 were bursting with resentment. The Defence Regulations dominated daily life – the Home Secretary, from 22 May 1940, had the right to imprison anybody he believed 'likely to endanger the realm'. These regulations, among other things, banned chinks of light in the blackout, wasting of food, talking of your fighting son's whereabouts in public or making inessential journeys, and enforced compulsory check-ups of those suspected of venereal disease. In 1943 187,000 people were found guilty of breaking Defence Regulations. About one in every fifty were found guilty of infringing the lighting regulations, and 300,000 were prosecuted in 1943. In industry 30,000 were prosecuted for breaking regulations, and 12,500 under the Control of Employment Act. In such conditions, which must always have seemed stressful, and sometimes unfair, it was not surprising that some turned all the more readily to the luxury-laden spiv.

One family in Chalk Farm, drawn to the forbidden fruit, remembers 'never going short'. As soon as the air-raid sirens sounded, their uncle was 'off on the loot'. While families abandoned their houses for the safety of the air-raid shelter, pilfering was as easy as robbing a piggy-bank. Their gran often had steak, and no questions asked, while toys and clothes were never a problem, and the booty was always shared with neighbours. A Stepney child, accustomed to a single toy car, remembers dashing home from the air-raid shelter during a lull in the bombing to fetch his cat (although pets were illegal in shelters) and discovering a toyshop blasted open to reveal a wealth of pre-war stock. He set to and collected everything he could, and 'Me and my mates had a good old time in the shelter after that.'

Large depots at docks, stations, canteens and military bases were the most obvious targets for the larger-scale racketeers, who charged exorbitant prices. 2,153 carcases were taken from five ships at the Liverpool docks, and sold for prodigious profits; chocolates changed hands at 2s 4d above their legally enforced price: fifty pound's worth of sugar sold for £162; a bunch of grapes could cost as much as a guinea; a 6d cigar would find a buyer prepared to pay 5s.

In 1941, the year that one man in a hundred went absent without leave from the Forces, the crime figures rose steeply and £200,000 worth of merchandise was stolen from the Great Western Railway (GWR), £160,000 worth from the Southern Railway, £300,000 from the London & North Eastern Railway (LNER) and more than £500,000 from the London, Midland & Scottish (LMS). *War Illustrated*, however, defended the railwaymen: 'It must be remembered that the railways have been largely denuded of their permanent, fully responsible staff, and have had to employ a number of temporary hands.'

As supplies dwindled and people's patience began to wear thin, it became increasingly common to turn a blind eye to some regulation or other, and much more or less innocent bartering went on. A Cambridge baker's wife saved a few bags of flour for the shoe-shop next door in exchange for children's footwear, and a farmer's wife happily wrung a hen's neck in her blacked-out barn in return for sugar and tea from the grocer she supplied with eggs.

The line between legal and illegal dealings was often a thin one. By 1945 people needed a respite, or at least a glimpse of a world without stress, overtime and shortages. Towards the end of the war 9 per cent of the London war crime figures were attributed to a dispirited band of soldiers absent without leave, and deserters. By October 1944 there were approximately 80,000 such men with no jobs to go to, forced to make a living on the side – a situation made even worse as the war entered what was to be its final year and the official demobilisation programme went into operation. And this situation continued after the war ended. Between 1945 and 1950 the crime wave, born of disillusionment, unemployment and frustration, rose staggeringly as not only did wartime restrictions continue but even bread and potatoes were added to the list of rationed foods.

GIs *stocking up on glossy, sellophaned packets of cigarettes and sweets, in very short supply in the Britain outside their barracks.*

13. Crossing the ocean doesn't make you a hero

THE GIs

During the first months of war, Mass Observation reported a marked change in people's evening activities. Although no bombs fell, the nation stayed at home, reading, listening to the wireless, playing card games, writing and smoking, and going to bed early. Visiting friends was made difficult by unreliable transport; dancing, cinema and theatre-going and attending meetings ceased until December when they were allowed to reopen.

> We learned to sit out an alert unless the 'roof spotter' gave the alarm and projection ceased. Films like 'Mrs Miniver' helped – our critical faculties did not function over much when we could 'escape' in this way. By watching the 'ordinary woman' we became heroic by accident.

By December 1939 a jazz song announced, 'There's no place like Home, but we see too much of it now'. Enforced home life for women especially was one of the hardest changes to get accustomed to at a period in history when theatre and cinema-going as well as dances were all the rage. A young Liverpool typist thought the circumstances of war had altered her leisure time more than the actual blackout.

> The absence of friends on active service has made more difference to me. I intended to play badminton this winter, but of course the club has been disbanded. I would have played tennis but that's been closed down too. I used to go to the Playhouse and theatre a lot with friends, but so many of them are now away.

With the pattern of leisure so drastically changed, mothers concentrated on new family pastimes. Many regretted their children's evacuation and recalled them, preferring to paint the walls of their Anderson shelter or cellar together during air raids to being separated. Some families made the most of their blacked-out windows, painting or embroidering moonlit scenes, or. autographing them. Others in hostels and grim billets painted imaginary curtains and wallpaper on empty walls to lend a cheery impression to their surroundings. Some lit candles as far from the window as possible in order to keep curtains open while still managing to avoid fines during the blackout. Neighbours shared heat and light, following government advice that it was better to have one room (the kitchen if possible, to make the most of oven heat) really warm and bright for two families than for each household to make its own depressing economies. Families accordingly took it in turns to share the comforts of each other's company and kitchens, often contributing a few pieces of coal or wood to the other's fire.

And there was the comfort of the wireless. A Croydon woman with two small children recalls:

> New sets soon became unobtainable and used ones fetched high prices. Charles Hill (now Lord) and Mabel Constanduros did a good job of uplift with the 'Radio Doctor' and 'Kitchen Front' programmes, as did Jack Warner, ITMA and many information programmes. A sort of lifeline was kept with the outside world – a world of rumours – by the 'Forces Favourites' (Jean Metcalfe and Cliff Michelmore being especially popular). Vera Lynn could generally be relied upon for tearful relief and I recall some annoyance when the siren put an end to our reception of 'Hamlet' (with I believe John Gielgud) when broadcasting stopped because we were told 'that enemy planes could travel on our sound waves'!! Nobody was terribly interested in tragedy or even in heroic war films, preferring a distraction to their own thoughts.

A sad song was sung at the time:

Saturday night is the loneliest night in the week,
'Cos that's the night my sweetie and I used to dance cheek
   to cheek.
I don't mind Sunday night at all,
'Cos that's the night friends come to call,
And Monday to Friday go fast and another week is past,
But Saturday night is the loneliest night in the week . . .

Until I hear you at the door
Until you're in my arms once more
Saturday night is the loneliest night in the week.

Gradually a minority of young married women, saddened, worried and depressed by their husbands' absence, joined the swelling ranks of young girls at dances and 'hops'. At first they danced with each other, or with trusty civilian acquaintances, but by early 1942 their partners included the more glamorous Australian, New Zealand and Canadian troops. It was in this, the third year of war, that the strain on marriages was found to be the greatest, and many foundered. Uniforms represented forgotten colour, glamour and status, much resented by the civilian male population, struggling with far lower wages and increasingly dowdy clothes. 'Over-sexed, over-paid and over here,' was their only comment on their American rivals.

The new songs from America were jazzy, seductive and abandoned. The uniformed men positively sparkled. The GIS were so smart that many people found officers and men indistinguishable unless they were familiar with rank markings. By 1944, 1,421,000 Allied troops were accommodated in Britain, the vast majority American.

French sailors, Dutch police, the Dominion air forces, the Russians, the Poles and the Chinese Navy as well as British uniforms all glittered at NAAFI dances, clubs, village halls or improvised ballrooms, casting British civilian men into careworn shadow.

There was rivalry between uniforms, as a former Land Girl Ann Waugh recalled at an 'old girls' reunion' at the Albert Hall in 1977.

> We had great times with the GIS as the WLA were more popular with them than the ATS or WAAF girls especially when we were lovely and brown and they were insipid at dances. We used to sit segregated with the ATS girls on one side, WAAF the other side and WLA on another side and civvies on yet another. When the dancing started up it was always the WLA on the floor first – naturally – which didn't go down well with the other girls so they took the micky out of us as we had to leave earlier than they did as we only had two late passes a week, one for eleven o'clock and one for twelve o'clock. The rest of the week we had to leave by ten o'clock and when it was announced that we had to go as the truck was waiting for us they would say, 'Come on girls your hot milk is waiting for you,' or 'Oh what a shame you have to get up so early.'

Dance places were improvised in strange quarters. Barns, fire-engine stations, schools, barrack rooms, halls of country houses all drew the local young. These 'hops' were often preferred to the more formal sort of town dance, now on the wane and anyway lacking the elegance of prewar days. The more official dances were held in NAAFI quarters and clubs, among the most popular being the American Red Cross Club with its transatlantic glamour, and the British Welcome Club. These provided accommodation as well as entertainment, and ranks of all nationalities, women as well as men, could relax in their bars and sitting rooms.

Festivities like Thanksgiving or Hallowe'en were obvious occasions for a dance. But the arrival of a new batch of orphans or wounded soldiers in a district was an equally good reason to hold a welcoming party. Precious nylons or silk stockings were the tribute that girls in uniform paid to these

'A careless word, another Cross', was another motto
in this campaign for National Security. Even
husbands and wives were not allowed to discuss
details of work. Stickers on telephones warned 'Think
before you speak.' A similar poster of a naked woman
with an American soldier was issued by the Nazis to
demoralise British men serving abroad.

occasions, taking extra care with their hair; while at fancy dress parties, carefully draped sheets would sparkle with sequins for an evening of styles ranging from Roman togas to clothing for ghosts.

At the more stylish dances at American and Canadian bases, girls were regaled with unaccustomed extravagances. Norman Longmate describes how glimpses into storerooms revealed a wealth of brightly coloured stock, all pre-packed and covered in cellophane, which shocked a young WRAF girl, reminded of the paper shortage. Piles of doughnuts, bowls of sugar, mounds of oranges, novelties like peanut butter, salad cream, Coca-Cola and *real* coffee astounded the girls. Fruit and tomato juice flowed freely, much resented by those that knew it was shipped 'over here' by the endangered British Merchant Navy. Some girls not only saved their oranges to take home, but scavenged the peel from others' plates for syrups, marmalades and flavourings. Many were horrified at the waste of delicacies left on GI plates, and, to add insult to injury, GIS were even seen stubbing their cigarettes out on mounds of food. To the British uniformed counterpart, a GI mess meal looked more like a week's rations.

Alcohol was the only commodity in short supply at GI camps, but many Americans were met by glares from British men after tracking down the local pub. The official leaflet for GIS tried to temper their natural reactions:

> Not much whisky is now being drunk. Wartime taxes have shot the price of a bottle up to about $4.50. The British are beer drinkers and can hold it – the beer is now below peacetime strength, but can still make a man's tongue wag at both ends. You will be welcome ... as long you remember one thing. The pub is the 'poor man's club' where the men have come to see friends not strangers.

Further advice warned them about 'shooting off' about lukewarm and watery beer, and after all this the bewildered GI was often surprised to find a serious lack of glasses as well. Small children would bound away to look for drinking vessels, usually jam-jars, in return for the usual candies, with the familiar password to favour, 'Got any gum chum?' Once in possession of both glass and watery drink, there was a further code of conversation to be mastered.

> Don't comment on politics. Don't try to tell the British that America won the last war. NEVER criticise the King or Queen. Don't criticise food, beer or cigarettes. Remember they have been at war since 1939 ... Neither do the British need to be told that their armies lost the first couple of rounds in the present war. Use your head before you sound off, and remember how long the British alone have held Hitler off. If the British look dowdy and badly dressed it is not because they do not like good clothes or know how to wear them. All clothing is rationed. Old clothes are good form.

A new barrage of government propaganda also beset the British. Families were encouraged to befriend GIS with invitations to their homes. The 1942 Ministry of Food pamphlet, *Entertaining the GIs*, reminded women:

> Many GI and Canadian soldiers are spending their first Christmas in the British Isles. Many of our housewives have sons in the Forces and they will know how homesick a soldier can feel far from his home. America is famous for its open-hearted hospitality to strangers. Let us show America that we are hospitable too. Let us all invite a soldier from overseas to share in the festivities.

But even the resulting cosy teatimes surprised both nationalities with the number of cultural differences. In spite of warnings, GIS found lettuce and margarine sandwiches, eggless and fatless cakes, and especially ersatz coffee hard to stomach, while the British housewife often had to plan rigorously to provide even these. When a rather more substantial tea of pilchard fingers, chocolate pinwheels and fruit jelly was proffered by an Exeter woman, she and her daughter watched amazed while three GI friends placed a little of each on the same plate and proceeded to eat.

There were many obstacles to understanding – including 'separation by a com-

mon language'.

As late as 1944 a British newspaper continued to offer advice, though very patronisingly, on successful amalgamation with our allies:

Remember:
1. That they are foreigners. Only a small percentage have British forbears.
2. That the similarity between our languages is misleading. Try out the word 'homely' on any American and you will see what I mean.
3. That they are all young in spirit as well as body, and that the mistakes they make are likely to spring from too quick enthusiasm and too little 'background'.
4. That though we may be spiritually far more civilised, materially they have the advantage. They know the value of comfort, we don't.
5. That they are no more superior to us than we are to them . . .
6. That like all children they are very sensitive. They mistake our British reticence and reserve for the cold shoulder and positive dislike. They come from a land where everybody knows everybody and everybody entertains everybody at sight. The contrast makes us seem unfriendly.

Americans over here celebrate Mothers' Day at the Salvation Army Anglo-American Services Club at Dunmow, Essex. Not having their own mothers in Britain, they had to fête adopted British mothers who had sons in the forces. American soldier sons had tea and a concert with their 'mothers' who also received a bunch of flowers.

Next page: Red Cross workers and GIs enjoy their free time on the Serpentine.

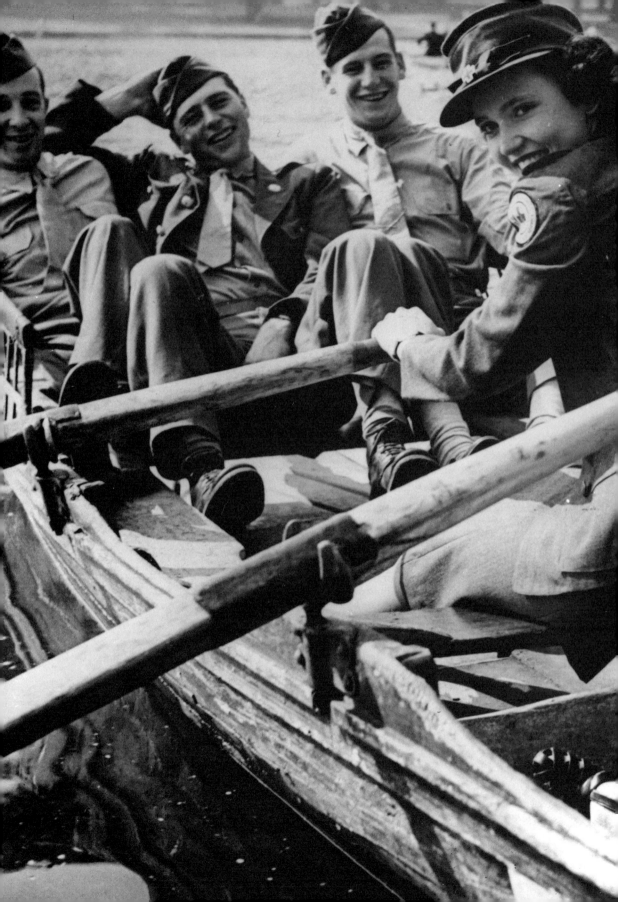

On the Kitchen Front the tone was a little more positive. Ministry of Food pamphlets for the housewife attempted to stretch the wartime ration into almost impossible recipes for coleslaw, waffles (more an ersatz sort of muffin), mussel (instead of clam) chowder, chilli sauce and milk shakes. Mock hamburger steaks (containing two-thirds potato), GI tripe, Allied Salad and Beano Mac Roosevelt were among the delicacies regarded as suitable for a visiting GI.

The Americans in their turn were advised to be careful:

> The British will welcome you as friends and allies. But remember that crossing the ocean doesn't automatically make you a hero. There are housewives in aprons and youngsters in knee-pants in Britain who have lived through more high-explosives in air-raids than many soldiers saw in first-class barrages in the last war . . . If you are invited into a British home and the host exhorts you to 'Eat up – there is plenty on the table', go easy. It may be the family ration for a whole week spread out to show their hospitality. You are coming to Britain from a country where your home is still safe, food is still plentiful and lights are still burning . . . Remember that the British soldiers and civilians have been living under tremendous strain. It is always impolite to criticise your hosts. It is militarily stupid to insult your allies.

Once GIS and Canadian troops fully understood the extent of rationing, some mistakenly refused to accept their hostesses' meals, but most responded with lavish generosity. One young girl, the daughter of an absent serviceman from a part of Lincolnshire 'littered with aerodromes', remembers never having to eat margarine, and enjoying the large boxes of candy given to her mother. Her grandmother, however, thought it shameful of her daughter to accept so much in the way of food and presents, and gave away many of the gifts. The young mother, employed at a munitions factory and typical of many young women, was never too tired to follow government advice and entertain the GIS, usually for tea with the delighted children.

Another girl from Hull remembers the fun of sitting on GIS' laps and being fed with unforgettable sweets. She remembers her mother making pretty underclothes and negligees from parachute silk to replace her severely rationed quota of Utility undergarments. She also remembers a very happy christening by the American chaplain after her mother had had a GI's child. The baby was brought up by the grandmother, as was often the custom.

A Devon boy received a bicycle from a group of local GIS his mother had made welcome. More commonly, any GI with access to the storeroom would bring large tins of corned beef, soup, pats of butter, grapefruit, bananas, dried fruit or unfamiliar American cigarettes, as well as soap, not only scented but wrapped. Occasionally they left their uniforms behind. One woman remembers her brother continually parading in a GI friend's forgotten uniform, 'to draw in the local talent'. Gradually the British, especially the women, became familiar with the land of electric razors, ice boxes, central heating and good plumbing – as much through films as through meeting the glamorous, well-pressed creatures themselves.

It was not all glamour. With the GIS came experiences of racism and segregation. British women were warned, on posters, that their friendliness towards black soldiers might easily be misinterpreted. The black GIS themselves often needed much persuasion to desegregate themselves, hesitant to share buses, pavements and cafés with whites. At American camps segregation was constantly enforced and consequences were harsh if they dared to mix with whites outside. Norman Longmate records a New Year's Eve dance at a black American base recalled by an Ipswich WVS member.

> No alcohol was allowed, so we had plenty of food. You talked and danced but were not allowed to leave the hall unless you were accompanied by another of the guests. All around the wall, while Military Police stood watching, there was a jazz band . . . When it was time to leave at twelve we were packed into the lorries. Of course our companions

wanted to see us go and that was the start of the trouble. The MP beat the boys unmercifully, so that any pleasure we may have had at the party was spoilt for us all.

Once in the freezing lorries, the girls had to persuade the shaken men to share their blankets and were humbly thanked. The women vowed never to go to another party run by or for Americans.

The language of Hollywood became a permanent part of British vocabulary. 'Snacks' replaced 'elevenses', children became 'kids', 'honey' became a form of endearment and girls said 'OK' to 'dates' with 'swell guys'. The Yanks, on the other hand, struggled with the technicalities of their explanatory handbooks:

> The top of the car is the hood. What we call the hood (of the engine) is the bonnet. The fenders are wings . . . A wrench is a spanner. Gas is petrol – if there is any . . . You will have to ask for sock suspenders to get garters and for braces instead of suspenders, if you need any. If you are standing in line to buy (book) a railroad ticket or a seat at the movies (cinema), you will be queuing (pron. cueing) up.

Americans adapted themselves quickly to the odd licensing hours, familiarised themselves with 'the impossible' £.s.d. system, with chemists instead of drugstores, flats instead of apartments, the oddities of football and cricket, and quiet Sundays advisedly to be spent in the country without disturbing church services, and learned not to say 'bum' or 'bloody' in British hearing. British reserve was explained to them in this way:

> With 45 million people living on a small crowded island, each man learns to guard his privacy carefully. Britain may look a little shopworn and grimy to you. The British people are anxious to have you know that you are not seeing their country at its best . . . the houses haven't been painted because factories aren't making paint, they're making planes. The famous English gardens and parks are either unkempt – there are no men to take care of them – or they are being used to grow vegetables. British taxi cabs look antique because Britain makes tanks for herself *and* Russia and hasn't time to make

Anglo-American Club Hallowe'en party 1944, given by the YWCA *in High Wycombe. Many met future wives and husbands at this club, and some held their wedding receptions here.*

new cars. British trains are cold because the power is needed for industry. There are no luxury dining cars because the war effort has no place for such frills. The trains are unwashed and grimy because men and women are needed for more important work.

There could be no denying that the GI became the very symbol of all that was glamorous. Many of the GIS themselves found it an attractive proposition to live up to the widely held view that they were brash, charming, generous and sexy. They were, after all, several thousand miles away from their own families, wives, and girl friends. They were also, in British terms, fabulously wealthy. A lower paid black GI would earn £15 a month, compared with the British private's 15s a week (the married ones would get 7s deducted for their wives). The young adventurous GI could certainly have some fun on his foreign posting to a country where the young women were beginning to feel sorely deprived of such a luxury. Besides, the GI was an ally – the fun and friendships almost had the government's stamp of approval.

A Land Girl in Worcestershire has a vivid memory of her group being wooed by a circling helicopter out of which parachuted several GIS who dropped in to make dates – much to the farmer's irritation. Another time the American soldiers flamboyantly tossed them two crates of grapefruit from their lorries over the hedge. Their style was appreciated as much as the forbidden fruit.

Mothers on trains were offered boxes of candies and watched in amazement as yet more were thrown out of the windows to waving, sweet-deprived children. One woman recalls how, as a ten-year-old child living at Chalk Farm in London, her schooling was non-existent, due to evacuation and the lack of teachers. Instead she spent hours with friends waving at passing trains in the hope of catching sweets. She was usually successful. It was by this method too that many children got to taste their first banana. The GIS found that such cheerful, often rough-and-ready gallantries were an easy way to the hearts of the British.

As in the country, London girls trekked long distances in as much finery as they could muster, suffering the inconveniences of slow and restricted travel on bus or underground for the bright lights of the Hammersmith Palais or the Paramount at Tottenham Court Road, to enjoy the Blackout Stomp and learn the latest jive steps. Formerly quiet provincial towns, now garrisoned, jitterbugged and tangoed into life, mostly to gramophone records at the smaller hops, with a huge surplus of partners – until the military units were posted overseas, leaving young women dancing with each other or with young civilian boys.

Even long hours in factories for women unaccustomed to manual labour were no deterrent. At a Hereford factory, Norman Longmate records, the office became a

beauty parlour until the coach arrived straight after work to take the girls to dances. 'We washed our hair at lunchtime, set it in steel clips, then all afternoon in the office we covered our heads with scarves made into the turban style and several people went to have their eyebrows plucked by colleagues, or painted their nails.'

Rumours preceded the GIS to remoter districts – that they would bring babies as well as nylons, that shop entrances would be littered with their official quota of contraceptives, and that venereal disease would spread like wildfire. But, quite apart from the 80,000 GI brides, memories seem to be of warm hearts and exuberant gestures. 'Good clean fun' is how a young woman scientist in London remembers the excitement:

So many nice lads – Norwegian, Polish, Canadian and of course the GIS. We all made dates that we could never possibly keep, and had the time of our lives, never expecting the war could be such fun. There was no question of settling down with anyone, just the sheer enjoyment of dancing with soldiers of different nationalities in different styles. We re-cut our mothers' dance dresses, wore as much make-up as we could, and loved every minute.

Nous t'aimons
et pensons sans cesse à toi.

0.506.G

A typical postcard sent to their families from men serving in France.

14. Airgraphs get priority

It is a well known fact that during a war the pressure of daily life brings this question [of sex] very much to the fore. Emotions are churned up, dramatic situations arise in all directions, and, between men and women, these emotions are often stronger because they are deprived of their normal outlets. Many men and women under the strain of war conditions and in spite of their ordinary . . . rule of rectitude, find they have become involved in a situation in which normally they would never have been entangled.

For many married couples, the normal securities of living together disappeared in wartime. Couples planning their futures were forcibly separated, and often from their children too. Sometimes their homes disappeared, either through bombing or because the wife could no longer afford to run it on insufficient wages and had to take cheaper lodgings. Women who joined the services often let their homes, uncertain whether they would remain intact. The fundamental structure of many lives was badly disturbed, however hard people strove to maintain a superficial sense of normality.

With occupations, family and surroundings all changed, normal patterns of behaviour often changed greatly. And the further removed from the familiar routines, the more extreme was the reaction. With husbands and wives subjected to long periods of separation, there was a good deal of strain. Even well-established marriages were severely tested. Apart from anxiety for the safety of their spouse, there was much room for misunderstanding in letters. A military psychiatrist, H.B. Craigie, wrote in July 1944 of his men in the Middle East: 'The very great importance of regular and reasonably rapid mail services was in constant evidence – delay, irregularities or non-arrival of mail were potent causes of anxiety and depression even in the most stable personalities.'

The same was true of their wives. The government ensured a quick, reliable postal service including an official form on which men were allowed to tick 'well', 'wounded but getting better', 'will write soon', etc. But many people had left school at the age of fourteen with little literary ability, and clumsy letters could lead to misunderstanding and suspicion. Although it was always tacitly understood that men befriended girls on leave, complete wifely fidelity was a necessity for most fighting men. Suspicion bred suspicion.

According to *Patterns of Marriage*, marriage bonds, if they were going to break, did so usually during the third year of absence. The brief leaves were often not enough to prevent the break-up. Couples often met as strangers, in unfamiliar surroundings and with personalities changed by their experiences. A special army welfare service dealt with soldiers' domestic problems, usually with the help of probation officers. One found adultery proved in 50 cases out of 171 he handled, and suspected it to be more. 'From all over the world came letters of enquiry and requests for help from the men and women themselves, or their commanding officers. "What about my wife?" "What about this man's home?" "Please reply, please enquire, urgent".' They were all urgent, and they were all treated as such. An officer from the Thames Police Court wrote in 1946:

Many excellent young mothers have been unable to stand the loneliness at home, particularly when their husbands are abroad, with not even spasmodic leave to break the monotony . . . Hasty war marriages, on embarkation leave, sometimes between com-

175

parative strangers with a few days or weeks of married life, have left both parties with little sense of responsibility or obligation towards one another.

With so many young men between the ages of 19 and 40 posted away, and the gap filled by millions of non-British troops (1,421,363 just before D-Day), relationships, as everything else, were improvised. Many isolated or uprooted women were encouraged away from their wireless sets and dutiful knitting on long dark evenings by organised get-togethers to maintain morale. Adolescent girls and lonely women found in these new situations that they had unsuspected appeal.

In an atmosphere of instability and uncertainty, people sometimes reacted uncharacteristically. Whereas some would become withdrawn and depressed by the news, for example, of a husband's death, others might react with a desperately care-free attitude, and temporarily lose any sense of responsibility. *Living Together Again* (written in 1946 to try and present the array of problems that families might have to face after the war) explained: 'The dangers and excitement of war often stimulate these [sexual] instincts and inflate them to quite an abnormal extent. Add to this the general loosening up of restraints due to the idea that if one does not take one's chances when one can, one may never have them again, and the stage is set for many mistakes.'

Women had no option but to concentrate on their patriotic duties, but men in the services were often unaware of the tedious and tiring work done by their women, since it was 'unpatriotic' to write anything to the men which might upset them. And however patriotic the war nursery or factory bench, many still found it dull and unsatisfying, although it was undertaken gladly to 'help the men'. *Living Together Again* described the woman's position:

The wife, unexpectedly left with all responsibility and anxious about her husband, feels forlorn and solitary. It is quite natural that she should draw nearer to her friends and maybe her husband's friends. Without any

These women are all wearing the same dress. Altogether it was worn seven times during the war.

Bride and bridesmaids. Note the simple civilian clothes jazzed up with frothy hats.

All these dresses were made from net curtains for a Plymouth wedding in 1941.

conscious desire or intention on her part . . . she finds herself looking forward to his visits. She saves up her problems and difficulties to discuss with him . . . She is sensitive to her man friend's sympathetic touch upon all her interests and problems . . . Very often the woman and man find they have, for the first time in their lives, really fallen in love.

The men who were posted long enough to form real friendships, and the Americans in particular, were, a girl in the WRNS remembers, usually also devoted to their wives and families. In general, both married and unmarried men posted away preferred a loyal friendship with one girl, akin to the one they were missing, to many casual relationships. One of the GI songs recalled by a WAAF girl suggests this loyalty:

My wife's a corker
She's a New Yorker
I buy her everything to keep her in style
She's got a pair of legs
Just like two whiskey kegs
Hot dogs, that's where my money goes

For unmarried women, thrust into hostel or lodging, the search for friendship and contact was equally necessary. Railway stations were full of separating young couples wondering whether they would ever meet again, and if they did, whether it would be as strangers. Sometimes this 'last dance' behaviour was strongly criticised. A girl at Bomber Command resented the reputation that prudish women held against them. 'They seemed to think that uniforms represented grimy morals, though it was far from true. Girls were called up from the age of eighteen, many practising Christians, and although no one could say that hostel life was anything but an eye-opener for the innocent, the pre-war sense of morality and respectability prevailed.' The girls in a WRAF camp near Newcastle were 'all for having a good time and meeting as many men as possible, but we all disapproved of any girl who went 'too far'.' One girl at the camp got married and just had time for a short honeymoon before her husband was posted abroad. Her friends were horrified when she had too much to drink at a NAAFI

dance and was found 'lying on the ground outside with another man', and gave her 'a good ticking-off'.

As the six-year war escalated, its tensions bound groups together – the only way to survive was by 'carrying on as usual' with tenacity, humour and kindness. Personal lives were more exposed in shelters, lodgings and the services, and further shared by a common and dreadful experience. The odd mixture of liberty and discipline that women coped with, combined with widespread sexual ignorance, was bound to lead to pregnancies, although sexual innocence and virginity before marriage were still held to be desirable. But women and men were often thrown, literally, into each other's arms: they were squashed into shelters, tackled anti-aircraft guns together, dug out friends from debris, clutched each other in the blackout, or simply enjoyed a dance together, possibly after years of self-denial.

At a period when sexual myths flourished, it was rumoured that you should never get into the bathwater after your brother or father since doing so could make you pregnant. Sitting on a man's lap could produce the same result. It was very difficult to find intelligent and straightforward information on sex, or indeed on bodily functions. The authors of *Our Towns 1939–42* discovered serious taboos surrounding menstruation. It was believed that butter would not set if churned by a menstruating woman, she should not touch meat in a pickle tub, and should not take baths or exercise. Menstruating women were refused the Pilot's B Certificate for flying on the grounds that they would be too incompetent to be trusted with the lives of passengers. The authors suggested that 'in the name of sense and humanity', sensible sex education on all functions of the body was an essential part of preparation for life. The moral atmosphere at the time was such that several national newspapers refused to publish the Ministry of Health's anti-disease campaign pleading 'Please wash your hands after using the WC'.

Although contraception had become more available during the inter-war period, there was still appalling ignorance and the subject was surrounded by myths and prudery. Although in the 1930s some birth control clinics were in existence, the Ministry of Health supported them only with reluctance, in cases where pregnancy was dangerous to a woman's health. Family doctors quite often advised women not to have any children, but without actually giving them any advice as to how to prevent it. But in popular women's magazines and on the problem pages advice began to be given for the first time on more explicit marital problems. The cinema and wireless too inadvertently advertised birth control clinics like Marie Stopes's by at least discussing their controversial existence.

A young actress from Leeds remembers looking with friends for 'the sort of books, you know, the word 'sex' wasn't *ever* mentioned' in order to find out more about the subject. 'None of us really had any idea about how our bodies worked. The first period was a dreadful shock for most of us, and of course in those days we used rags that had to be washed out. I didn't even *hear* about sanitary towels until I joined the WRNS.' On finding a 'seedy bookshop' at last, she described the information that she and her friends were able to share.

> One described a sort of Dutch cap you could improvise by soaking a bath sponge in oil, or was it vinegar? That would have stung anyway, and then inserting it. Another book explained how to fake virginity on your wedding night by getting a small bladder from the butcher, filling it with blood and inserting it! Just imagine . . . but really, there was no one else to turn to.

The state wanted no part in dealing with the 'distasteful subject' of contraception until the rubber supply from Japan was cut off in 1943. It was almost a year before the shortage improved, and then the demand was for rubber teats, prams, wheels and wellington boots. But pressure from the birth control clinics, as well as the very obvious problems

of illegitimacy, forced the government to face the problem.

The Directorate of Medical Supplies, the Rubber Control and the Board of Trade argued. The Rubber Control had believed there to be a surplus of rubber in 1942, and had cut allocations to manufacturers without taking advice on the state of the contraceptive market (or indeed the increased need for rubber teats if mothers were working). 'At one stage the Rubber Control cut off all supplies for the manufacture of those appliances that were used purely for contraceptive purposes, and not as preventatives against VD.' In other words, rubber was supplied, not to prevent women's pregnancies, but to protect men from venereal disease, particularly those in the Forces where rubber sheaths were issued as a matter of course. At last the chief medical officer for the Ministry of Health took a more positive line and declared that 'On social and medical grounds a shortage of any of the main types of rubber contraceptives was most undesirable.'

As in the First World War, the high statistics for both syphilis and gonorrhoea shocked the government. In 1941 it was calculated that syphilis infection for women had risen by 63 per cent and for men, both civilian and servicemen, by 113 per cent. By 1943, with the incidence of venereal disease 139 per cent higher than in 1939, the government was propelled into action with a vigorous propaganda campaign.

A new Defence Regulation 33B impelled any person suspected of infecting more than two people to undergo treatment, while taboos were lifted and the subject was debated in Parliament. Posters warned men about 'easy girls', and women of sterility and dangers to unborn children. The Ministry of Health and the Central Council of Health mounted the campaign, and the Chief Medical Officer for the Ministry even mentioned the subject in a broadcast in the autumn of 1942. A very real problem among the brief encounters that led to over-hasty marriages was presented in one poster, dark

QUESTIONS ANSWERED

Why are Venereal Diseases a growing menace?

Wartime conditions have brought about an increase in venereal diseases which are spread through free and easy sex relations. Many sufferers put off seeking medical advice and meanwhile spread the disease to others.

Why does this problem concern everybody?

Venereal diseases damage the nation's health, threaten the future of the race, cause wasted hours and reduced efficiency in the factories and Services. They are highly contagious. Husbands infect wives (and vice versa) and the infection may be passed on to unborn children, condemning them to a life of misery and ill-health.

Can Venereal Diseases "just happen?"

No. They are caused by germs which cannot grow in the human body of their own accord. Usually they enter the body during intercourse with an infected person.

What are the Danger Signals?

Syphilis first appears as a small ulcer on or near the reproductive organs from 10 to 90 days after infection; usually 21 days. The first sign of gonorrhœa is a discharge from the reproductive organs 2 to 10 days after infection.

hands outstretched to receive the unsuspecting bride:

> Here comes the bride.
> A man suffering from venereal disease who infects his wife commits a vile crime against her and her children yet unborn.
> Treatment is free and confidential.

Another poster showed a skull in a frothy pink hat inviting the kiss of death. 'The "easy girlfriend" spreads syphilis and gonorrhoea, which *unless properly treated* may result in blindness, insanity, paralysis, premature death. If you run the risk, get skilled treatment at once.' A woman scientist remembers the procedure very well. Taxi drivers and prostitutes worked together, so that any man who jumped into a taxi would be propositioned and shown a 'clean bill of health', the official seal of approval. If, during her check-ups, the woman was found to have a venereal disease, the scientist recalls that it was quite usual for the doctor to insert some purple potassium permanganate so that the colour would be an evident sign to any man she went to bed with.

Between 1939 and 1940, in a record marriage boom, 22.5 people per thousand got married. This fell to 14 per thousand in 1943 and rose to 18.7 in 1945. Three out of ten brides were under twenty-one, reflecting not only a peacetime trend, but also the 'last dance' atmosphere of a population facing war. The birthrate for married women actually fell, probably because of a new awareness of contraception among the young, as well as the obvious absence of their husbands.

Richard Titmuss suggests a 'parents' revolt' in his book of the same name, a sense of disillusionment with a failing capitalist system at war. He calculated the falling birth rate of 1940 to be 25 per cent lower than replacement level. Between Dunkirk in June 1940 and the end of the Blitz, the most threatening period of the war, he reckoned the number of conceptions to be the lowest ever recorded, at 13.9 per thousand of the population. But by 1942, however, the birth rate had shot up to the highest number recorded for eleven years, to 15.6 per thousand. The numbers continued to rise: 16.2 in 1943, 17.9 in 1944, a halt in 1945 just before demobilisation, and up to 20.6 per thousand in 1947.

Why did women have more children after 1942? Pregnancy was described as 'the prevailing disease' at the time. Loneliness might have been a factor, as well as the breakdown of home life and a need to restore it. And pregnant women had a new status. Apart from the green ration book and extra rations for nursing mothers and small children (often more useful for the rest of the family than for the baby), women with young children were immune from conscription, which was a serious fear for some. A popular song, sung at the YMCA Anglo-American clubs, suggests the continuation of a relationship with a man by having his child:

Oh give me something to remember you by
When you are far away from me,
Some little something little something
When you are far across the sea.

The experiences of delivery of these 'little somethings' were as varied as those of the war itself. Some idyllic memories of evacuated married mothers recall spacious and clean nursing homes. Norman Longmate describes the effect of wartime anxieties on breast feeding. Many women were unable to feed their babies with the strain of sirens and air raids, or news of injured relatives. A woman from Purley was delivered prematurely after a holiday with 'soldiers digging trenches on the beaches' and 'explosions on the far side of the Channel', while news of her soldier husband's and her mother's injuries in March 1941 'prevented me from feeding her any more and I had to put her on to artificial food at once'. Three years later another child was delivered to the sound of falling shrapnel, 'and I had to wean him at four months owing to exhaustion on my part'.

Other women describe stillbirths. A Newcastle woman, hearing a siren 'leapt out of bed to save my daughter and brought

Every night London's Underground stations are crowded with people seeking shelter.

Hitler's enemies. A bombed out child and his foster mother look at the ruins of their home.

a miscarriage'. Others were delivered by doctors still wearing their helmets after rushing to the delivery ward from tending street casualties. One woman, after longing for a baby for sixteen years, spoke highly of

> the Wandsworth Borough Maternity Home where my first son was stillborn, an extended breech baby, after a seventy-eight-hour labour. Two of these three nights were spent in shelters at the Maternity Hospital with intense bombing and fireraids etc. We had a number of carryings out to the shelter... strapped to our mattresses like corpses ready for burial at sea... The straps always lay ready across the bed springs under the mattresses so that we only had to fold our arms under the covers, get strapped up and away we went.

Mothers were full of praise for nurses and doctors. A London woman remembers the sister regularly mounting a small metal staircase to sweep incendiary bombs off the roof, while the ambulance attendants drove through air-raids to hospitals, and doctors and midwives braved raids to reach mothers who were then delivered by torch or candle-light.

The attitude to illegitimate birth, however, was far less tolerant, and statistics illustrate the grim ordeal faced by many young mothers. Illegitimacy was paramount to prostitution in the eyes of those brought up by Victorian mothers, and was judged as the depth of shame and moral impurity. The less tolerant of all classes shunned the disgrace of an illegitimate grandchild, and the young mother might have to cope with prejudice on all sides from birth. Family outrage might be overcome by 'giving 'er a good hiding' but never turning their backs on her. Or ingenious stories were woven about adopting long-lost cousins. Many people quite rightly put these pregnancies down to the war, since in normal times many of the conceptions would have been legalised by marriage. Women all over Britain remember it being quite common for the grandparents to bring up the child, while a Lincolnshire child remembers the muddle she used to get into by being obliged to call her mother 'Aunt' in company. They didn't keep the secret for very long after the war, she recalled, and she even remembered a pair of GI trousers in her dressing-up box for many years afterwards.

The illegitimate birthrate almost doubled between 1940 and 1945, rising to an unprecedented 255,460, almost a third of all births, compared with 153,075 in the six years before the war.

			Total maternities conceived out of wedlock		
Year	Illegitimate maternities	Pre-maritally conceived legitimate maternities	Numbers	Per cent of all maternities	Percentage of illegitimate maternities regularised by marriage before birth
1	2	3	4	5	6
1938	28,160	66,221	94,381	14.6	70.2
1939	26,569	60,346	86,915	13.8	69.4
1940	26,574	56,644	83,218	13.7	68.1
1941	32,179	43,362	75,541	12.7	57.4
1942	37,597	40,705	78,302	11.8	52.0
1943	44,881	32,271	82,152	11.8	45.4
1944	56,477	37,746	94,223	12.3	40.1
1945	64,743	38,176	102,919	14.9	37.1
1946	55,138	43,488	98,626	11.8	44.1
1947	47,491	59,633	107,124	12.0	55.7

Legitimate and illegitimate maternities
England and Wales, 1938–1947

Whereas 70 per cent of illegitimate conceptions were regularised before the war, only 37 per cent were in 1945. Hence the high figures for illegitimacy which alarmed the moralists. Whereas before the war (when the importance of virginity was still upheld, at least in public) many women would only have had intercourse with a man they were fairly certain of marrying, brief love affairs and premature engagements, later broken, were bound to occur with so many men in transit. The pre-war habits of courtship broke down completely in wartime, when almost half the men were posted away, with little or no chance of legalising births.

A rare survey was kept in Birmingham. The Public Health Department observed that during the last two years of war, nearly a third of all illegitimate children were born to married women. Of the 520 married women recorded in 1945 who had illegitimate children, 283 had husbands in the Forces, while of the remainder, almost half were widowed, separated or divorced. A further five husbands were prisoners of war. As a married woman's child assumes her husband's name, unless otherwise stated, it is hard to judge the figures, although roughly 50 per cent of children born to married women were judged to be illegitimate during the first half of 1945 in Birmingham. The distress of married women on discovering their pregnancies was all the more acute as the husband's consent was needed for the adoption papers. Between 1934 and 1938, over 26,500 adoption orders were made: between 1940 and 1944, the number was 50,000 with a peak of 21,000 in one year.

Because of the outbreak of war the Adoption of Children (Regulation) Act of 1939 was not enforced in its attempts to restrict adoption advertisements and sending children abroad for adoption. By 1943, with so many illegitimate children, the Press reported a haphazard disposal of babies by word of mouth in public houses and fish queues. Only then did the Ministry of Health and Home Office enforce the Act whereby the welfare authorities should be informed.

For those women who found themselves pregnant, abandoned and unmarried, the appearance of a bulge, concealed for as long as possible, usually resulted in discharge from the service, factory or job where they were employed. Older landladies could not tolerate the 'shame' of lodging an unmarried mother, and would most commonly give her notice to leave. In hostels, women were asked to go as soon as they stopped work, usually about two months before birth. Other women were shunned by their families or were too ashamed to tell them, preferring to manage alone until the child was adopted. The National Insurance scheme at the time gave a small maternity grant of £2 to the wives of employed men (although it excluded the self-employed and the well-paid), with £4 for an employed woman with an insured husband. Otherwise it was necessary to contribute to a hospital saving scheme. The alternatives were hospitals financed by charities or from local rates in voluntary or local authority hospitals.

For the unmarried mother there was little alternative but to continue work for as long as possible or to resume work soon after the birth. Although the Factories and Public Health Act prohibited women's employment within four weeks of childbirth, unsupported women often had to circumvent this rule. Married women with babies found it hard enough to find billets due to the severe housing shortage, and unmarried mothers had even less chance. Relatives likely to foster in normal times were liable to be involved in war work, and the girls themselves were often away from home. War nurseries were crowded, making the possibility of work more difficult.

A complete cross-section of women were affected, of all classes and ages. Many young girls had drifted away from insecure homes, and a surprising number of fourteen- and fifteen-year-old girls, eager for the affectionate attentions of uprooted service-men for whom they seemed to hold a special fascination, became pregnant. In Home Office language 'even a completely plain and unattractive girl stood a chance'. A pro-bation officer's report from London's dock-land in the Home Office survey mentions this age group:

> All that seems to be necessary is for the girl to have a desire to please . . . Those girls who are misfits at home and at work, or who feel in-ferior for some reason or other, have been very easy victims. Their lives were brightened by the attention . . . and they found that they had an outlet which was not only a contrast, but was a definite compensation for the dull-ness, poverty and sometimes unhappiness of their home life.

Many were thought to be semi-prostitutes, some already had venereal disease, some were unequipped to deal with a child. Other women were seriously attached to the men, hoping to marry them. Then there were the lonely servicemen's wives and the 'good-time girls' who had jumped on to the band-wagon of sometimes unusual prosperity with great *joie de vivre*.

For many of these pregnant women the only alternative was abortion – a criminal offence, although in 1939 the Inter-departmental Committee on Abortion had suggested a more humane attitude to un-married mothers after estimating that be-tween 16 per cent and 20 per cent of their pregnancies would end in abortion.

Sometimes the only relief for women who wanted to keep their children was pro-vided by the homes for unmarried mothers. Many were forbidding, prison-like insti-tutions still run very much on workhouse lines, although far-sighted welfare officers were pressing for greater and unprejudiced tolerance. As late as 1950, a survey of eleven assistance institutions revealed that a pro-portion of women had been admitted under section 24 of the Lunacy Act 1890, only because they had illegitimate children, and one woman of forty had been admitted in late adolescence. These women were the only inmates not permitted to take walks

for fear of further pregnancies.

Although the wartime Ministry of Health allowed no official discrimination against unmarried mothers, it was not prepared to 'grant them any favours', such as evacuation, for example, unless they were in the care of a welfare officer. Voluntary homes and mater-nity hospitals had few places, and beds were kept for casualties and evacuees; many unmarried mothers were discharged with-out money or billets. Moral welfare homes preferred to accept girls for a minimum of three months. A Ministry of Health report stated:

> In most of the homes, inmates are required to wear some sort of uniform, at least a coloured overall, or something of the kind; corres-pondence is supervised; attendance at prayers is expected; inmates are not allowed to go out alone and there is a definite restriction on 'comings and goings'; help in the routine household duties is required according to the health and capabilities of the individual. Mis-understanding on the question of these sim-ple rules . . . which vary in different homes, but are always to be found in some degree or other, leads to trouble, and it is most im-portant that any unmarried expectant mother who is to be transferred to such a home should know something of what is to be expected of her.

Furthermore, only the public assistance in-stitutions and the Salvation Army hostels would accept women expecting subse-quent illegitimate babies.

This was the atmosphere that unmarried mothers faced during the war. Those with a new, independent spirit, bearing their child-ren and facing hardship openly, surprised the authorities. For the first time, some unmar-ried mothers refused to be cowed by the shame inflicted on them by society, and were determined to avoid the homes at all costs. Parallel to this, though also in a minority, was a new breed of social worker, attempting for the first time to help women understand their pregnancy, prepare for the birth, and find lodgings, nurseries, work and independence.

And sometimes public opinion was more sympathetic, as in the kindly tone of one

WOMEN

please lend your support a little longer…

let's work together for

PROSPERITY

ENQUIRE ABOUT JOBS AVAILABLE NOW AT YOUR NEAREST EMPLOYMENT EXCHANGE

popular song, remembered by an ATS girl:

Round and round the park she pushed a perambulator,
She pushed it in the springtime and in the month of May.
And if you asked her, why the hell she pushed it,
She pushed it for a sailor/soldier/airman,
Who is far, far away,
Far away. Far away.
She pushed it for a sailor/soldier/airman,
Who is far, far away.

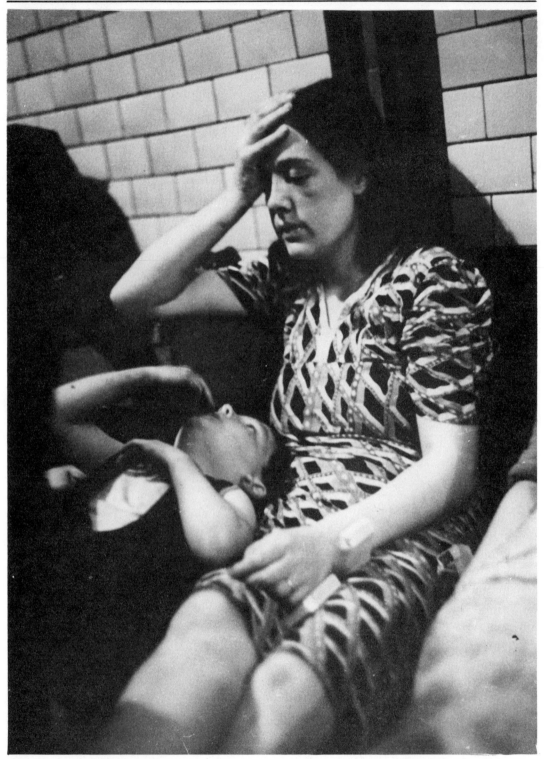

Nerve tonics, aspirins and bedtime drinks were all heralded as the best way to get through sleepless nights. By the end of the war, the message had worn thin.

15. Living together again

During the first three years of war more civilians died than soldiers, and nearly half of these 60,595 deaths were in London. For the entire war a low estimate of civilian injuries was 237,000; of these, 86,000 were serious. By 1945 a further 264,000 members of the armed forces (women as well as men) had been killed, leaving grieving families all over the world.

Numbers of British Civilian Deaths from Enemy Action

Year	London	Elsewhere	Total
1940	13,596	10,171	23,767
1941	6,487	13,431	19,918
1942	27	3,209	3,236

Medical books advised nurses and doctors on psychological disturbances in wartime. In 'War Wounds and Air-Raid Casualties', published in 1939 in the British Medical Journal, Maurice Wright, MD, wrote:

> It is recognised that the psychiatric casualties of the present war ... may have even more far-reaching effects than physical casualties, loss of life or material destruction. It is a problem that everyone in our large towns is having to face – not so much 'Shall I be killed or injured?' but 'Can I face it? Shall I break down? Shall I keep sane or normal under the conditions I may have to endure ...?' It is impossible to estimate with any certainty the number of psychiatric casualties that will have to be dealt with if any civilian population is exposed to frequent intense or unexpected aerial bombardment.

Doctors were advised on the best ways to deal with panic and hysteria, the worst cases, if 'infectious', to be removed to hospital. In fact comparatively few 'psychiatric air-raid casualties' were reported, apart from those who had been buried alive or had suffered directly from a blast or a near miss. On the whole it was a matter of honour to keep going and care for others first, and the attitude 'we can take it' often helped people to overcome their anxieties.

But many suppressed their state of shock in order to 'keep going' until the end of the war. Many people who had been buried alive, for example, even for a few hours (and many had to wait beneath the rubble for days) had recurring nightmares, developed phobias or could not bear to go to boxed-in, darkened cinemas for years after: some would fling open doors and windows even during gales. One woman was taken to the doctor by her fiancé because she frequently fainted and suffered a kind of heart attack:

> In the end she reached the consulting room of a psychologist where it was discovered that three years before she had been buried in the debris of a bombed house for many hours. The rest of the inhabitants were killed, but she was rescued, apparently unhurt ... It had been so awful that she had thrown up the strong defence of 'forgetting'. But whenever any emotional upset or memory touched her even slightly she reacted in a subtly convulsive way, affecting the physical heart and causing the pseudo-real fainting-fit.

Others, dazed by the loss of their home or relations, might worry obsessively about a coal delivery, that they would be late for work or that they had to do a neighbour's shopping, such was the need for normality under these conditions.

The effect on the children varied too. Schooling, which might have been a lifeline, was haphazard, to the serious detriment of many children's education. Those in cities and towns where schools had been evacuated suffered the most, wandering about or playing in bomb craters during the day or going to work with their mothers. Many schools were evacuated to large houses or hotels where beds were crammed into dining rooms and desks were nose to nose among an awkward assortment of armchairs in the hotel lounge. Steady routines in these conditions were often out of the question. Teachers might be moved from school to school according to evacuation programmes, while air-raid warnings could make consistent school work impossible. After the war it was found that over half of all junior school children were backward readers.

Absenteeism in what schools there were reflected mothers' dependence on their older children for domestic responsibilities, including care of the youngest members of the family. The pressures and strains that mothers were under were visible in a horrifying rise of accidents in the home during the war. More young children suffocated in their cots or choked to death while eating. Impetigo, lice and scabies increased to epidemic proportions, finally affecting seven million children. More suffered fatal falls or burns, and more children

Hospital for War Nerves.
Therapy took the form of pottery, carpentry, toy making and weaving. 'They learn to think of themselves not only as individuals but as part of a community.' Courses were also run to 'civilianise' institutionalised women in the Services. The home-making course was the most popular.

were drowned than usual, particularly in the huge civic emergency water tanks. Although fewer cars were on the road because of petrol rationing and the hazards of driving in the blackout, more children were knocked down and injured than in peacetime.

Between 1939 and 1941 juvenile delinquency increased by one third in England and Wales, petty thefts rose by 20 per cent and figures for malicious damage by 70 per cent. Some magistrates returned to the unpopular punishment of birching. By the time these children were ready to embark on their post-war National Service, a large proportion of them were dismally uneducated after their years of familial and educational disruption. In Bristol it was found from teachers' reports that psychological disturbance was eight times higher than usual, and particularly among those who stayed in the city during the Blitz rather than in the tunnel shelters on the outskirts – though others seem to have thrived on the excitement. A London nurse in a children's ward described their reactions to distant gunfire, 'dumb through terror, whimpering like a puppy, stiff as a ramrod and mouth open but no screams'.

Children, even those not separated from their mothers, remember the speechless terror with which they listened to the scream of v-1 rockets and the awful silence that meant it was dropping, as well as the even bigger v-2s, which could appear with almost no warning to flatten groups of houses. In an article called 'Children and Death' for the *Guider*, the Girl Guides' Magazine, Margaret Graham explained:

Since September 1939 children . . . have been brought face to face with death in a way probably unprecedented in history. And it is not only in the heavily raided areas that children have to face the problem. Those who are evacuated must constantly ponder the idea, and in fact do, whether they speak of it or not. One child whose mother assured me that the war passed over her head and made no impression on her whatsoever, told me that she dreamed constantly of her mother being killed

in a raid . . . the fear is of the pain and shock which may bring about death, of the terror to be endured from which death alone can bring release. The fear is of suffering rather than dying.

With the possibility of invasion from 1940 onwards children shared the strains of war in their roles of auxiliaries to the Services in the Girl Guides and Boy Scouts. In the Home Emergency Service and with Message Corps work, children were trained to 'absolute punctuality, accuracy, self control and instant response to orders'. They were taught to take messages from 'vague and hysterical' people as well as normal people, to memorise the essentials, in spite of interruptions: 'For instance, it is of little use to remember a message from a village whose telephone lines have been cut, to another, if you have forgotten on arrival the number to which the message is to be telephoned.' Throughout the Blitzes on various towns older children bicycled with urgent messages, sometimes returning with a mangled bike. Young boys willingly involved themselves, so that in the absence of enough lecturers at Osterley Park for the Home Guard, thirteen-year-old Boy Scouts demonstrated the use of trip-wires to dismount and, if possible, kill Nazi motorcyclists.

Mothers, already concerned at their children's involvement, now discovered a leaflet on guerrilla warfare 'to be left at the post office'. The instructions must have been surprising for the unsuspecting person queueing for stamps:

The enemy is bound to confiscate and use any private cars that have not been destroyed or disabled. And sometimes he may have a British civilian, male or female, driving him. In Brussels the Germans forced Belgian women to drive their officers' cars (to reduce the likelihood of attack). If you happen to be standing in a ditch or behind a tree or some other position of safety, and you have some kind of grenade or bomb in your hand, and a car comes along with enemy officers, driven even by your best friend, YOU MUST LET THEM HAVE IT. It is what your friend would want you to do.

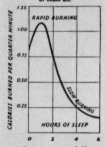

Other leaflets from the Ministry of Information and the County Invasion Committee had titles like: 'If the Invader Comes: What to Do and How to Do It', 'If Your House is Bombed', 'It Might be You', 'After the Raid', and 'Denial of Resources to the Enemy', which announced that all bicycles, cars and lorries should be sabotaged, all maps should be burnt, and petrol and transport refused. However, much of this advice was considered by women as 'just so much red tape', since no emergency ever went according to rule and in the worst crises even reassuring regulations could not help.

After the war came the problems of accustoming children subjected to the strains of separation or the unnatural demands of wartime existence to normal family life again. Children who had been evacuated began to imagine life with their parents as a permanent party, full of treats. Their homecoming was often a severe disappointment, as parents too had to readjust to the daily routine of school hours and bedtime, and they picked up the remaining pieces of family and home life with a wary eye on the grim future that held little promise. Then too there were siblings of the 'wartime bulge' to be presented to the newly returned children, and whose birth might have left scars in the mother's memory – born in an air-raid perhaps or months after the father's death.

Returning children were confused between their Mum and the 'Auntie' who had looked after them for so long. Mothers were advised to anticipate problematic behaviour to win them back:

It does not just happen. There have been cases where serious problems of behaviour have cropped up, *not* from any wickedness or defect in the child but simply from the shock of being uprooted and planted down again too suddenly... Sleepwalking, night-terrors, a recurrence of bed-wetting, pilfering, playing truant from school and home – all of them have been known to occur as a direct result, as well as the more obvious signs of misery, discontent and loss of appetite... If understanding and sympathy are not enough, help should be sought from the nearest Child Guidance Clinic.

Six years after their first transplantation, children who had been evacuated for the entire war now had to readapt to town life. If they had left at six years old they returned as adolescents. Those who had settled down away from familiar streets to a world of weasels, field mice, cows and carthorses now had to face the extraordinary return to new homes, faces, families and attitudes. 'There are no rabbits in the Old Kent Road, and while a bunch of flowers picked in the country is welcomed and admired, if he picks them in the Battersea Park, he is likely to get a scolding or worse, for stealing.'

As for the effects of the war on the women themselves, a London woman described it as 'a sort of dreadful guessing game, without rules, rhyme or reason. It was always the woman who suffered, always working or waiting. Husbands were often silent and, afraid of writing too much, wrote practically nothing. They were inhibited, too, by the knowledge that their letters would be censored, and spelling was often very strange.' Six years of war work, often with sleepless nights in shelters and, as more homes were bombed, with shared accommodation and no real family life, left women exhausted.

> Having to live in a small space hemmed in by other people is another cause of things going wrong in the home . . . It is not only that working, housework and washing have to be

Changing Face!
Yesterday it was a block of offices. Today it's a mass of rubble. A man has got to be prepared for changes these days. Thank goodness something is always the same—maybe the grocers' boys couldn't resist helping themselves to a few drops of H.P. Sauce.

These grocer's boys might well have used bicycles to take messages through air raids if other communications were damaged. Stories abound of children returning with mangled bikes. Girl Guides and Scouts were also trained for these emergencies.

Here today, gone tomorrow.
Shopping in Canterbury in June 1942.

191

done under uncomfortable conditions, but the atmosphere gets overcharged, restless, chaotic... Many a tired woman sits down and cries because she feels she cannot live another day in the difficult atmosphere pervading the house; or a weary man blows up in a gust of irritation because 'this house gets on my nerves'.

The juggling of good humour and generosity with danger and tragedy left women longing for the normality of peace. Crime and prostitution were increasing as disillusioned men deserted from the Forces and women tried to earn more money. During a hushed-up spate of murders (mostly for women's purses) in London towards the end of the war, a Red Cross nurse on solitary air-raid missions remembered the blacked out streets and the awful pre-raid silences:

I do not think one was afraid for oneself – better to die as the result of action of a brave foe than at the hands of a greedy petty thief. I would have accepted, almost welcomed a bomb or the shrapnel that so battered and dented my tin hat – I was so tired, so sickened by the sights of sadness, so weary of the noise, the NOISE, in particular the guns, the cold, the disbelief of ever being warm again, the perpetual dark, the sadness of hospitals in dim daylight, of men gurgling through ghastly glass tubes (I never minded the spitoons of the cheerful TB men), of the cheers when brave men (human Germans) hurtled to death in a shot-down aircraft – that I longed for peace. But I wanted it to be a clean death – how egotistical – a grain of sand wanting special treatment.

In the more comforting public atmosphere of the shelters, ARP notices remained encouraging

ARP
(ALL RIGHT PRESENTLY)

Air raid precautions can be fun if we're cheerful – everyone.
Don't be dismal, wear a smile, t'will be quite OK in a while.

But by the end of the war the smiles were wearing thin. Rationing continued. In mid-austerity, with shortages at a peak and rations at their most severe, even whalemeat and the infamous snoek were reluctantly accepted by a dispirited population. The taste of whalemeat was described as similar to 'cod liver oil', 'fishy liver', and 'a meaty biscuit with overtones of oil'. One man observed that even his dogs refused to eat it, though the Ministry of Food was delighted to find that a single Lyons Corner House was serving 600 whale steaks a day. But eventually 4,000 tons of whalemeat lay unwanted in Tyneside warehouses. Snoek was another dubious taste which continued to be inflicted on the public after the war. 'I have never met a snoek', said one Minister, 'so I cannot tell you much about it. It is long and slender and weighs up to eighteen pounds.' It cost 1s 4½d and one coupon point a tin, but by this time the Ministry of Food was infamous for its preference for quantity, not quality, in its choice of food. For a long time the nature of the fish was only surmise. Cartoonists and song-writers were delighted when an even more unpleasant form of salted snoek arrived, inedible except as fish paste. £857,000 were spent on eleven million half-pound tins of snoek. Snoek sandwich spread, snoek pasties, snoek with salad, and 'snoek piquante' were some of the recipes launched by the Ministry. 'Research finally revealed that the snoek was a large ferocious, tropical fish like a barracuda; that it was dangerous to bathers, had rows of fearsome teeth, and when displeased hissed like a snake and barked like a dog.'

Stringent rationing and unpalatable food were not the only rigours suffered by post-war Britain. There were more serious problems. Resistance to illness was low. Simple cases of septicaemia and conjunctivitis were taking weeks to cure. The dismal visions people faced were of bomb craters, wrecked and empty shops, mutilated men and orphanages. In spite of bonfires on V-E day, the war ended with a whimper, as women queued for advice at the Citizens' Advice Bureaux. A glimpse of their day-to-day problems in 1945 is revealed in the records of some of the requests for help.

Mrs W. Has adopted child: Can she get extra clothing coupons?	Yes. Given form CRSC/1.
Mrs F. Regulations about parcels to New Zealand	Advised about regulations.
Miss S. Still worried about poor quality of war damage repairs – house damp and lodger is leaving on this account. (Poor Man's Valuer says house very shoddily built originally)	Explained that Poor Man's Valuer can't help any further. Referred to Poor Man's Lawyer to see if any action possible against builder.
Mrs R. (1) Where to get vaccinated and inoculation against yellow fever? (2) Light job wanted while waiting passage.	Dr P. for inoculation, advised Bureau of Scientific Disease. Will go on our list of child minders.
Mrs P. Having difficulty with daughter-in-law who is waiting for council house. Thinks daughter-in-law is not making sufficient effort.	As daughter-in-law has been repeatedly to us and we have approached council on her behalf, advised that everything possible has been done.
Mr M. Wife has had twins. Home help wanted – two other children.	Will ask Mrs H how soon she will be free and notify him.
Mr D. Returning to rebuilt house. Electricity department are treating him as a new customer and ask 12s 6d which he was paying when bombed.	Would like to discuss this with rehousing minister before taking any action. He will call back.
Mrs W. Has now had notice to quit from father. Does this affect advice given her earlier by Poor Man's Lawyer on getting possession of their own house (post-1939 purchase)?	It makes no difference. To ask for further appointment with lawyer when summons issued.
Mrs O. Husband in Forces and insured herself until August. Do they get two maternity benefits?	Yes.
Mrs McR. Situation with husband is deteriorating. He now says baby she is expecting is not his and is refusing to maintain her.	Referred Poor Man's Lawyer. Monday next.
Mrs O'L. Can she get her licence for leaded lights?	Council at present not granting licences for this but advised to apply as licences are deferred not refused.
Mrs B. Living with daughter and very unhappy. Furniture in store and firm say she must remove it by end of week as they are giving up depository.	Possible candidate for old people's hostel. She will consider this. Arranged with another firm to store furniture.
Gunner M. To hear what arrangements we have made for confinement of his wife and subsequent adoption of baby (not his). Has got extension of leave.	Told him of suggestions made by moral welfare worker. He will discuss them with wife and come in again.
Mrs L. Has son of eighteen who is 6′ 4″ and she can't keep him clothed.	She has all the coupons to which he is entitled.
Mrs S. Still no reply from County about help with Home Help expenses.	Rang County again who assure us action is being taken. They are waiting for report of health visitor.
Mrs T. To say can find no correspondence to help in dispute with Ministry of Pensions about arrears of rent allowance.	We will refer cases to LCSS for advice as to further action.

List of requests and answers at a Citizen's Advice Bureau on a day picked at random.

FREEDOM to Listen!

Under 'Harder Problems' came cases like war widows and deserted wives. Or Mrs D. who was interned in France during the German occupation and whose husband subsequently died. After her repatriation she found her husband's assets were only £12, and she was sleeping on her sister's sofa. The Citizens Advice Bureau was able to find her a job and even a week's holiday 'which she greatly appreciated'. 'Lesser' problems were often handled as far as they could be with inadequate social service by unpaid women like those of the WVS.

This was the brave new world that women had fought for, and now at last with the return of the men, they were warned of the difficulties they should expect with their fathers, brothers and spouses – a far cry from the comforting harmony they had looked forward to. Some worried about the lines in their own faces, their lack of energy, or even about their young daughters, for they were warned, 'It is a natural enough thing for a man to like to make much of an attractive woman – even if that woman is his own daughter. And in his pride and affection for her he may very well upset his wife, especially if she has aged and feels she has lost some of her personal attraction.'

Living Together Again, written in 1946 by a doctor and his wife, was a remarkable attempt to deal with the array of problems that families might have to face after the end of the war. Shell-shocked or disfigured husbands, disturbed and disrupted children who had rarely or never seen their fathers, exhausted wives and marital infidelity were just some of the situations that people had to cope with as well as the housing shortage and rising prices.

For those over thirty-five, this was their second experience of the difficulties of reunion. Now they were warned to prepare themselves for long periods of silence and depression from their husbands and brothers, for outbursts of tears and violence and for the need to be extra tranquil with those returning from active campaigns.

Those who had been interned in prisoner-of-war camps were returned more gently through the civil settlement hospitals (actually psychiatric hospitals) for rehabilitation.

Often difficult questions from children had to be dealt with:

> To tell a child about a dead parent roughly or with uncontrolled emotion does real damage to the child's sensitive mind and feelings.
>
> When the circumstances of life have been sordid or tragic it is better to leave out all detail and just quietly state the facts, taking the child's attention forward to something new and interesting, such as 'If Daddy were here now he would have loved to see that new wireless set you have just made.'

This attitude was also suggested on the subject of separations, so that through 'gentle tactics' a mother could explain a father's absence with, 'Daddy prefers to live with Alice. He loves her and is happier with her.'

With more civilian injuries than in any previous war, women and children as well were among the disfigured, the mutilated, the blinded and the crippled who were reunited with their families at the end of the war. After the pain and the severe shock of the injury and its aftermath, the smaller agonies and frustrations of daily life had to be dealt with as families faced possible reactions of horror and disappointment in their loved ones. *Living Together Again* tried to prepare women at least for disfigurement in returning soldiers.

> Tim, a naval patient, minded so much about his disfigured face that he deliberately avoided thinking about his accident. Least of all would he allow himself to think about the lovely girl he had just met before he left England on his last submarine trip. Tim was a grand person, aged twenty-three and had been handsome and attractive.

For women the book was encouraging, if perhaps daunting in its requirements: 'It is a hard task for those who love these men to get through the self-made barriers, but infinite patience, gentleness and an exquisite tact, will gradually wear thin the resistance and enable the truly loving wife

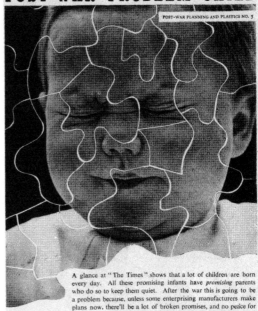

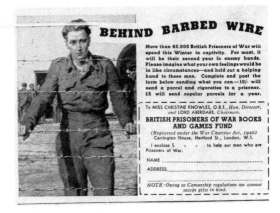

or sweetheart to get emotionally near enough to the man to deal quietly with his resistance.'

Women were told that their men might need a lot of mothering and might behave 'strangely', even if only at night with

> nightmares, sleepwalking, talking or shouting. Once more we are faced with the difficulty of deciding what is normal behaviour and what may be due to shock. For if John marries Joyce, who had always seen him sober, then takes to drink, or if, having previously been a quiet person, he has fits of rage and moodiness, Joyce needs to find out whether she is now seeing John in his true colours or whether he is suffering a form of mental illness due to shock, and is still really the decent fellow she knew.

Another husband cited had had a bad time for three years in a prisoner-of-war camp.

> When he got home to his wife whom he had been fond of, he could not stay in the house. He seemed happy only when he was roaming the hills and wandering from inn to inn drinking all the beer he could drink with two other men who had been in the same camp. It was obvious that he still loved his wife and children but he was inclined to snap and be impatient. Then he would be penitent . . . Then one day when Megan had told him to bring his friends home . . . the three of them suddenly grabbed at the loaf and tore it to pieces.

The truth is that the institutionalised soldier, trained to kill on demand, was not a good civilian or husband.

> They had to learn to do things which they have been taught to hate and to unlearn many other things which were part and parcel of civilised life. Killing and the use of force are much discouraged in civilian collective life; here the use of force and the infliction of a maximum amount of death and damage on the enemy became a desirable aim . . . Now the process was once more to be reversed.

And it must have been hard for toughened men returning (often clutching teddy bears) to a more civilised world than their barracks. Many had enjoyed their time in the services and faced the return to 'civvy street' with trepidation:

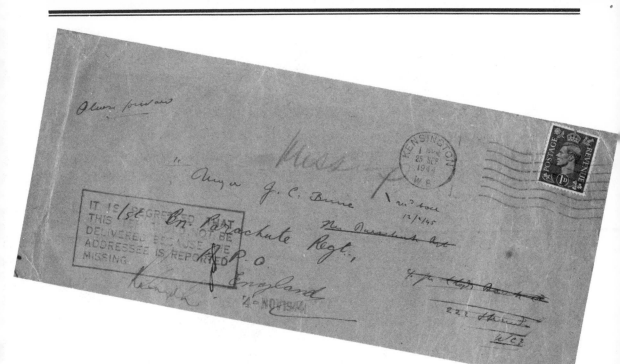

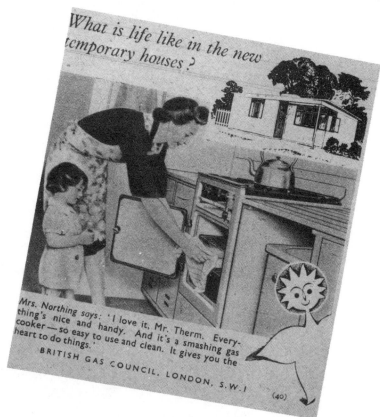

What is life like in the new
temporary houses?

Mrs. Northing says: 'I love it, Mr. Therm. Everything's nice and handy. And it's a smashing gas
cooker—so easy to use and clean. It gives you the
heart to do things.'
BRITISH GAS COUNCIL, LONDON, S.W.1   (40)

I've had such a grand time with the chaps – they are a fine lot. We yarn or smoke and have a drink just when we like, and a chap need never feel dull or lonely... Nell is a good soul and the children are fine, only it's different and it rather scares me. One forgets one's manners in the Army and I may do things she won't like at first. If I get the blues sometimes she'll think I'm bored with her... and there'll be the bother of getting a job or a little shop and seeing I make enough money to go round. It almost makes one wish the war weren't over!

If they were returning to dull homes and boring desk jobs they might well 'feel lonely and cramped and cooped up and some are inclined to break loose' women were warned. And with the disillusionment of a post-war world of drab food, uncared-for and unsightly accommodation, disrupted relationships, shortage of jobs, and with no new world in sight, the divorce rate soared to double the 1930 figure. 58 per cent were filed by husbands and about 75 per cent of these were on grounds of adultery.

In all respects, the war had affected women's lives dramatically. The war economy had depended heavily upon their involvement – in the battle zones, servicing the armed forces, in voluntary organisations, in the Land Army, and in kitchens and homes. The war had also been instrumental in revealing large inequalities in wealth and opportunity, and the new Labour government voted into power in July 1945 began to lay the foundations of a welfare state. But peacetime did not bring an immediate end to hardship and austerity. The inevitable after-effects of a world war included inadequate housing and shortage of jobs, as well as considerable disruption of lives which required often formidable psychological adjustments to be made. Readjustment to a post-war society was not always easy for women who had got used to working, coped with ghastly emergencies, and cared for their relatives for six difficult years. The fact was that for many, their wartime activities had resulted in a new and fierce independence. Yet there was little official recognition of this.

It is doubtless true that there are many jobs done during the war (by women) for which men are better suited, both mentally and physically. And, if there is to be a nation in the future, there must be children and children mean homes and endless chores. So that there must naturally be a drift back from the Services and the factories to domestic work.

Six years of deprivation and disruption had at least provided women with some financial advantages. But in 1945 many of them had to face and adapt to a society which expected them to relinquish much of their recently acquired skills and independence. With men returning from fighting needing jobs, suggestions from psychologists that mothers should be with their children full-time in the early years, and a dramatic reduction in nursery schools after the war, it was thought that many women would be thrust back into their former position in the home. Some welcomed this. For others, new jobs became available after the war. But the possible implications of forcing unwilling women back into the home did not pass unnoticed by the more far-sighted. The authors of *Living Together Again* summed up some of their feelings. They suggested that although, after the strain of the previous years, many women would welcome a return to the old order, 'many will also feel that they are going back to prison, unless they have some life away from sinks and brooms and washtubs.'

Select Bibliography

BOOKS

Bendit, P & L, *Living Together Again*, Gramol 1946

Beveridge, Sir William, *Social Insurance and Allied Services*, HMSO 1942

Beveridge, Sir William, *Voluntary Action*, Allen & Unwin 1946/7

Boyd Orr, Sir John, *Food, Health and Income*, Macmillan 1937

Briggs, Susan, *Keep Smiling Through*, Weidenfeld & Nicholson 1977

Brittain, Vera, *England's Hour*, Macmillan 1941

Brittain, Vera, *Testament of Experience*, Virago 1979

Brockway, Fenner, *Bermondsey Story*, Allen & Unwin 1949

Cadogan, Mary & Craig, Patricia, *Women and Children First*, Gollancz 1978

Calder, Angus, *The People's War*, Panther 1971

Cassandra, *The English at War*, Secker & Warburg 1941

Central Statistics Office, *Statistical Digest of the War*, HMSO 1951

Chambers, Rosalind, *A Study of Three Voluntary Organisations*, Routledge & Kegan Paul 1954

Crompton, Richmal, *William and the Evacuees*, George Newnes 1940

Crompton, Richmal, *William Carries On*, George Newnes 1942

Dent H.C., *Education in Transition*, Routledge & Kegan Paul 1944

Ferguson, S.M. & Fitzgerald, H., *Studies in the Social Services*, HMSO 1954

Foot, Michael, *Aneurin Bevan*, MacGibbon & Kee 1962

French, Philip & Sissons, Michael, (eds.) *The Age of Austerity*, Hodder & Stoughton 1963

Glass, D.V., (ed.) *Social Mobility in Britain*, Routledge & Kegan Paul 1954

Grant, I & Maddren, N., *Countryside at War*, Jupiter 1975

Graves, Charles, *Women in Green*, Heinemann 1948

Gollancz, Victor, (ed.) *The Betrayal of the Left*, Gollancz 1941

Haldane, Charlotte, *Truth Will Out*, Weidenfeld & Nicholson 1949

Hammond, R.J., *Food, Vol. 1, The Growth of Policy*, HMSO 1951

Hammond, R.J., *Food and Agriculture in Britain 1939–45*, Stanford University Press 1954

Hargraves, E.L. & Gowling M., *Civil Industry & Trade*, HMSO 1954

Harrisson, Tom & Madge, Charles, *People in Production*, Murray 1942

Harrisson, Tom & Madge, Charles, *War Factory*, Penguin 1942

Harrisson, Tom, *Living Through the Blitz*, Penguin 1978

Hayes, Dennis, *Challenge of Conscience*, Allen & Unwin 1949

Holden, Enez, *Nightshift*, Bodley Head 1941

House of Commons Debates (Hansard), fifth series

Isaacs, Susan, *The Cambridge Evacuation Survey*, Methuen 1941

Joseph, Shirley, *If Their Mothers Only Knew*, Faber 1946

Katin, Zelma, *Clippie*, Gifford 1944

Kops, Bernard, *The World is a Wedding*, MacGibbon & Kee 1963

Laird, Sydney M., *Venereal Disease in Britain*, Penguin 1943

Leavy, Bert, *Guerilla Warfare*, Penguin 1940

Lehmann, John, *I Am My Brother*, Longmans 1960

Longmate, Norman, *How We Lived Then*, Hutchinson 1971

Marchant, Hilde, *Women and Children Last*, Gollancz 1941

Mass Observation, *War Begins at Home*, Chatto & Windus 1940

Mass Observation, *Home Propaganda*, Advertising Service Guild 1941

Mass Observation, *The Tube Dwellers, The Saturday Book 3*, Hutchinson 1943

Moran, Lord, *Winston Churchill, The Struggle for Survival, 1940–1965*, Constable 1966

National Federation of Women's Institutes, *Town Children Through Country Eyes*, Dorking 1940

Nicholson, Harold, *Diaries and Letters 1939–45*, Collins 1967

Nicholson, Jenny, *Kiss The Girls Goodbye*, Hutchinson 1944

Nixon, Barbara, *Raiders Overhead*, Lindsay Drummond 1943

The People's Convention, *Alliance for Victory*, Dorset County Chronicle 1941

The People's Convention, *Factory Front*, Grafton Press, Leicester 1941

The People's Convention, *Series*, Marston Printing Company, Watford 1941

The People's Convention, *More Food & How to Get It*, Marston Printing Company, Watford 1941

The People's Convention, *Women Want A Square Deal*, Marston Printing Company Watford 1941

(*The above People's Convention material is to be found in the Imperial War Museum Library.*)

Phipps, Kate, Diaries (unpublished)

Priestley, J.B., *Postscripts*, Heinemann 1940

Sackville-West, Vita, *The Women's Land Army*, Michael Joseph 1944

Spring-Rice, Margery, *Working Class Wives*, Virago 1981

Thomas G., *Woman at Work*, Wartime Social Survey 1944

Titmuss, R.M. & Titmuss, K., *Parent's Revolt*, Secker & Warburg 1942

Titmuss, R.M., *Problems of Social Policy*, HMSO 1950

War Wounds and Air Raid Casualties, articles from the British Medical Journal, Lewis 1939

Waugh, Ann, private diaries (unpublished)

Waugh, Evelyn, *Put Out More Flags*, Penguin 1943

Williams-Ellis, Amabel, *Women in War Factories*, Gollancz 1946

Women's Group on Public Welfare, *Our Towns*, Oxford University Press 1943

COOKERY

Baker, Gertrude, *Rational Recipes*, Cardiff 1941

BBC Kitchen Front broadcasts

Carter, F.W.P., *The Penguin Book of Food Growing, Storing and Cooking from Seed to Table*, Penguin 1941

Craig, Elizabeth, *Gardening in Wartime*, Literary Press, Glasgow 1943

Constandinos, Mabel & Grisewood, Freddie, *The Kitchen Front*, MOF

Eyles, Leonora, *Eat Well in Wartime*, Gollancz 1940

Harben, Philip, *The Way to Cook*, Bodley Head 1945

Heath, Ambrose, *Meat Dishes without Joints*, Faber 1940

Heath, Ambrose, *Wartime Recipes*, Eyre & Spottiswoode 1941

Heath, Ambrose, *Cook with Cheese*, Faber 1943

Hill, Charles, *Wise Eating in Wartime*, HMSO 1943
Hill, Charles, *Wartime Food for Growing Children*, HMSO 1942
Over 100 Famous People, *The Kitchen Goes to War*, John Miles Ltd. 1940
Spry, Constance, *Come into the Garden*, J.M. Dent 1942
Terry, Josephine, *Food Without Fuss*, Duckworths 1941
Terry, Josephine, *Food for the Future*, Duckworths 1941
Webb, Mrs Arthur, *Farmhouse Fare*, Farmers' Weekly, 1946
Webb, Mrs Arthur, *Wartime Cookery*, J.M. Dent & Sons 1939
Woolton Lord (foreword), *Food Facts for the Kitchen Front*, Collins n.d.

There were dozens of leaflets, some free, some costing 2d, 3d or 6d, issued by the Board of Education, the Gas & Electricity Boards, the National Association of Maternal & Child Welfare, the Ministry of Food – as well as by the brand names such as Stork, McDougalls etc, written to educate the cook in both thrift and nutrition. These are just a few of them.

Certo, *Why Jams and Jellies Are Fresher when made the Certo Way*
Croft, Susan, *The Stork Wartime Cookery Book* (Stork)
Food Education Menus, *Good Fare in Wartime*, HMSO
Gurney, Ann, *Vegetable Variety*, Medici Society 1940
Johnson, Janet, *What to Give Them?*, (McDougalls)
Ministry of Food Publications: 'Preserves from the Garden'; 'How to Plan Meals for Children'; 'Jam Making at Preservation Centres'; 'Oats & Barley'; 'Food Without Fuel'; 'Canteen Catering'; 'Mushrooms'; 'Fruits of Summer'; 'Food Facts for the Kitchen Front'; 'How Britain was fed in Wartime'; 'Entertaining the GIs'; 'The Market Square – the Story of the Food Ration book'; 'Green Vegetables'; 'All About Herrings'; 'How to Fry' – and many others.
National Association for Maternal & Child Welfare, *Feeding the Young Family*; Radiation Ltd., *Cooking Today the Regulo Way*, (MOF approved)
Webb, Mrs Arthur, 'Seasonal Recipes' from the *Farmer's Weekly*

PAMPHLETS, ARTICLES, LEAFLETS, REPORTS

I have read numerous reports, pamphlets, leaflets, statistics, advertisements, some long, some short, some issued by the government, some by other organisations. My account of the pressures and demands on women in the war is based in part on an assessment of these. There are too many to mention all of them. The following is a list selected from the mass of available material.

Annual Abstract of Statistics (Divorce) 1947
Annual Report of the Medical Officer of Health for the City of Birmingham, 1945
ARP notices
Camden History Society, 'Hampstead at War', 1947
Collection of debates from the London Parliament of Women (*in the Fawcett Library*)
Fire Party Handbook
Headley National Council of Social Services Report 1940
Imperial War Museum War Posters
League of Nations Report on Nutrition, Bell & Son 1937
Ministry of Defence: Posters & leaflets, including defence regulations issued to householders; 'Denial of Resources to the Enemy'
Ministry of Health: Summary Reports; Growmore Bulletins

Ministry of Home Security: 'Front Line, The Story of Civil Defence', HMSO 1942
Ministry of Information: 'Roof Over Britain', HMSO 1943; 'British Women at War', HMSO 1944; 'Land At War'; Form 20B
Ministry of Works & Ministry of Supply Notices and Advertisements
Reading, Lady, 'Memorandum for the National Council of Maternity and Child Welfare', March 1941
Records of the Waifs and Strays Society
Report by the National Council for the Unmarried Mother, 1941–46
Royal Commission on Equal Pay 1944–46, HMSO 1946
Schofield, S., 'Women's Organisations in Wartime', unpublished minutes (*in Imperial War Museum*).
TU Women's Advisory Committee 'Annual Conference of TU Women', 1943
Williams Ellis, Amabel, 'Is Woman's Place in the Home?', Labour Publications Department 1946
Wolfenden, John, *Memorandum on Probation during the War*, 1946
Women in War Jobs, HMSO 1943

MAGAZINES, NEWSPAPERS AND PERIODICALS

Bristol Evening News, *Bulletins of the WVS*, *British Medical Journal*, *Daily Mail*, *Daily Mirror*, *Daily Sketch*, *Farmer's Weekly*, *Housewife*, *Illustrated London News*, *Lancet*, *Lilliput*, *Manchester Guardian*, *News Chronicle*, *Parade*, *Peace News*, *Picture Post*, *Punch*, *Teacher's World & Schoolmasters*, *Listener*, *The Times*, *The War Illustrated*, *Vogue*, *Woman and Beauty*, *Woman's Own*, *Woman's World*, *Women's Newspaper*, *Worker's Fight*.

Index

Page numbers in italics refer to illustrations. Unless otherwise indicated, 'war' refers to the Second World War. All recipes appear together under 'recipes'. Acts of Parliament are together under 'Parliament'.

abortion, 184
accidents, 8, 39, 81, 188–9
adoption, 183, 193
advertisments, 49–51, 60, 144; examples of approach, *13, 24, 36, 41, 44, 47, 49, 50, 56, 60, 76, 82, 123, 136, 140, 150, 156, 171*; for birth control, 179; for unobtainable goods, 153, (examples) *13, 18, 72, 128, 148, 152, 155, 164*
Age of Austerity, The, ed. French and Sissons, 93
agriculture, 10, 75–83, 95–7, 99–101
Air Raid Precautions, 6, 55, 57, 192
air raid shelters, 66–8, 69; Anderson, 6, 59, 66, 163; life in, 37, 54–5, 66–8; types, 6, 7, 68
air raids, *see* Blitz, bombing
alcohol, 85, 134, 151, 166, 170
animals: farm, 7, 23, 75, 76, 77–81, (kept in towns) 99–101, 111, (slaughter) 88, 100–1; pet, 7, 69, 192; zoo, 98
anti-aircraft devices, 47–9, 53, 95
armed forces, British, 4, 37, 53; desertion, 161, 192; effect on personality, 196–9; envy of, 43, 69; mixed batteries, 48–9; serviced by women volunteers, 73; and countryside, 7, 76; women's auxiliaries, 9, 43–51
armed forces, foreign, 164, 166, 176, 178; *see also* US Army
arms, 9, 32, 33–4, 40, 55, 189
Ashby, Margery Corbett, 10–11
Attlee, Clement, 41
Austerity Regulations, 152, 153–4

Baldwin, Stanley, 53
bartering, 97, 99, 161
beer, 85, 151, 166
bees, 101, 122
Bendit, Phoebe and Laurence, *Living Together Again,* 29, 176–8, 194, 195, 199
Bevin, Ernest, 13
Birmingham, 20, 24, 59, 65, 183
birth-rate, *90,* 180–1, 182
Black Market, 59, 89, 149, 157, 159–61
blackout, 8, 36, 76, 91, 163
Blitz, 24, 54–5, 57–63, 65–73
Bolan, Constance, 32
bombing, 7, 27, 57–60, *61–2,* 97, 182; effects, 62–3, 65–73, 149, 187; *see also* Blitz
bread, 135–6; teabreads, 126–7
Bristol, 18, 189
BBC, 8, 17; programmes, 32, 37, 91, 163; reactions to, 22–3, 106

British Medical Journal, 187
British characteristics, 1, 166, 170, 171–2
British Restaurants, 23, 37, 73, 86, 118
Brownies, 19, 29, 89, 143, 144
building, 34, 65, 70; skills, 57–9
burial (alive), 62–3, 187

cakes, 122, 124; recipes, 124–8, *136,* 140
Calder, Angus, 1
canteens, 37, 118
censorship, 9; *see also* secrecy
Chamberlain, Mary, 109
Chamberlain, Neville, 3, 8
chemical warfare, 5, 57
childbirth, 59, 181–2
childcare, 25, 40, 193; *see also* nurseries
children: attitudes to, 22, 195; and men, 29, 63, 166, 173, 194; responses of, 68, 69, 153, 161, 189; doing war work, 75, 89, 95, 144, 189; *see also* Brownies, Cubs, evacuation, Guides, mothers, nurseries, schooling, Scouts
Christmas cards and presents, 100, 122, 144, 152
churches: groups, 3; buildings, 21
Churchill, Winston, 33, 41, 48–9, 86
Citizens Advice Bureaux, 69, 192–4
Civil Defence, 4, 5, 11, 53, 56–63
class: clashes, 21–2, 25; distinctions, effect of war on, 3, 85–6, 144, 147; and health, 85; *see also* poverty, privilege
cleaning materials, 3, 73, 86, 149; recipes, 132–3
clothing, 63, 77, 151, 153–7; for armed forces, 43, 45, 154; donations, 19, 73; shortage, 143, 149, 151, 152; *see also under* prices, rationing
Commonwealth, British, 154, 164, 166
communications, 49–51, 57
compensation, 39, 63
conscientious objectors, 32, 57, 75, 108
conscription, 4, 9; of women, 13, 15, 43, 45, 53, 181; post-war, 189; *see also* mobilisation
contraception, 173, 179, 180
cookery, 1, 81, 103–41; commercial, 123–4; low-fuel, 103–5, 109; large-scale, 73, 107, 117, 118; *see also* food, recipes
Cooper, Susan, 93
Corsellis, Mary, 37

countryside: use by armed forces, 7, 76; reactions of townspeople to, 22, 23, 29, 80–1
Coventry, 10, 20, 24, 59
Craigie, H.B., 175
crime, 161, 189, 192; *see also* offences, sentencing
Cripps, Stafford, 152, 154
Cubs, 19, 75, 143

Daily Worker, 26
dances, 36, 83, 157, 164, 170, 173
deaths, 43, 57, 59, 62, 65, 187, 192; infant, 85, 89, *90,* 111
decorating, home, 144, 150, 163
Defence Regulations, 4, 32, 160, 179
diet, 23, 83, 85, 86, *116,* 118; improved in wartime, 89, 96–7, 111–2, 119, 122–3
diets, recommended basic, 86–8
Dig for Victory campaign, 95–101
divorce, 197

Eat Well in Wartime (Eyles), 119
education, *see* schooling, training
eggs, 60, 81, 86, 91–2, 100; dried, 86, 136; mock, *88,* 137, 140; preserved, 100; as fire extinguisher, 61; recipes, 110, 120, 139
emigration, 19
employment: hours, 12, 15, 31, 33–4, 39, 81; key to normality, 70; part-time, 15, 31, 34; of people with disabilities, 34; *see also* working conditions *and under* women
Encyclopaedia Britannica, 159
Entertaining the GIs, 166
entertainments, 9, 37, 163; *see also* dances
evacuation, 7–8, 19–25, 66, 163; children's responses to, 20, 23, 29, 190; effects, 187–8, 190–1; of hospitals, 63; and nurseries, 26, 29; preparation for, 17
eyesight, 97
Eyles, Leonora, 119

factories, 3, 11–12, *12–13,* 32, 33–9, 40; conversion of, 33, 34, 149, 179
families broken up, 13, 15, 19–20, 22, 29, 175
Farmer's Weekly, 96, 109
farming, 10, 75–83, 95–7, 99–101
fingers and toes, parcel of, 62
fire service, 5, 53, 57, 59–61
first aid, 62–3
fish, 89, 91, 108–9, 192; mock, 109, 140; recipes, 109–10, 138

fishing, 108
food, 1, 23, 26, 46, 75–141, 166, 170;
for animals, 76, 77, 99–101, 147;
in emergency, 6, 17, 51, 70–3,
106; imports, 10, 75, 89, 135;
preserving, 100, *120*, 129, 130;
waste, 47, 75, 91, 136, 166, 192;
wild, 81, 83, 89, 95, 99, 118–9,
129, (for pigs) 101; *see also* British
Restaurants, cookery, diet,
farming, recipes *and under*
rationing
Food Facts for the Kitchen Front
(Ministry of Food), 117, 118
Food for the Future (Terry), 137
Food without Fuel (Ministry of Food),
103
fruit: drying, *120*, 134; homegrown,
95, 96–7; scarcity, 85, 89, 95,
97– 8, 122, 129; recipes, *99, 123*,
124– 8, 130–1, 133
fuel, 86, 103–5, 143

GIS, *see* US Army
gas masks, 5, 7, 8, 67, 160
gas warfare, 5, 57
Germans, reactions to, 60, 62, 135,
192
Glasgow, 20, 59, 65, 85
Graham, Margaret, 189
Graves, Charles, *Women in Green*, 62
guerilla warfare, leaflet on, 189
Guider, The, 95, 189
Guides, 19, 51, 75, 89, 95, 189
'Gypsy Petulengro', 95

hairstyles, 157
Hamlyn, Calmody, 11
Hammerton, John, 147
Harrisson, Tom, 3; *see also* Mass
Observation
health, 18, 27, 29, 179–80, 188, 192;
improved by rationing, 111–2,
122–3; poverty and, 18, 85; *see also*
hospitals, nursing
Heath, Ambrose, 105, 106, 109, 111,
113
Herbert, A.P., 60
herbs, 99, *120*, 133, 134
holidays, *77*, 81
Home and County, 22–3
Home Guard (*earlier* Local Defence
Volunteers), 9, 51, 56, 57, 189
homelessness, 6, 24, 25, 65, 66, 69,
70, 149–50
hospitals, 7, 17, 43, 44, 62, 63;
emergency, 5; maternity, 181–2;
mental, 21, 184, 195
household goods, shortage of, 19, 40,
144, 149–57
housework, 32, 37, 40
housing, 65, 81, 183, 193, 199; costs,
149; *see also* homelessness

Hull, 20, 59, 65
hysteria, 7, 20, 22, 187

identity papers, 4, 5, *88*
ignorance, 178–9
illegitimacy, 170, 179, 182–5
imports, 99, 147; *see also under* food
inflation, 89, 108, 149, 154
ingredients, ersatz or substitute, 93,
135; unusual, (animal) 81, 105,
108, 117, 137, 138, 139, 192,
(eggs) 81, 86, 100, (vegetable) 83,
89, 93, 95, 99, 118–19
intelligence work, 51
invasion of Britain, threatened, 5, 33,
53, 55, 56, 77, 189–90

jam-making, 98–9, 129; extra sugar
ration, 86, 98, 122; low sugar,
130, 131; use of scum, 124, 130;
recipes, *99, 120, 131*, 133
jokes, 24, 66, 89, 137, 149

Kitchen Goes to War, The, 109, 110

Labour Government, 197
Land Army, Women's, 75, 77–83,
164, 199
language: American, 167, 171; sexist,
6, 10, 13, 91
Leeds, 20, 59
Lend-Lease scheme, 75–6, 89, 112,
136–7
Liverpool, 18, 20, 59, 72
Living Together Again (Bendit), 29,
176–8, 194, 195, 201
London, 6–7, 18, 53, 65, 187, 191; *see
also* Blitz
Longmate, Norman, 1, 36, 40, 166,
170–1, 173
looting, 59, 61

make-up, 149, 157, *171*
malnutrition, 18, *90*
Manchester, 20, 24, 59
Marchant, Hilda, 63, 69–70
marriage, 164, 173, 175–8,
179–80, 199
Mass Observation, 1, 3 (note);
reports, 13, 24–5, 32, 54–5, 163;
women's statements to, 11, 15,
29, 37, 40
maternity benefits, 183, 193
meat, 111–3, 119; recipes, 112–7,
138, 139
medicines and medical supplies, 62,
99, 133, 134
men: attitudes to women, 40–1, 59;
effects of war on, 195–7;
responsible for war, 3
menstruation, 19, 178, 179
mental illness, 22, 187, 189, 190, 196

military equipment, production of, 3,
9, 32, 33–4, 40
milk, 86, 88–9; *see also* farming
mining, 103
Ministry of Food, 75, 95, 108–9,
135–6, 170, 192; publications, 75,
76, 91, 99, 103, 117, 118, 137,
166
Ministry of Health, 27, 62, 178,
179–80, 184
Ministry of Information, 15, 34, 36
mobilisation, 9, 11, 31–3, 53;
insensitivity of, 11, 15, 36
mock foods, recipes for, 88, 110, 112,
121, 128, 137, 140, 141, 170
moral attitudes, 178–9, 182–3
morale, 1, 20, 48–9, 65–6, 68, 149,
157
mothers, 5, 19–25, 29, 188, 190;
desire for employment, 25; Home
Helps for, 73, 193; pregnant,
rations for, 85, 88; seen as war
workers, 9, 17; unmarried, 183,
184; *see also* evacuation
mugging, 59, 192
museums, 17
music, 37, 68, 149, 164, 170

Nixon, Barbara, 53, 68
non co-operation, 5, 32, 48
nurseries, 13, 19, 24, 183, 201; call
for, 25, 54; numbers, 25, 26, 29;
residential, 26–9
nursing and nurses, 59, 62–3, 68, 73,
182, 192; in auxiliary forces, 43–4,
effect of war on, 8, 12

Observer, the, 154
occupations: reserved, 4, 9, 10, 31; *see
also under* women
offences, petty, 5–6, 8, 75, 95, 160;
see also sentencing
onions, 95–6
Our Towns 1939–42, 29, 178
Oxford, 17

pacifism, 32, 57
pacifist organisations, 3
Parents' Revolt (Titmuss), 180
Parliament, Acts of, and Orders:
Adoption of Children
(Regulation) Act (1939), 183;
Civil Defence Act (1939), 57;
Control of Employment Act
(1945), 41; Control of
Employment Orders (1939,
1943), 31; Defence Regulations
(various), 4, 32, 160, 179;
Emergency Powers Act (1939), 4,
8; Limitation of Supplies Order
(1940), 149; Military Training Act
(1939), 4; National Insurance Act
(1911), 12; National Service (No.
2) Act (1941), 13; National
Services (Armed Forces) Act
(1939), 9; Personal Injuries

(Emergency Provisions) Act (1939), 12–13, 39; Public Health Act (1936), 183; Registration of Employment Order (1941), 43

Patterns of Marriage, 175

People's War, The (Calder), 1

Phipps, Kate, 8, 44

Picture Post, 144

plants, 99; *see also under* food

Plymouth, 59, 65

Portsmouth, 20, 24, 59

potatoes, 96, 97, *100*, 118; recipes, *88*, *100*, *106*, 107, 117–8, 121, 128

poverty, 18–19, 20, 23, 27, 65, 85; of servicemen's wives, 13, 25

pregnancy, 19, 21, 31, 59, 181; *see also* illegitimacy, mothers

prescriptions, unusual, 152

presents, 100, 122, 152

prices, 89, 149; Black Market, 157, 161; examples, (clothes) 89, 149, 154, (food) 23, *24*, *56*, *60*, *82*, 86, 88, *93*, 108, *128*, *136*, (soap and cosmetics) *41*, *47*, *77*, *123*, *151*, *171*, (miscellaneous) 5, 25, 26, 39, *76*, *77*, 83, 147, 196

prisoners, 17, 19; of war, 43, 73, 75, 195, 196

privilege, 85, 86, 147, 149, 154, 159; *see also* class *and under* US Army

propaganda, 19, 24, 32, 91, 92, 199; examples, 34–6, *77*, 91, 101, 110; reactions to, 3–4, 22

prostitution, 59, 184, 192

protests, 3–4, 32; *see also* women's anger

pubs, 151, 166

puddings, 122; recipes, 124–8, 140–1

racism, 170–1

Raiders Overhead (Nixon), 68

railings, removal of, 147

ration books, 66, 85–6, *88*

rationing, 5, 60, 86, 149–51; after war, 86, 161, 192; clothes, 73, 77, 152, 153–4, 193; farm animals, 75; food, 23, 40, 43, *60*, 81, 83, 85–92, 111, 122–4, *137*; petrol, 5; soap, 3, *56*, 73, *77*, 86, *123*, 149; ways round, 86, 153, 159

Reading, Lady Stella, 68, 143–4

recipes given in full (* denotes vegetarian recipes): *Apple Bombes, 128; *Apple and Blackberry Jam, *99*; *Apple and Elderberry Jam, *120*; *Apples, Dried, *120*, 134; *Apricot (Dried) Jam, 131; *Beans, Salted, 120; *Bean and Tomato Pie, 120; *Beet the Cold, 120; Beef, Haricot, *111*; Beef, Spiced, *116*; Beefsteak Pudding, 113; Black Pudding Toast, 138; *Blackberry and Apple Jam, *99*; *Bread, Health, 127; *Bread Pudding, 125; Bread Soup, 141; *Butter, to double, 132; *Butterbur Spikes, Baked, 95; Cabbage Soup, 106;

*Cake, Beehive, 125; *Cake, Cherry, *136*; *Cake, Christmas, 127; Cake, Siege, 126; *Cake, Trench, 124; *Cake, Walnut, 126; *Carrot Jam, 131; *Cheese, Cottage, 131; *Cheese Muffins, 126, *Cheese, Potted, 131; *Cheese and Potato Custard, 121; *Cheese Pudding, 121; *Cheese Sauce, *120*; *Cherry Cake, *136*; Chestnut Soup, 107; Chicken, Stuffed Legs of, 114; Chicken, Two Dishes from One, 113; Chicken Liver Paste, 114; Chops, Stuffed, *112*; *Christmas Cake, 127; *Christmas Pudding, 127; Corned Beef with Cabbage, *111*; Corned Beef Hash, *111*, 113; Crow, 138; *Custard, Baked, 139; *Date and Nut Loaf, 126; Duck, 139; Eggs, Imitation, 140; Eggs, Scrambled, with Haddock, 110; *Elderberry and Apple Jam, *120*; *Fish, Mock, 140; Fish and Leek Pudding, 109; Fish Puffs, 110; Fish Soup, 106; Fowls, Stuffed Legs of, 114; Fowl, Two Dishes from One, 113; *Ginger beer, 135; Haddock, Scrambled Eggs with, 110; Haggis, Mock, 91; Ham Bone Purée, 108; Hare Soup, 107; Hasty Pudding, 139; Herrings, Stuffed, 109; *Honey Nut Tartlets, 125; *Ice Cream, 124; *Jam, Apple and Blackberry, 99; *Jam, Apple and Elderberry, *120*; *Jam, Apricot (Dried), 131; *Jam, Carrot, 131; Jam, Family, without sugar, 131; *Jam, Marrow and Pineapple, 131; *Jam, Medicinal, 133; Kale, Braised, 119; Kidneys with Horseradish, 117; *King-Cup Pickle, 85; Lentil Chick, 121; Liver Mould, 114; *Margarine, Flavouring, 132; *Marmalade, Orange Skin, 130; *Marrow and Pineapple Jam, 131; *Marrow Surprise, *120*; *Marrow and Walnut Cutlets, 121; *Marzipan, Mock, 128; *Mash, Spotted, 117–8; *Mayonnaise, 138; Meat Pudding, Trench, 113; Meat Stew with Mixed Vegetables, 117; *Mincemeat, 131; *Muffins, Cheese, 126; *Mushroom Puffs, 120; *Nut and Date Loaf, 126; *Oatmeal and Herb Sausages, 121; *Oslo Meal, 119; Oysters, Mock, 110; *Pancake, Potato, *100*; Pancakes, Sardine, 109; Pancakes, Sausage, 113; *Pancakes, Sour Milk, 125; *Parsley Honey, 130; *Pastry, fatless, 118; *Pastry, Potato, 121, 128; *Pea Soup, Cold Cream of, 107; *Pears, Dried, *120*, 134; Pig's Cheek, Baked, 117; (Pilchard) Snack, 110; *Pineapple and Marrow Jam, 131; *Plum Pudding, Mock, 141; *Plums, Dried, 134; Pork and Cabbage Soup, 106; Porridge, Leftover, 140; *Potato and Cheese Custard, 121; *Potato Eggs, *88*; *Potato Pancake, *100*; *Potato Pastry, 121, 128; Potato Soup, *106*; Potato and Watercress or Sorrel Soup, 107; Pudding, Emergency, 141; Rabbit Pudding with Mushrooms, 113; Roe Butter, Hard, 131; *Rolls, Baking Powder, 126; Rook Pie with Figgy Paste, 138; *Rosehip Syrup, 133;

*(Salad) Oslo Meal, 119; *Salad, Whit, *88*; Salmon in Custard, 110; Sandwiches, 'All Clear', 132; Sardine Pancakes, 109; Sausage Pancakes, 113; Sausages en Surprise, 113; Sheep's Head Broth, 107; Snoek Piquante, 138; *Sorrel and Potato Soup, 107; Sparrow Pie, 139; *Sponge, Victory, 140; Sultana Pudding, 124; *Summer Pudding, *123*; *Sweet Corn Pudding, 120; Thrushes, 139; Toad Special (Veal), 114; *Tomato Jam, Green, 130; Tops, 119; *Trifle, 125; Veal (Toad Special), 114; *Vegetable (Woolton) Pie, 118; Vegetable Roll, Baked, 121; *Vegetables, white, cooked in blanc, 138; *Walnut Cake, 126; *Walnut and Marrow Cutlets, 121; *Watercress and Potato Soup, 107; Woodpigeons, 117; *Woolton Pie, 118

recipes referred to, 83, 86, 91, 93, 97, *100*, 105; patriotic names, 91, 126, 132, 140, 170

reserved occupations, 4, 9, 10, 31

restaurants, 86, 109

Restaurants, British, 23, 37, 73, 86, 118

sabotage, 5, 65, 190

salvage, 19, *142*, 143–7, 149, *173*

Salvation Army, 10, 17, 184

sanitary towels, 19, 77, 157, 179

sanitation, 18, 29, 34, 36, 66; key to destroying London, 65

saving, 7, 108, 159, *160*

Schofield, S., *Women's Organisations in Wartime*, 3

schooling, 19, 25, 173, 175, 187–8

Scotland, 20, 25, 108, 136–7; poverty in, 10, 65, 85

Scouts, 189

secrecy, 5–6, 44, 51

sentencing, 32, 57, 101, 136, 149; inconsistency of, 160; *see also* offences

sexual relations, 15, 20, 170, 175–85

shampoo, home-made, 157

Sheffield, 18, 20, 24

shelters for homeless, 66–7, 69; *see also* air raid shelters

shock, 69, 73, 187, 189, 194–5, 196

shopping, 40, 63, 89–91, 149

shortages, 19, 40, 144, 149–57, 192

signposts, 6, 49

snoek, 138, 192

'Snoek Piquante' (Cooper), 93

soap, 3, *56*, 73, *77*, 86, *123*, 132, 149

social services, 6, 9, 13, 17, 68–9, 184; after war, 192–4, 200–1; for army, 175

songs, 55, 144, 163; words of, 31, 37, 66, 80, 83, 164, 178, 181, 185

soups, 105–6, 118; recipes, 106–8, 141

Southampton, 18, 20
Spanish Civil War, 24, 68
Spry, Constance, 91, 105
Squanderbug, 131, 135, *160*
strikes, 83
suffrage campaign, women's, 19
Summerskill, Edith, 12
surveys, 66, 85; *see also* Mass
 Observation
sweets, 86, 124, 170, 173

tea flavoured with bromide, 46
Terry, Josephine, 137
Thomas, Diana, 32
Times, The, 147, 159
Titmuss, Richard, 180
tobacco, 83, 152
total objectors, 32
toys, 144, 152
trades unions, 31, 37–9
training, 5, 34, 62, 81, 83; in armed
 forces, 4, 45, 47, 49–51
transport, 5, 20, 40, 49–51, 60
trenches, 6, 7, 68

Underground, London, 6–7, 37, 66
unemployment, 10, 15, 161, 199
USA: British imports from, 75; finance
 and supplies from, 27, 56, 72, 73,
 154; influence on British, 157,
 171; *see also* Lend-Lease scheme,
 US Army
US Army, 75, 164–73, 178; privileges
 of, 70, 122, 154, 157, 166, 172;
 view of Britain, 3, 150, 151–2,
 166, 171–2

vegetables, 83, 91, 95–7, 105, 117–9,
 139; drying, *120*, 134; to replace
 fruit, 97, 122, 124, 127, 129;
 recipes, *88*, 91, 95, *100*, *106*, 107,
 117–21, 130–1, 138
vegetarianism, 85, 119; vegetarian
 recipes, *see* recipes
venereal disease, 173, 179–80
Vogue, 147, 157
voluntary work by women, 5, 9, 17,
 33, 68–9, 73, 129, 147;
 compulsory, 57, 63; fund-raising,
 68; Sunday, 33; *see also* Civil
 Defence, Women's Voluntary
 Service

wages, 10, 15, 18, 31, 154; examples,
 11, 26, 56–7, 60, 63, 81, 83; in
 armed forces, 13–15, 43, 44, 47,
 172; increased in wartime, 34, 40,
 108, 159, 201; women's less than
 men's, 13, 31, 37, 39, 41
Wales, 10, 17, 34
war, *see* Spanish Civil War, World
 War I, World War II
War Agricultural Committees, 75

War Illustrated, 147, 159–60, 161
War Service Grants, 15
'War Wounds and Air Raid
 Casualties' (Wright), 187
water supply, 5, 6, 18, 65, 70–2; key
 to destroying London, 6; mobile,
 69; rationed, 86
Webb, Mrs Arthur, 96, 97, 109
weddings, 60, 151; *see also* marriage
Wilkinson, Ellen, 66
wine, *93*, 134
Woman Today, 12
Woman's World, 33, 36, 49, 51, 60
women: authority of, 67–8; capable
 of heavy work, 47; desire to fight,
 48, 51, 56; generosity of, 19, 144,
 149; 'human or women first?', 23
women's anger, 10, 11, 12–13; at
 conditions of work, 81, 83; at
 dependence on men, 10; at
 evacuation, 21, 22–3, 25; at
 government, 11, 15, 70, 81, 190;
 at refusal of their work, 53; as
 unmarried mothers, 184;
women, effects of war on: 'fighting
 for men', 63, 73, 170; hardship, 1,
 10, 191–9, (from bombing) 59,
 65–73, 191–2, (from laws and
 regulations) 8–9, (from poverty
 and shortages) 13–15, 93, 135,
 143–7, 149, (from separations) 26,
 175, 194; independence
 increased, 201
women and employment: attitudes to
 war work, 10, 37, 40; numbers in
 war work, 15, 32–3; women's
 labour, (needed) 25, 32,
 (inefficiently directed) 10, 11–12;
 difficulties in employment, 40,
 (discrimination) 11, 31, 41, 53,
 199; variety of work, 13, 31, 32,
 47, 49, 51, 62, 77; lack of
 occupation when evacuated, 24;
 women's work better than men's,
 34, 41, 48, 49, 51, 83;
women, government attitudes to: 10,
 13, 93, 199; classified 'mobile' or
 'immobile', 9, 15, 31, 73;
 discrimination (in compensation),
 39, 63, (against unmarried
 mothers), 183, 184
women, married: discrimination
 against, 10, 12–13, 53; lack of
 communication with husbands,
 69, 176, 191, 195–6; to
 servicemen, 13, 25, 32; sacrifice
 food to men, 91, 111
Women and Children Last (Marchant),
 63, 69–70
Women in Green (Graves), 62
Women in War Jobs, (HMSO), 31
women's armies, private, 55
Women's Freedom League, 3, 11
Women's Group on Public Welfare,
 Our Towns 1939–42, 29, 178

Women's Home Defence Corps, 56
Women's Institutes, 9, 21, 22–3, 98,
 129
Women's Newspaper, 10
women's organisations, 3, 9–10, 17,
 39, 68, 81; *see also* Women's
 Institutes, Women's Voluntary
 Service
Women's Organisations in Wartime
 (Schofield), 3
Women's Parliament, London, 37, 63
Women's Voluntary Service, 9–10,
 17, 72, 143–4; attempts to arm,
 55; examples of work, 20, 23, 51,
 62, 69, 73, 98, 194; formation, 68;
 under-5s department, 26, 27
Woolton, Lord (1st Earl), 19, 83, 85,
 86, 88, 101
working conditions, 34–9, 43, 46–7,
 51, 63, 81–3; *see also* employment
World War I, 3, 8, 31, 99, 179
World War II, *passim*; preparations
 for, 5; 'phoney war', 8, 9; effects
 on women, 1, 191–9; 'fought by
 women and children', 63, 73, 170;
 objections to, 3; women's desire
 to fight in, 48, 51, 56
Wright, Maurice, 'War Wounds and
 Air Raid Casualties', 187